McGraw-Hill Ryerson

MathLinks 9
PRACTICE AND HOMEWORK BOOK

Authors

Ralph Backé
B.Ed., P.B.C.E.
The Winnipeg School Division
Manitoba

Eric Balzarini
B.Sc., B.Ed., M.Ed.
School District 35 (Langley)
British Columbia

Darlene Couwenberghs
B.Ed., M.Ed.
School District 37 (Delta)
British Columbia

Brad Epp
B.Sc., M.A.
School District 73
   (Kamloops/Thompson)
British Columbia

Victor Epp
Hon. B.A., M.Ed.
School District 5
   (Southeast Kootenay)
British Columbia

Blaise Johnson
B.Sc., B.Ed.
School District 45
   (West Vancouver)
British Columbia

Tricia Licorish (Perry)
B.Ed.
St. James-Assiniboia School
   Division
Manitoba

Dean Wiersma
Dip. Eng., B.Ed.
Calgary Roman Catholic
   Separate School District No. 1
Alberta

Get Ready Authors

Bruce McAskill
B.Sc., B.Ed., M.Ed., Ph.D.
Mathematics Consultant
Victoria, British Columbia

Wayne Watt
B.Sc., B.Ed., M.Ed.
Mathematics Consultant
Winnipeg, Manitoba

Developmental Team

Chris Zarski
Evergreen Catholic Separate
   Regional Division No. 2
Alberta

Emily Kalwarowsky
Edmonton Catholic Separate
   School District No. 7
Alberta

Michael Webb
Mathematics Consultant
Toronto, Ontario

Cheryl Makokis
Kitaskinaw Education Authority
Alberta

Reg Fogarty
School District 83
   (North Okanagan/Shuswap)
British Columbia

Rick Wunderlich
School District 83
   (North Okanagan/Shuswap)
British Columbia

Robert Wong
Edmonton Public Schools
Alberta

Ian Strachan
Calgary Board of Education
Alberta

Sandra Harazny
Regina Roman Catholic Separate
   School Division No. 81
Saskatchewan

Ron Kennedy
Mathematics Consultant
Edmonton, Alberta

Toronto   Montréal   Boston   Burr Ridge, IL   Dubuque, IA   Madison, WI   New York
San Francisco   St. Louis   Bangkok   Bogotá   Caracas   Kuala Lumpur   Lisbon   London
Madrid   Mexico City   Milan   New Delhi   Santiago   Seoul   Singapore   Sydney   Taipei

COPIES OF THIS BOOK
MAY BE OBTAINED BY
CONTACTING:

McGraw-Hill Ryerson Ltd.

WEB SITE:
http://www.mcgrawhill.ca

E-MAIL:
orders@mcgrawhill.ca

TOLL-FREE FAX:
1-800-463-5885

TOLL-FREE CALL:
1-800-565-5758

OR BY MAILING YOUR
ORDER TO:
McGraw-Hill Ryerson
Order Department
300 Water Street
Whitby, ON L1N 9B6

Please quote the ISBN
and title when placing
your order.

McGraw-Hill Ryerson
MathLinks 9 Practice and Homework Book

Copyright © 2009, McGraw-Hill Ryerson Limited, a Subsidiary of The McGraw-Hill Companies. All rights reserved. No part of this publication may be reproduced or transmitted in any form or by any means, or stored in a data base or retrieval system, without the prior written permission of McGraw-Hill Ryerson Limited, or, in the case of photocopying or other reprographic copying, a licence from the Canadian Copyright Licensing Agency (Access Copyright). For an Access Copyright licence, visit www.accesscopyright.ca or call toll free to 1-800-893-5777.

Any request for photocopying, recording, or taping of this publication shall be directed in writing to Access Copyright.

ISBN-13: 978-0-07-097344-2
ISBN-10: 0-07-097344-X

http://www.mcgrawhill.ca

5 6 7 8 9 MP 1 9 8 7 6 5

Printed and bound in Canada

Care has been taken to trace ownership of copyright material contained in this text. The publishers will gladly accept any information that will enable them to rectify any reference or credit in subsequent printings.

EXECUTIVE PUBLISHER: Linda Allison
ASSOCIATE PUBLISHER: Kristi Clark
PROJECT MANAGER: Helen Mason
CONTENT MANAGER: Susan Till
DEVELOPMENTAL EDITORS: Kelly Cochrane, Richard Dupuis, Ann Firth, Adrienne Montgomerie, Rita Vanden Heuvel
MANAGER, EDITORIAL SERVICES: Crystal Shortt
SUPERVISING EDITOR: Jaime Smith
COPY EDITOR: Laurel Sparrow
EDITORIAL ASSISTANT: Erin Hartley
MANAGER, PRODUCTION SERVICES: Yolanda Pigden
TEAM LEAD, PRODUCTION: Paula Brown
COVER DESIGN: Valid Design & Layout
COVER IMAGE: Corbis Canada

Contents

To the User 1

CHAPTER 1
Symmetry and Surface Area

Get Ready 2
1.1 Line Symmetry 4
1.2 Rotational Symmetry and Transformations 6
1.3 Surface Area 8
Chapter Link 10
Vocabulary Link 11
Chapter 1 Review 12

CHAPTER 2
Rational Numbers

Get Ready 14
2.1 Comparing and Ordering Rational Numbers 16
2.2 Problem Solving With Rational Numbers in Decimal Form 18
2.3 Problem Solving With Rational Numbers in Fraction Form 20
2.4 Determining Square Roots of Rational Numbers 22
Chapter Link 24
Vocabulary Link 25
Chapters 1–2 Review 26

CHAPTER 3
Powers and Exponents

Get Ready 28
3.1 Using Exponents to Describe Numbers 30
3.2 Exponent Laws 32
3.3 Order of Operations 34
3.4 Using Exponents to Solve Problems 36
Chapter Link 38
Vocabulary Link 39
Chapters 1–3 Review 40

Contents • MHR iii

CHAPTER 4

Scale Factors and Similarity

Get Ready 42
4.1 Enlargements and Reductions 44
4.2 Scale Diagrams 46
4.3 Similar Triangles 48
4.4 Similar Polygons 50
Chapter Link 52
Vocabulary Link 53
Chapters 1–4 Review 54

CHAPTER 5

Introduction to Polynomials

Get Ready 56
5.1 The Language of Mathematics 58
5.2 Equivalent Expressions 60
5.3 Adding and Subtracting Polynomials 62
Chapter Link 64
Vocabulary Link 65
Chapters 1–5 Review 66

CHAPTER 6

Linear Relations

Get Ready 68
6.1 Representing Patterns 70
6.2 Interpreting Graphs 72
6.3 Graphing Linear Relations 74
Chapter Link 76
Vocabulary Link 77
Chapters 1–6 Review 78

CHAPTER 7

Multiplying and Dividing Polynomials

Get Ready 80
7.1 Multiplying and Dividing Monomials 82
7.2 Multiplying Polynomials by Monomials 84
7.3 Dividing Polynomials by Monomials 86
Chapter Link 88
Vocabulary Link 89
Chapters 1–7 Review 90

CHAPTER 8

Solving Linear Equations

Get Ready 92
8.1 Solving Equations: $ax = b$, $\frac{x}{a} = b$, $\frac{a}{x} = b$ ... 94
8.2 Solving Equations: $ax + b = c$, $\frac{x}{a} + b = c$ 96
8.3 Solving Equations: $a(x + b) = c$ 98
8.4 Solving Equations: $ax = b + cx$, $ax + b = cx + d$, $a(bx + c) = d(ex + f)$ 100
Chapter Link 102
Vocabulary Link 103
Chapters 1–8 Review 104

CHAPTER 9

Linear Inequalities

Get Ready 106
9.1   Representing Inequalities 108
9.2   Solving Single-Step Inequalities 110
9.3   Solving Multi-Step Inequalities 112
Chapter Link 114
Vocabulary Link 115
Chapters 1–9 Review 116

CHAPTER 10

Circle Geometry

Get Ready 118
10.1 Exploring Angles in a Circle 120
10.2 Exploring Chord Properties 122
10.3 Tangents to a Circle 124
Chapter Link 126
Vocabulary Link 127
Chapters 1–10 Review 128

CHAPTER 11

Data Analysis

Get Ready 130
11.1 Factors Affecting Data Collection 132
11.2 Collecting Data 134
11.3 Probability in Society 136
11.4 Developing and Implementing
       a Project Plan 138
Chapter Link 142
Vocabulary Link 143
MathLinks 9 Practice Final Exam 144

0.5 Centimetre Grid Paper 150

Answers 153

Contents • MHR **v**

To the User

Welcome to the *MathLinks 9* Practice and Homework Book. This print resource provides additional opportunities for you to develop the skills you used in the *MathLinks 9* student resource.
- Each chapter begins with a Get Ready that can be used to help you reinforce the skills you will need to be successful with that chapter.
- The chapter content is divided into sections. Each section starts with a review of the Key Ideas. This is followed by a series of questions that allow you to practise and apply the skills and concepts from that section in the *MathLinks 9* student resource.
- The end of each chapter includes a Chapter Link page that challenges you to combine the skills and concepts you learned during the chapter to solve problems.
- The final page of each chapter is a Vocabulary Link that reviews the key words and other important words from each chapter in the form of a word puzzle of some kind.
- The final spread of each chapter provides a cumulative review. This will reinforce the skills and concepts you learn throughout the *MathLinks 9* program.
- There is a Practice Final Exam for the year starting on page 144.
- Answers for all questions appear at the end of the practice and homework book starting on page 153.

 Additional activities, as well as games and puzzles, are available in McGraw-Hill Ryerson's Online Learning Centre. Go to **www.mathlinks9.ca** and follow the links to the Student Centre or to the Parent Centre. The Parent Centre also includes suggestions for helping your child in mathematics.

Authors
MathLinks 9 Practice and Homework Book

Using Translations

Transformations include translations, reflections, and rotations. A *translation* is a slide along a straight line. The slide can be horizontal, vertical, or oblique.

A'B'C' is used to label the image of ABC after the translation. A'B'C' is read "A prime, B prime, C prime."

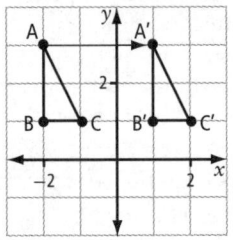

This is a translation 3 units horizontally to the right.

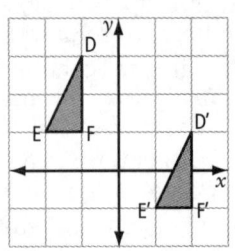

This is a translation 3 units horizontally to the right and 2 units vertically down.

1. Describe the translation.

   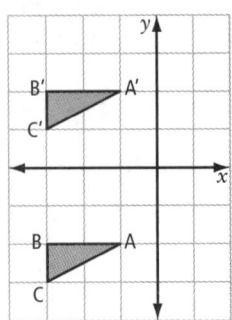

2. If figure PQRS is translated 6 units horizontally to the right, what are the coordinates of P'?

   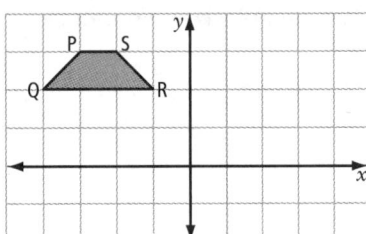

Drawing Reflections

A *reflection* is a mirror image in a line of reflection. A point and its reflection are the same distance from the line of reflection.
The line of reflection here is a horizontal line at $y = 1$.
Both N and N' are 1 unit from the line of reflection.

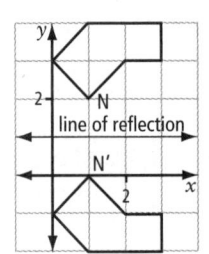

3. Draw the reflection image for each figure.

   a)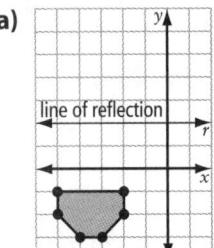

   b)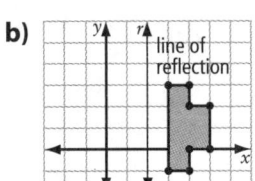

2 MHR • Chapter 1 978-007-097344-2

Drawing Rotations

A *rotation* is a turn about a point or centre of rotation. The rotation can be clockwise or counter-clockwise.
The centre of rotation here is at A.
The rotation is 180° counter-clockwise about A.

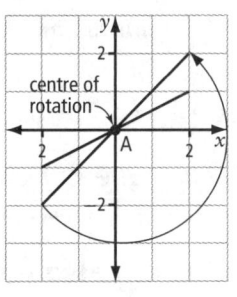

4. Figure DEFG is rotated 90° clockwise about its centre of rotation, A.

   a) Draw the rotation image D'E'F'G'. Label the coordinates.

   b) Describe the rotation if it had been in a counter-clockwise direction.

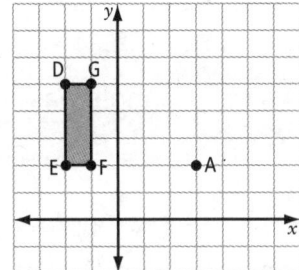

Using Surface Area

Surface area is the sum of the areas of all the faces of a 3-D object.
A right rectangular prism has six faces. Three of its faces are different sizes.
Front and back have the same area: $A = 6 \times 8 = 48$
Top and bottom have the same area: $A = 6 \times 2 = 12$
Two ends have the same area: $A = 2 \times 8 = 16$
Total surface area $= 2(48 + 12 + 16) = 152$
The surface area is 152 cm².

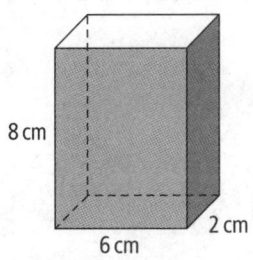

5. Calculate the surface area of the right rectangular prism.

   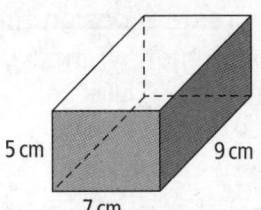

6. How many faces does each solid have?

   a) right triangular prism

   b) cylinder

1.1 Line Symmetry

MathLinks 9, pages 6–15

Key Ideas Review

Decide whether each of the following statements is true or false. Circle the word True or False. If the statement is false, rewrite it to make it true.

1. **True/False** A strategy for completing a symmetric drawing is folding one half in the line of symmetry.

2. **True/False** An isosceles triangle has no line of symmetry.

3. **True/False** You can find a line of symmetry using a grid.

4. **True/False** A shape that has a line of symmetry is asymmetrical.

5. **True/False** A curved shape cannot have lines of symmetry.

Check Your Understanding

6. Draw two lines of symmetry in the following figure.

7. Use the first letter of your name or use a number to create a design that uses at least two lines of symmetry. Example:

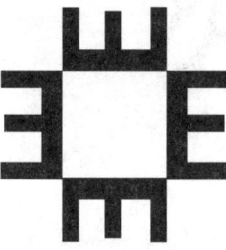

Date: _____

8. How many lines of symmetry does an equilateral triangle have? Show them.

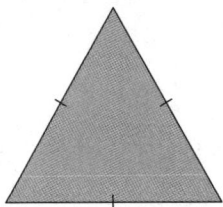

9. a) How many lines of symmetry does a square have? Show them.

   b) How many of the lines are oblique?

10. a) The Olympic rings are a symbol based on five circles. Draw the line or lines of symmetry. How many are there?

   b) When the 1988 Winter Olympic Games were held in Calgary, the organizers used the Olympic rings to create a new design. Draw the line or lines of symmetry. How many are there?

11. Use the coordinate grid to complete the following questions.

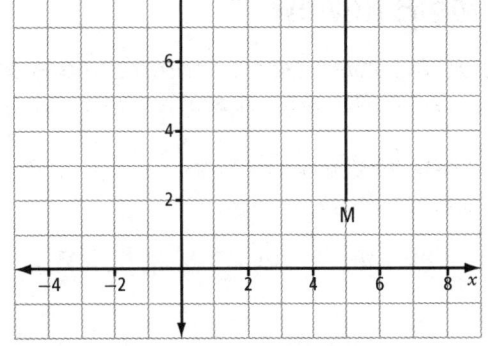

   a) What are the coordinates of figure KLM?

   b) Translate the figure 6 units to the left.

   c) What are the coordinates of the new figure K'L'M'?

   d) Do the original figure and the translated figure show symmetry with each other? Explain.

   e) For the combined image of the original figure and the translated figure, where is the line of symmetry?

1.1 Line Symmetry • MHR 5

1.2 Rotation Symmetry and Transformations

MathLinks 9, pages 16–25

Key Ideas Review

Unscramble the words to complete the sentences below.

1. a) _____ symmetry means that a figure can be turned and fitted over itself.
   NRTAIOTO

   b) The number of times a figure can be placed over itself is called the _____.
   DEORR

   c) A line of _____ divides a figure into two reflected parts.
   YYSRMTEM

   d) A _____ is a point on which a figure turns.
   RETNEC

   e) The number of degrees in a _____ is 360.
   ELCRIC

Check Your Understanding

2. Look at the design shown. Explain if the design has line symmetry, rotation symmetry, or both.

   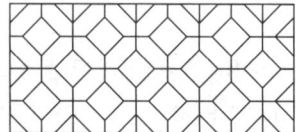

3. Using the design shown above, complete the table.

Shape	Lines of Symmetry	Order of Rotation	Angle of Rotation
Small square			
Octagon			

4. a) Choose a letter from the alphabet. Create a design using this letter at least four times. Repeat using two other letters.

   b) Which letters that you chose have line symmetry? Explain.

   c) Which patterns show rotational symmetry? Justify your response.

 coleann   Date: _____

5. a) Use the figure below to create a tessellation, repeating the figure at least six times to establish the pattern.

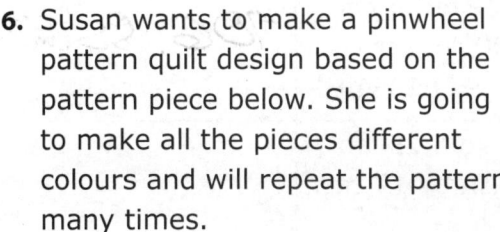

b) Through what angles did you have to turn your figure to rotate it as you built your tessellation?

6. Susan wants to make a pinwheel pattern quilt design based on the pattern piece below. She is going to make all the pieces different colours and will repeat the pattern many times.

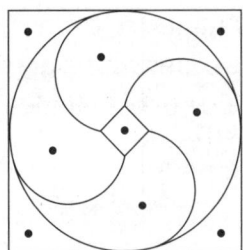

a) Determine the order of rotation for the pattern shown above.

b) Can Susan create a quilt design with more than one type of symmetry? Explain your answer.

7. Draw a large capital letter H on a blank piece of paper. Place a point in the middle of the letter H. Use your point as a centre and turn your letter H on this point.

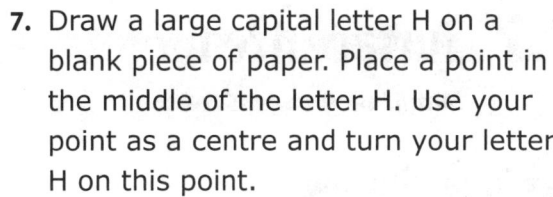

a) What is the order of rotation for the letter H?

b) Fold the letter through the centre point. How many lines of symmetry can you find by folding your letter H?

c) Repeat the exercise using the capital letter X. What is the order of rotation for the letter X?

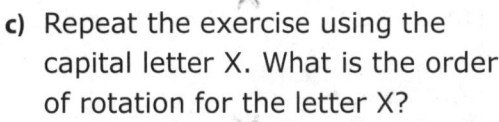

d) How many lines of symmetry can you find by folding your letter X?

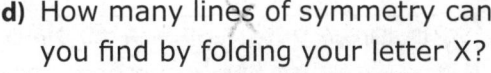

e) What other block letters have rotation symmetry?

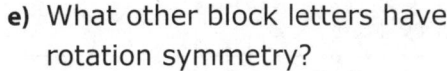

f) What other block letters have line symmetry?

1.2 Rotation Symmetry and Transformations • MHR 7

Date: _____

1.3 Surface Area

MathLinks 9, pages 26–35

Key Ideas Review

1. Complete the chart below, using the first row as a sample. Show your answer to the nearest tenth.

Shape	Formula	Example	Surface Area
Square	$A = l \times w$	One side of a paper napkin: 10 cm by 10 cm	100 cm²
a) Rectangle	$A = l \times w$	One side of an envelope: 30 cm by 22.5 cm	66.6 cm²
b) Circle	$A = \pi r^2$	One side of a clock face: 30 cm across, or radius of 15 cm	706.85 cm²
c) Rectangular prism	$A = 2(\text{area of base}) + (\text{perimeter of base}) \times \text{height}$	Tissue box: 25 cm by 12 cm by 12 cm	
d) Cylinder	$A = 2\pi r^2 + 2\pi r h$	Candle: 15 cm high and 8 cm across	
e) Triangle	$A = \frac{1}{2} b \times h$	End wall of a tent: 2 m along base and 1.5 m high	

2. Define *surface area* in your own words.

Check Your Understanding

3. Which container has the greater surface area? How much more surface area does one have than the other? Show your answer to the nearest tenth.

5 cm
14 cm

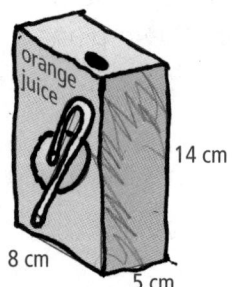
14 cm
8 cm
5 cm

Date: _____

4. The diagram shows a right rectangular prism.

   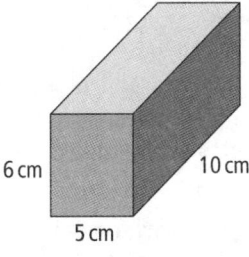

   a) Determine the surface area of the prism.

   b) If the height is doubled, what is the new surface area?

5. Silvio wants to cover the stairs to his basement. There are 14 treads, or steps, and 14 risers. Each step is 90 cm wide and 24 cm deep. Each riser is 90 cm wide and 18 cm high. The diagram shows some of the stairs.

   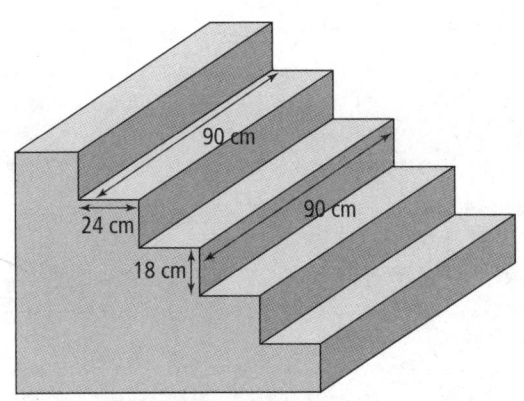

   a) What is the surface area of the step treads?

   b) What is the surface area of the risers?

   c) What is the total surface area of the part of the stairs Silvio plans to cover?

6. The Great Pyramids at Giza, Egypt, are one of the greatest engineering accomplishments ever. The largest pyramid is 146.7 m high. The length of each side of the square base is approximately 230.6 m. Show all answers to the nearest tenth.

   a) What is the surface area of the base of the pyramid?

   b) What is the surface area of each triangular side?

   c) What is the total surface area of the pyramid?

7. The rectangular box has a tube running through it. What is its total surface area to the nearest tenth?

   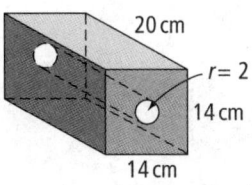

8. a) This object has been constructed from centimetre cubes. Calculate its surface area.

   b) If the length of the object is increased from five cubes to eight cubes, what is the new surface area?

1.3 Surface Area • MHR 9

Chapter Link

You have been hired to create a rug design that will be used in homes all over the country. Your design must
- have at least two lines of symmetry (vertical, horizontal, or oblique)
- have a minimum order of rotation of 2
- use at least two different shapes

Label the dimensions of your design. The design will be repeated to create the finished rug. The finished rug must fit in a room that is 4.5 m by 6.5 m. The design shown here is one example that would meet all criteria. What can you design?

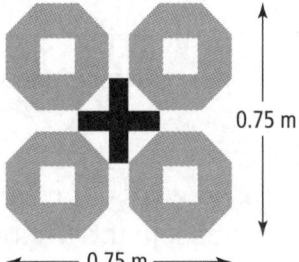

1. How many lines of symmetry does your design have? Show them.

2. What is the order of rotation of your design?

3. What is the maximum number of times your design can be repeated, without exceeding the size of the room?

Vocabulary Link

Unscramble the letters of each term in column B. Use the clues in column A to help you. Each term is one to three words long.

A	B
1. 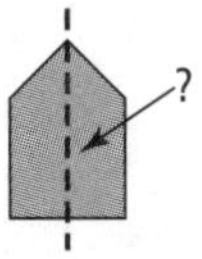	LMYIFYSEMNTOER
2. a type of symmetry in which an image or object can be divided into two identical reflected halves by a line of symmetry	LRYENYSITMEM
3.  this figure has	TINOEOYYRRAMMSTT
4. an object or image has this if it is balanced and can fit onto itself either by reflection or rotation	ERYMMYST
5. 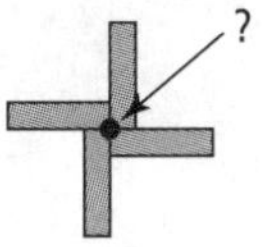	IFOANEROETOTNTRC
6. 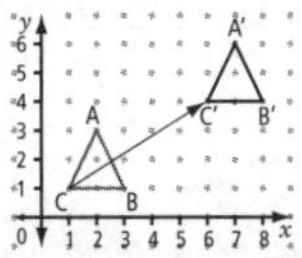 the graph shows a	ANOSRNLAITT
7. the minimum measure of the angle needed to turn a shape or design on itself	NELOOTAGOFAINRT
8. the sum of the areas of all faces of an object	AERUSAFRAEC
9. adjective to describe a shape or design that has symmetry	MSMYRETLIAC

Chapter 1 Review

1. Describe the types of symmetry in each figure. Use the terms *vertical, horizontal, oblique,* and *rotational*.

   a)

   b)
   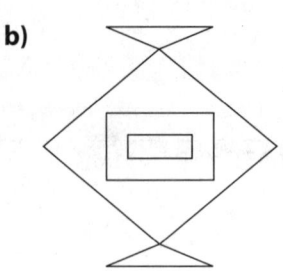

   c) oblique symmetry

   d) rotational symmetry

2. Using the given line of symmetry, complete the drawing.

   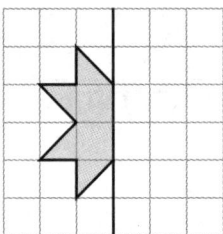

3. Describe each of the following types of symmetry. Make your own sketch of each type. Label the lines of symmetry.

   a) vertical symmetry

   b) horizontal symmetry

4. Does each design have line symmetry, rotation symmetry, both, or neither? For the designs with symmetry, mark the line(s) of symmetry and/or the centre of rotation. For the designs with no symmetry, describe what changes would make the designs symmetrical.

   a)
   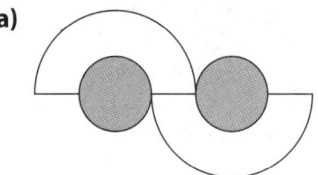

   b)
   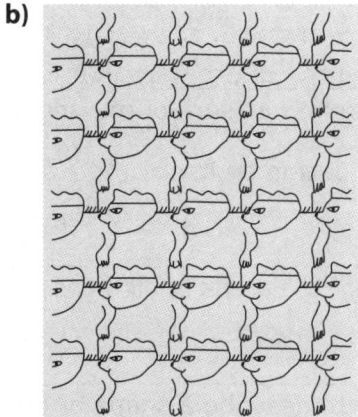

Date: _____

5. A parallelogram was drawn on a coordinate grid.

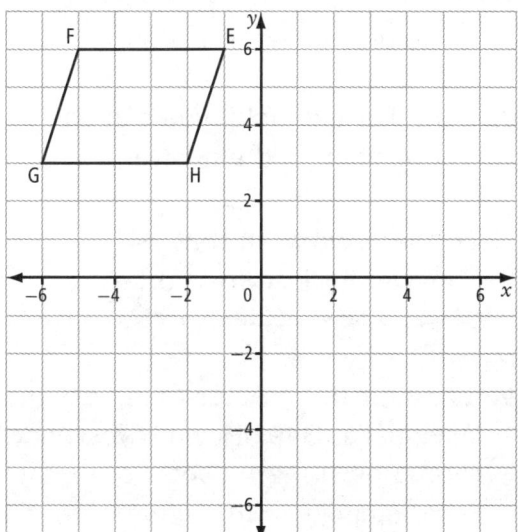

a) Complete the diagram so that it has rotation symmetry of order 2 about the origin. Label the vertices and coordinates of the new image.

b) Use line symmetry to make two new images. First, use the y-axis and then use the x-axis as the line of symmetry. Label the vertices and the coordinates of the vertices of each new image.

6. Calculate the surface area of each of the following shapes. Show your thinking. Show your answer to the nearest tenth, where necessary.

a)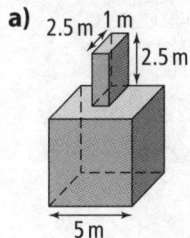

b)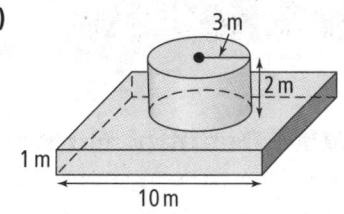

7. A contractor needs to put new siding on a house. There are eight identical windows that measure 1 m by 0.5 m and a door that measures 2.1 m by 0.75 m. Siding does not go on the roof.

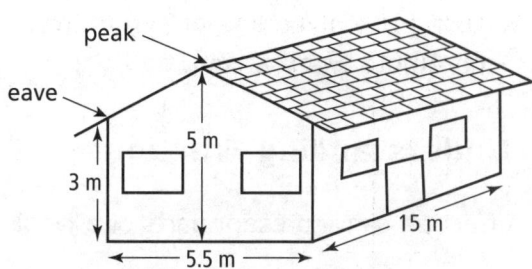

a) What is the area of the house that needs new siding?

b) One piece of siding covers 1 m by 0.1 m. How many pieces of siding does the contractor need? Assume that there is no overlap or wasted material.

Chapter 1 Review • MHR **13**

Working With Decimal Numbers

Estimation can help you work with decimal numbers. For example, you can use estimation to place the decimal point in the correct position in the answer.

16.94 + 3.41 + 81.07 = 10 142
Estimate: 17 + 3 + 80 = 100
Calculation: 101.42

Place the decimal so that the answer is close to 100.

1. Without calculating the answer, place the decimal point in the correct position to make a true statement.

   a) 149.8 ÷ 0.98 = 152.85714

   b) 2.7 × 100.9 = 272.430

   c) 40.6 × 9.61 = 390.16600

2. Is 349 × 0.9 greater than, less than, or equal to 349? How do you know?

   it greater

Understanding Fractions

A fraction can represent parts of a whole.

The shaded part of the diagram shows $\frac{4}{8}$ or $\frac{1}{2}$ or 0.5.

Compare $\frac{3}{8}$ and $\frac{2}{6}$. Use denominators that are the same.

$$\frac{3}{8} \stackrel{\times 3}{=} \frac{9}{24} \qquad \frac{2}{6} \stackrel{\times 4}{=} \frac{8}{24} \qquad \frac{9}{24} > \frac{8}{24}, \text{ therefore } \frac{3}{8} > \frac{2}{6}$$

3. Give the fraction and decimal value for the shaded part of each diagram.

   a)

   b)

4. Compare each set of fractions by arranging them from smallest to largest.

   a) $\frac{3}{4}$ and $\frac{7}{10}$

   b) $\frac{3}{8}, \frac{2}{7},$ and $\frac{1}{3}$

Adding or Subtracting Fractions

When adding or subtracting fractions, work with parts of the whole that are of equal size. You can

- use diagrams

$$\frac{2}{3} + \frac{1}{6}$$
$$= \frac{4}{6} + \frac{1}{6}$$
$$= \frac{5}{6}$$

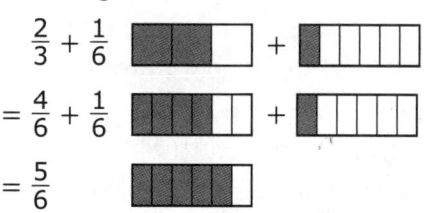

- use a common denominator

$$\frac{2}{3} - \frac{5}{8}$$
$$= \frac{16}{24} - \frac{15}{24}$$
$$= \frac{1}{24}$$

5. Write each statement shown by the fraction strips.

   a)

   b)

6. Determine the sum or difference. Give your answer in lowest terms.

   a) $\frac{1}{2} + \frac{3}{8}$

   b) $\frac{5}{6} - \frac{3}{4}$

Multiplying and Dividing Fractions

To multiply two proper fractions, you can multiply the numerators and multiply the denominators. $\frac{1}{2} \times \frac{2}{3} = \frac{1 \times 2}{2 \times 3}$

$$= \frac{2}{6}$$
$$= \frac{1}{3}$$

To divide two fractions, you can

- use a common denominator and divide the numerators

$$\frac{7}{10} \div \frac{2}{5} = \frac{7}{10} \div \frac{4}{10}$$
$$= \frac{7}{4} \text{ or } 1\frac{3}{4}$$

- multiply by the reciprocal of the second fraction

$$\frac{7}{10} \div \frac{2}{5} = \frac{7}{10} \times \frac{5}{2}$$
$$= \frac{35}{20} \text{ or } \frac{7}{4} \text{ or } 1\frac{3}{4}$$

7. Multiply. Give your answer in lowest terms.

   a) $\frac{3}{4} \times \frac{5}{6}$

   b) $\frac{11}{2} \times \frac{3}{4}$

8. Divide.

   a) $\frac{15}{2} \div \frac{3}{4}$

   b) $1\frac{2}{3} \div \frac{1}{2}$

Get Ready • MHR 15

2.1 Comparing and Ordering Rational Numbers

MathLinks 9, pages 46–54

Key Ideas Review

1. a) Circle the rational number(s).

   (2.1) $-\frac{3}{2}$ (π)   3 $\sqrt{2}$ −55

   b) Circle the numbers that are equivalent to 3.

   $-\frac{9}{3}$ 3.0 $-\left(\frac{-15}{3}\right)$ $\sqrt{9}$ $\frac{-21}{-7}$ $\frac{3}{1}$

Choose from the following rational numbers to complete #2.

$\frac{3}{4}$ −2.1 $\frac{5}{4}$ $\frac{0}{3}$ $-\frac{3}{4}$ 1.8 $-\frac{14}{5}$ $\frac{6}{4}$

2. a) Fill in the blanks to identify the rational numbers.

   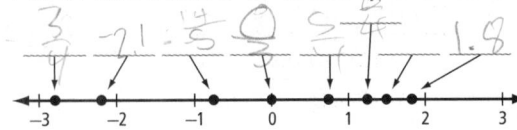

   b) Circle the opposite numbers.

   c) Which rational number lies between 0 and 1? .8

Check Your Understanding

3. Match each rational number to a point on the number line.

   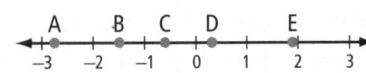

   a) −0.6 C
   b) $-\frac{3}{2}$ B
   c) $-2\frac{3}{4}$ A
   d) 1.9 E
   e) $0.\overline{3}$ D
   f) Explain your thinking.

4. a) Fill in each blank using the correct rational number from the list.

   $\frac{7}{8}$ −2.2 $\frac{11}{6}$ −1.$\overline{1}$ $\frac{10}{8}$

   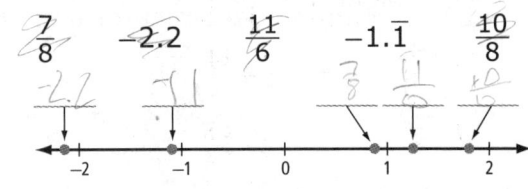

   b) Place the opposite of each number on the number line.

5. What is the opposite of each rational number?

   a) $\frac{3}{2}$ $-\frac{3}{2}$ b) $-6.\overline{8}$ 6.8   c) $-2\frac{1}{5}$ $2\frac{1}{5}$

6. Compare $\frac{9}{8}$, 0.511, $-1\frac{2}{3}$, -1.7, and $\frac{6}{11}$.

   a) Write the fractions in decimal form.

   b) Write the numbers in ascending order.

7. Compare $\frac{5}{6}$, 0.7, $-\frac{12}{5}$, -2.1, and $-1\frac{3}{4}$.

   a) Write the fractions in decimal form.

   b) Write the numbers in descending order.

8. Express each fraction as an equivalent fraction.

   a) $-\frac{3}{4}$ b) $-\frac{4}{6}$

   c) $\frac{12}{8}$ d) $-\frac{5}{3}$

9. Write each rational number as an equivalent fraction.

   a) $\frac{5}{-8}$ b) $\frac{-7}{-9}$

   c) $\frac{-1}{4}$ d) $-\left(\frac{-8}{-7}\right)$

10. Circle the greater value in each pair.

    a) $\frac{1}{3}, -\frac{1}{3}$ b) $-\frac{4}{5}, \frac{3}{5}$

    c) $-1\frac{1}{6}, -1\frac{1}{3}$ d) $-\frac{3}{4}, -\frac{7}{8}$

11. Circle the smaller value in each pair.

    a) $\frac{2}{3}, \frac{4}{5}$ b) $-\frac{5}{6}, -\frac{11}{2}$

    c) $-\frac{5}{4}, -\frac{7}{4}$ d) $-2\frac{4}{5}, -2\frac{5}{6}$

12. Change each fraction to a decimal. Then, identify a decimal number between the given numbers.

    a) $\frac{1}{4}, \frac{1}{8}$

    b) $-\frac{2}{3}, -\frac{4}{5}$

13. The table lists the average low temperature of the coldest month in eight Canadian cities.

City	Average Low (°C)
Winnipeg	−23.6
Regina	−22.1
Edmonton	−17.0
Calgary	−15.7
Vancouver	0.1
Victoria	6.5
Whitehorse	−23.2
Yellowknife	−32.2

    a) Write the temperatures in descending order.

    b) What is the difference in temperature between Victoria and Calgary? Show your work.

14. Fill in each ☐ with >, <, or = to make each statement true. Show your thinking.

    a) $-\frac{3}{4}$ ☐ -0.8 b) $-\frac{5}{3}$ ☐ $-\frac{11}{6}$

    c) -0.81 ☐ $-\frac{4}{5}$ d) $-\left(\frac{-12}{-5}\right)$ ☐ -2.4

2.1 Comparing and Ordering Rational Numbers

2.2 Problem Solving With Rational Numbers in Decimal Form

MathLinks 9, pages 55–62

Key Ideas Review

Circle the correct response to complete each statement.

1. One way to model the subtraction of rational numbers is by (**adding**/subtracting) the opposite on a number line.

2. The product or quotient of two rational numbers with different signs is (positive/**negative**).

3. The product or quotient of two rational numbers with the same sign is (**positive**/negative).

4. The order of operations for calculations involving rational numbers is:

   a) Perform operations inside parentheses (**first**/last).

   b) Divide and (subtract/**multiply**) in order from left to right.

   c) Add and (**subtract**/multiply) in order from left to right.

Check Your Understanding

5. Estimate and calculate. Show your work.

   a) 3.75 − 1.25

   2.50

   b) −7.05 − 10.82

   −17.87

   c) −4.51 + (−9.33)

   −13.84

   d) 8.04 + (−1.25)

   6.76

6. Estimate and calculate. Show your work.

   a) −6.2 × (−4.3)

   24

   b) 16.12 ÷ (−3.1)

   −4

   c) −3.9(8.9)

   −36

7. Calculate. Express your answer to the nearest thousandth, if necessary. Show your work. *calculator

   a) −3.2(7.8)

   −24.96

   b) −6.7 ÷ (−1.3)

   5.1538

   c) −5.7 ÷ 0.34

   −16.7647...

Date: _____

8. Calculate. Show your work.

a) $-3.2(3.6 - 7.1)$

b) $-1.8 \times 6.1 + 3.8(-0.9)$

c) $-2.2[4.8 - (-1.7)]$

d) $9.7 + 4.8 - 19.24 \times 5.2$

e) $(7.04 - 9.26)(9.13 - 4.78)$

f) $8.07 + 3.1[9.5 - (-8.7)]$

9. Samir owns some company shares. The value of each share rose and dropped over a week, as shown in the table. What was the total change in value of each share after the week? Show your work.

Mon	Tues	Wed	Thurs	Fri
+0.21	−0.03	−0.11	−0.09	+0.02

10. Complete each statement.

a) $-12.5 - \square = -5.6$

b) $2.7 + \square = -7.1$

c) $-8.58 \div \square = 3.9$

d) $-3.2 \times \square = 24$

11. Determine the average of each set of numbers. Express your answer to the nearest hundredth, if necessary.

a) −3.6, 0.9, −4.5, −2.7, −0.5, 3.6, 1.7

b) 9.6, −8.9, −12.6, −2.7, −7.5, 23.6

12. The average high temperature in January in Winnipeg is −12.7 °C. In Victoria, it is 6.9 °C.

a) Write an expression to represent the difference between these temperatures.

b) Calculate the answer.

13. A submarine was floating on the surface of the water. It then descended at a rate of 0.5 m/s for 3 min. Then, it ascended at a rate of 0.7 m/s for 1 min and 15 s.

a) Write an expression to determine the depth of the submarine after these two moves.

b) Calculate the answer. Show your work.

2.3 Problem Solving With Rational Numbers in Fraction Form

MathLinks 9, pages 63–71

Key Ideas Review

Select words from column B to complete the statements in column A.

A	B
1. The addition of rational numbers can be modelled on a ___e___.	a) adding the opposite
2. Subtraction can be modelled on a number line by ___c___.	b) improper fractions
3. Rational numbers expressed as mixed numbers can be added, subtracted, multiplied, and divided by first writing them as ___b___.	c) multiplication and division
4. Rational numbers expressed as proper or improper fractions can be added, subtracted, multiplied, and divided in the same way as ___d___.	d) positive fractions
5. The sign of the product or quotient can be predicted from the sign rules for ___a___.	e) number line

Check Your Understanding

6. Estimate and calculate. Show your work.

a) $-\frac{3}{10} + \left(-\frac{7}{10}\right)$

$\frac{-3 + -7}{10} = \frac{-10}{10} = -1$

b) $\frac{1}{3} + \frac{5}{6}$

$\frac{2}{6} + \frac{5}{6} = 1\frac{1}{6}$

c) $3\frac{1}{2} + \left(-1\frac{3}{4}\right)$

$\frac{7}{2} + \frac{-7}{4}$

$\frac{14}{4} + \frac{-7}{4} = \frac{7}{4}$ → $1\frac{3}{4}$

d) $3\frac{1}{4} - \left(-4\frac{5}{12}\right)$

$\frac{13}{4} - \frac{-43}{12}$

$\frac{39}{12} + \frac{43}{12} = \frac{30}{12}$ ... $2\frac{6}{12}$

7. Estimate and calculate. Show your work.

a) $\left(-\frac{3}{5}\right) \times \frac{2}{3} = \frac{-6}{15}$ → $\frac{-2}{5}$

b) $\left(-\frac{4}{9}\right) \times \left(-\frac{3}{8}\right) = \frac{-12}{72}$

c) $\left(-\frac{6}{7}\right)\left(-\frac{5}{12}\right) = \frac{30}{84}$

d) $-\frac{5}{6} \times 2\frac{1}{4}$

$\frac{5}{6} \times \frac{9}{4} = \frac{-45}{24}$

20 MHR • Chapter 2 978-0-07-097344-2

8. Estimate and calculate. Show your work.

   a) $-\frac{7}{8} \div -\frac{3}{4}$

   b) $1\frac{1}{2} \div \left(-1\frac{3}{8}\right)$

   c) $-3\frac{2}{3} \div \left(-1\frac{1}{6}\right)$

   d) $\frac{1}{3} \div \frac{3}{4}$

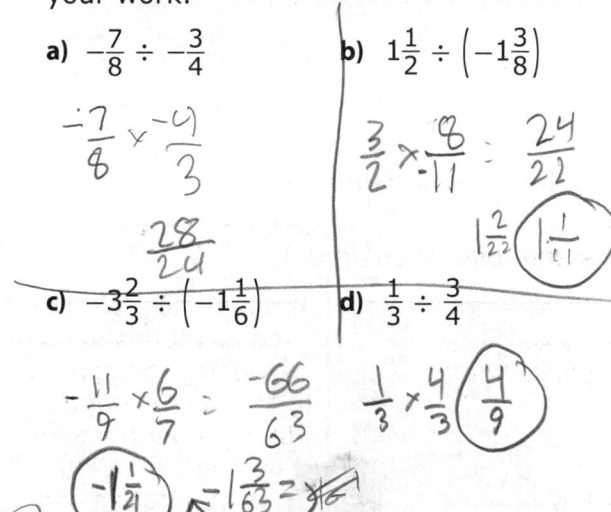

9. Luc has 1 h of homework to do. He has assignments to complete for social studies and math, and a science test to begin studying for. He spends $\frac{2}{5}$ of the time completing the social studies assignment, and $\frac{1}{3}$ of the time on math. How much time does Luc have left to study for the science test? Show two ways of answering this question.

10. Alyssa purchased 120 shares of ElecTeck stock for $1\frac{1}{4}$ dollars per share. She also purchased 200 shares of Apexal stock for $\frac{4}{5}$ of a dollar per share. After six months, the value of ElecTeck stock went up by $1\frac{1}{2}$ and Apexal lost $\frac{1}{4}$ of its value. What was the total value of Alyssa's stock after six months?

11. A pine tree growing on shallow soil has roots extend one-eleventh of its height below the surface. The roots extend 0.87 m deep. How high is the tree, to the nearest tenth? Draw a diagram to represent the situation. Justify your answer.

2.4 Determining Square Roots of Rational Numbers

MathLinks 9, pages 72–81

Key Ideas Review

Select words from column B to complete the statements in column A.

A	B
1. The side of a square is equal to _____ e _____.	a) the product of two equal rational factors
2. The area of a square is equal to _____ d _____.	b) an exact answer
3. The square root of a perfect square is _____ c _____.	c) an approximation
4. The square root of a non-perfect square determined with a calculator is _____ b _____.	d) the square root of the area
5. A perfect square can be expressed as _____ a _____.	e) the square of the side

Check Your Understanding

6. a) Use the diagram to identify a rational number with a square root between 5 and 6.

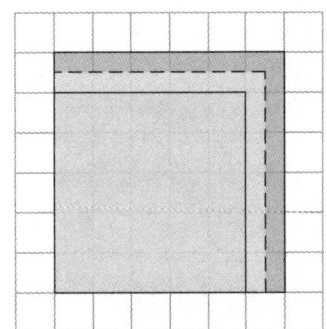

   b) Using the same thinking, what rational number has a square root between 3 and 4?

7. Estimate and calculate the number that has the given square root.

   a) 2.2 (6)   b) 8.7 (7%)
   2 = 4   9 = 81

   c) 11.3 (124)   d) 0.92 (.83)
   11 = 121

8. Estimate and calculate the area of each square, given its side length.

   a) 14.7 cm   b) 2.3 km
   14.7×14.7   2.3×2.3
                  ≈ 7

9. Is each of the following rational numbers a perfect square? Explain.
   a) $\frac{4}{9}$
   b) 0.4
   c) 0.81
   d) $\frac{1}{2}$

10. Determine whether each rational number is a perfect square. Show your thinking.
    a) 0.16
    b) $\frac{90}{49}$
    c) 0.001
    d) $\frac{8}{18}$

11. Evaluate.
    a) $\sqrt{289}$
    b) $\sqrt{0.0361}$
    c) $\sqrt{1225}$
    d) $\sqrt{5.29}$

12. Calculate the side length of each square from its area.
    a) 2.25 cm²
    b) 361 m²

13. Calculate each square root.
    a) $\sqrt{25}$, $\sqrt{36}$
    b) $\sqrt{49}$, $\sqrt{64}$
    c) $\sqrt{0.16}$, $\sqrt{0.25}$
    d) $\sqrt{0.64}$, $\sqrt{0.81}$

14. Use your answers to #13 to help estimate each square root to the specified number of decimal places.
    a) $\sqrt{30}$, to the nearest tenth
    b) $\sqrt{52}$, to the nearest tenth
    c) $\sqrt{0.18}$, to the nearest hundredth
    d) $\sqrt{0.78}$, to the nearest hundredth

15. A water fountain has a square pool with a surface area of 5.29 m². What is the length of the side of the pool?

16. A square has an area of 225 cm². What is the radius of the largest circle that can fit inside the square? Show your thinking.

17. Chu needs carpet for a square room with an area of 15 m². The store sells carpet from rolls 3.8 m wide. Will the store be able to install the carpet without a seam? Justify your answer.

Chapter Link

Ken has trouble sleeping and is trying some new strategies to get a better night's rest. Answer the questions below to help him evaluate his progress.

1. Experts say adults should sleep about $\frac{3}{8}$ of a 24-h day. How many hours of sleep are recommended?

2. Ken's doctor is reviewing his sleep record for the last week.

Monday	$\frac{2}{3}$ the recommended sleep
Tuesday	7.5 h
Wednesday	$\frac{3}{4}$ of the recommended sleep
Thursday	$4\frac{2}{8}$ h
Friday	6 h 30 min
Saturday	$\frac{9}{10}$ of the recommended sleep
Sunday	$\frac{4}{9}$ of the recommended sleep

   a) Arrange the values from longest sleep to shortest. Show your thinking.

   b) On what day did Ken get the most sleep?

3. A new bed may help Ken's sleep. He is admiring a square king-size bed that has sides $1\frac{9}{10}$ m long.

   a) Estimate, then calculate, whether the bed will fit in his square bedroom with an area of $11\frac{11}{50}$ m².

   b) Ken can choose from the following square rugs.
   - flower rug: 10 m²
   - checker rug: 4-m sides
   - geometric rug: $\frac{22}{10}$-m sides

   Which one will stick out beyond the sides of the bed and still fit in the room? Explain.

4. Now that Ken is sleeping the recommended amount, he would like to make up the loss of sleep he recorded. How much extra sleep will he have to get each day over the next two weeks? Calculate the answer to the nearest minute.

Vocabulary Link

Use the clues to identify the Key Words from Chapter 2. Then, write the Key Words in the crossword puzzle blank.

Across

6. These cannot be expressed as the product of two equal rational numbers. Examples include 7, 8, 3.5, and $\frac{11}{13}$.

Down

1. One set of these includes $\frac{24}{-6}$, $\frac{-32}{8}$, -4, and $-\left(\frac{-4}{-1}\right)$.

2. This is another name for brackets.

3. This is an answer to a division question.

4. Examples of this include -3, 4.5, $-\frac{1}{3}$, $2\frac{7}{13}$, and 0.

5. Examples of this include 0.36, 0.49, $\frac{16}{25}$, and $\frac{49}{81}$.

Chapters 1–2 Review

1. Compare 2.5, $-\frac{7}{4}$, $-3\frac{2}{5}$, $1\frac{1}{3}$, -0.7, and -2. Write the numbers in ascending order. Show your thinking.

2. Draw the lines of symmetry in the following figure. Identify each type of symmetry. If there is rotational symmetry, name the order and the size of the angle of rotation.

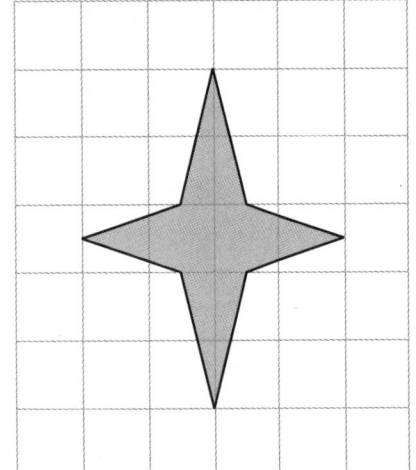

3. Replace each ☐ with >, <, or = to make each statement true.

   a) $-\frac{1}{3}$ ☐ -0.3

   b) $1\frac{5}{8}$ ☐ $\frac{-13}{-8}$

   c) $-\frac{10}{15}$ ☐ $-\frac{12}{16}$

   d) 1.75 ☐ $\frac{17}{10}$

   e) $-\frac{8}{6}$ ☐ $-\frac{4}{3}$

4. Use the coordinate grid to complete the following questions.

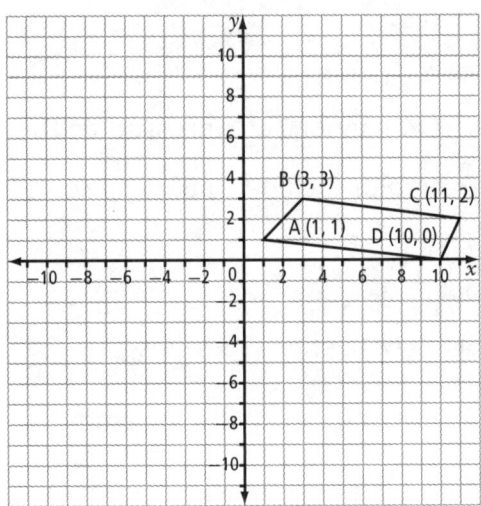

   a) What are the coordinates of figure ABCD?

   b) Rotate the figure about point A order 2.

   c) What are the coordinates of the new figure A'B'C'D'?

5. On January 15, 1972, Chinook winds in Loma, Montana caused the greatest recorded temperature change in 24 hours. The temperature rose from −48 °C to 9 °C. How many degrees did the temperature rise?

Date: _____

6. Estimate and Calculate.

   a) $-1.3 \times 2.4 + 5.6 \times (-2.5)$

   b) $(5.76 - 3.45)(2.34 - 1.57)$

7. Estimate.

   a) $\frac{2}{3} + \frac{1}{6}$ b) $-1\frac{1}{7} - \left(-2\frac{1}{5}\right)$

   c) $-\frac{7}{4} + \frac{1}{8}$ d) $-\frac{2}{9} - \frac{2}{9}$

8. Calculate.

   a) $\frac{4}{7} \div \frac{7}{8}$ b) $\left(2\frac{2}{3}\right)\left(1\frac{2}{5}\right)$

   c) $\left(-1\frac{2}{5}\right) \div \left(3\frac{1}{2}\right)$ d) $-\frac{3}{4} \times \left(-\frac{2}{5}\right)$

9. This shape was constructed out of centimetre cubes and a triangular wedge. Calculate the exposed surface area of the entire shape.

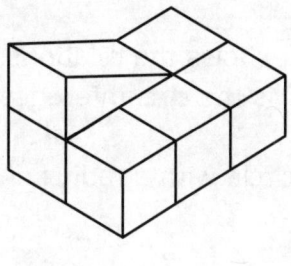

10. Quentin has 96 retaining wall blocks. He uses $\frac{1}{4}$ of the blocks on the first day. The second day he uses $\frac{4}{9}$ of the remaining amount. How many does he have left over? Show your thinking.

11. Is each of the following numbers a perfect square? If it is, calculate the square root.

    a) $\frac{1}{25}$ c) 0.0001

    b) $\frac{7}{16}$ d) 0.49

12. Estimate each square root. Then, calculate it to the specified number of decimal places.

    a) $\sqrt{52}$, to the nearest tenth

    b) $\sqrt{0.67}$, to the nearest thousandth

13. You need to replace the fence in your backyard. It costs $75 to build each metre of fence, including new materials and labour.

    a) If your garden is square with an area of 18 m², how much would it cost to replace the entire fence?

    b) Can you enclose a larger area without paying for more fencing? Why or why not?

Date: _____

Squares and Square Roots

You can think of the *square* of a number as the area of a square.

Area is $3^2 = 3 \times 3$
$ = 9$

The area is 9 cm².

You can think of the *square root* of a number as the side length of a square.

$s = \sqrt{16}$
$ = 4$

The side length is 4 cm.

1. What is the area of each square?

   a)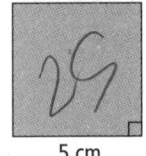
   5 cm

   b)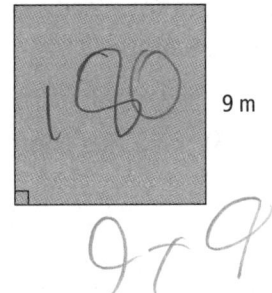
   9 m

2. What is the side length of each square?

   a)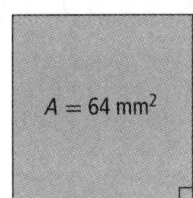
   $A = 64 \text{ mm}^2$

   b) area of 36 cm²

Substituting Into Formulas

A formula is a mathematical statement that shows the relationship between specific quantities. An example is $C = 2\pi r$, where C is the circumference and r is the radius of a circle.

What are the circumference and area of a circle with a radius of 10 cm?
Use 3.14 as an approximate value for π.

$$C = 2\pi r \qquad\qquad A = \pi r^2$$
$$ = 2\pi(10) \qquad\qquad = \pi(10)^2$$
$$ \approx 20(3.14) \qquad\qquad \approx 3.14(100)$$
$$ \approx 62.8 \qquad\qquad \approx 314$$

The circumference is approximately 62.8 cm. The area is approximately 314 cm².

3. When a certain chemical is added to water, the water gets hotter. A formula for the water's temperature, t, in degrees Celsius, is $t = 24 + 8m$, where m is the amount of chemical added, in kilograms. Complete the following table of values for the missing values of m and t.

m (kg)	0	12	5	8	9
t (°C)		48		72	81

Volume and Surface Area

You can determine the volume, V, of a right prism using the formula $V = Ah$, where A is the area of the base and h is the height of the prism.

What is the volume of the rectangular prism?

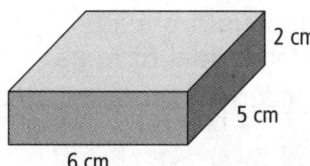

$A = (5)(6)$
$\quad = 30$
$h = 2$
$V = Ah$
$\quad = 30(2)$
$\quad = 60$

The volume of the prism is 60 cm³.

4. Determine the volume of the rectangular prism.

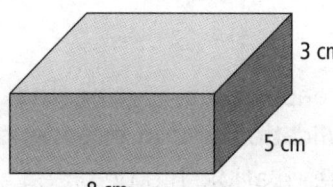

$8 \times 5 \times 3$
15×9
$\overline{112}$

5. Determine the volume of the triangular prism.

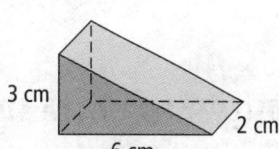

$6 \times 2 = 12 \text{ cm}^3$
$= 36$

3.1 Using Exponents to Describe Numbers
MathLinks 9, pages 92–98

Key Ideas Review
Choose from the following terms to complete #1.

base   exponent   multiplication   power

1. a) A __power__ is a short way to express repeated __multiplication__.

   b) In a power, the __exponent__ represents the number of times you multiply the __base__.

Check Your Understanding

2. Write each expression as a power. Then, evaluate.

   a) $3 \times 3 \times 3 \times 3$ $3^4 = 81$

   b) $(-5) \times (-5) \times (-5)$ $(-5)^3 = 125$

   c) $2 \times 2 \times 2 \times 2 \times 2 \times 2 \times 2 \times 2 \times 2$
   $2^9 = 512$

3. Write each expression as a power and evaluate.

   a) $4 \times 4 \times 4$ $4^3 = 68$

   b) $(-7) \times (-7) \times (-7) \times (-7)$
   $(-7)^4$

   c) $8 \times 8 \times 8$
   $8^3 =$
   64

4. Rewrite each exponential form as repeated multiplication, then evaluate.

   a) 6^3
   $6 \times 6 \times 6 = 133$

   b) $(-10)^5$
   $(-10) \times (-10) \times (-10) \times (-10) \times (-10)$

   c) -4^4
   $-4 \times -4 \times -4 \times -4$

5. Show each value as repeated multiplication and in exponential form.

   a) 81 9×9

   b) 256
   2^9

6. What alternative answers can you suggest for #5?
   a. $3 \times 3 \times 3 \times 3$

   b

7. Evaluate each power.
   a) 4^5 $4 \times 4 \times 4 \times 4 \times 4$
   b) $(-5)^4$ $(-5)^4 \times (-5)^4 \times (-5)^4$
   c) -8^2 -8×-8

8. Does $-3^6 = (-3)^6$? Explain how you know.

   no second has brackets

9. Write the volume of the cube in exponential form. Then, evaluate.

   8 mm

   $8 \times 8 \times 8$
   $8^3 = 468$

10. Arrange the powers from greatest to least value: $5^2, 4^3, 3^4, 2^5$. Show your thinking.

    $2^5, 4^2, 3^4, 5^2$

11. Explain why 45 cannot be expressed as a power in the form y^x.

    five is not an exponent

12. Michelle will load and unload the dishwasher every day of the week. In return, her parents will pay her 2¢ for the first week, and twice as much as the previous week for each week thereafter. Use the expression 2^w to determine her weekly rate of pay, where w represents the number of weeks. How much will she earn, in dollars, in week 7, week 15, week 25, and week 30?

13. The volume of a cube with an edge length of 9 cm is 729 cm³. Write the volume in repeated multiplication form and exponential form.

    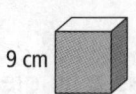
    9 cm

3.1 Using Exponents to Describe Numbers • MHR 31

Date: _____

3.2 Exponent Laws
MathLinks 9, pages 99–107

Key Ideas Review

Match each exponent law in column A to an equation in column B.

A	B
1. You can simplify a quotient of powers with the same base by subtracting the exponents.	a) $(a \times b)^m = a^m \times b^m$
2. You can simplify a power that is raised to an exponent by multiplying the two exponents.	b) $a^m \div a^n = a^{m-n}$
	c) $a^0 = 1, a \neq 0$
3. When a product is raised to an exponent, you can rewrite each number in the product with the same exponent.	d) $(a^m)^n = a^{mn}$
4. When the exponent of a power is 0, the value of the power is 1 if the base is not equal to 0.	

Check Your Understanding

5. Write each expression as a single power. Then, evaluate.

  a) $3^2 \times 3^3$ b) $(-2)^4 \times (-2)^3$

  c) $4 \times 4^3 \times 4^4$ d) $[(-3)^2]^4$

6. Rewrite each expression as a single power. Then, evaluate.

  a) $7^6 \div 7^4$ b) $(-5)^8 \div (-5)^5$

  c) $\dfrac{8^2 \times 8^7}{8^5}$ d) $\dfrac{(-6)^2(-6)^4}{(-6)^3}$

7. Write each expression in exponential form.

  a) $(5 \times 5 \times 5) \times (5 \times 5 \times 5) \times (5 \times 5 \times 5) \times (5 \times 5 \times 5)$

  b) $[(-9) \times (-9)] \times [(-9) \times (-9)] \times [(-9) \times (-9)] \times [(-9) \times (-9)] \times [(-9) \times (-9)]$

8. Write each expression as a quotient of two powers, and then as a single power.

  a) $(5 \times 5 \times 5 \times 5) \div (5 \times 5 \times 5)$

  b) $\dfrac{(-2) \times (-2) \times (-2) \times (-2) \times (-2) \times (-2)}{(-2) \times (-2) \times (-2) \times (-2)}$

9. Tony was asked to solve $\dfrac{6^8 \times 6^4}{6^2}$. Find and explain the mistake in his solution. What is the correct answer?

$$\dfrac{6^8 \times 6^4}{6^2} = \dfrac{6^{8+4}}{6^2}$$
$$= \dfrac{6^{12}}{6^2}$$
$$= 6^{12} \div 2$$
$$= 6^6$$
$$= 46656$$

12. The province of Saskatchewan has a population of approximately 1 million (10^6). There are approximately 100 billion (10^{11}) cells in the human body. Estimate the number of human cells in Saskatchewan. Write your answer in exponential and standard form.

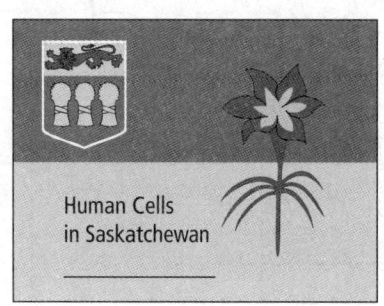

Human Cells in Saskatchewan

10. Using $\dfrac{4^3}{4^3} = 4^{3-3}$ as an example, explain the exponent rule $b^0 = 1$, $b \neq 0$.

13. Write three different products. Each product must be made up of two powers and must be equal to 6^7. Justify your choices.

11. a) Write $(5^2)^3$ as a single power. Evaluate.

   b) Write $[(-4)^3]^2$ as a single power. Evaluate.

3.3 Order of Operations

MathLinks 9, pages 108–113

Key Ideas Review

1. Use the following words to label the table headings. Then, complete the table.

coefficient　　power　　repeated multiplication　　value

Expression	coefficient	power	repeated multiplication	value
$-3(7)^2$	-3	7^2	$-3 \times 7 \times 7$	-147
$2(5)^4$				

2. Column A shows the solution to $5(-2) - (2 + 4)^2$. Match each step in column A to its description in column B.

A	B
Step 1 $= 5(-2) - (6)^2$	a) Evaluate the power.
Step 2 $= 5(-2) - 36$	b) Add and subtract from left to right.
Step 3 $= -10 - 36$	c) Simplify inside the brackets.
Step 4 $= -46$	d) Divide and multiply from left to right.

Check Your Understanding

3. Evaluate each expression.

　a) $3(6)^2$

　b) $2(-4)^2$

　c) $7(10)^5$

　d) $4(-3)^3$

4. Write each expression using a coefficient and a power.

　a) $2 \times 3 \times 3 \times 3$

　b) $5 \times (-7) \times (-7) \times (-7) \times (-7) \times (-7)$

　c) $-2 \times 8 \times 8 \times 8 \times 8$

　d) $6(9)(9)(9)(9)$

5. Evaluate. Where necessary, express your answer to the nearest tenth.

   a) $5^2 - 3^2$

   b) $7 + 3(-2)^3$

   c) $4 - (2 + 3)^2 \div 25$

   d) $45 \div (-2)^6$

6. Identify the step where Susan made an error. Explain her mistake. What is the correct answer?

   $12 + 2(3 + 5)^2$

   $= 12 + 2(8)^2$ Step 1

   $= 12 + 2(16)$ Step 2

   $= 12 + 32$ Step 3

   $= 44$ Step 4

7. Evaluate.

   a) $-5(2 + 5^2) + (-4)^3$

   b) $[(-7)^2 - (-2)^6]^2$

   c) $\dfrac{-16 + (-3)^2}{(6 - 2)^2 - (-4)^2}$

   d) $5(4)^3 \div (-2)^4$

8. Evaluate the expression $7a^2 - 3b^3$ when

   a) $a = 4, b = -2$ b) $a = -8, b = 5$

9. Write an expression with powers to determine the difference between the surface areas of the two cubes. Then, solve.

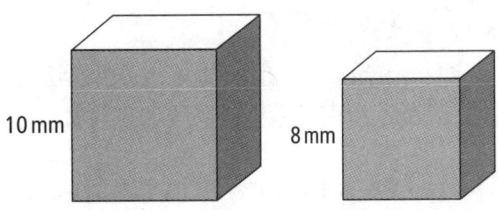

10. The cube of the sum of 5 and 2 is decreased by the square of the product of 6 and 4. Write an expression that models this statement. Then, solve.

11. a) Evaluate -5^2 and $(-5)^2$.

    b) Using the words *coefficient*, *base*, and *exponent*, explain why the two answers are not the same.

3.4 Using Exponents to Solve Problems
MathLinks 9, pages 114–119

Key Ideas Review

Decide whether each of the following statements is true or false. Circle the word True or False. If the statement is false, rewrite it to make it true.

1. **True/False** A power in a formula represents a measurement.

   _____
   _____

2. **True/False** Powers are often used to keep formulas as short as possible.

   _____
   _____

3. **True/False** Patterns involving repeated multiplication can be modelled by an expression that contains only coefficients.

   Patterns involving Repeated multiplication can be modelled by a power

Check Your Understanding

4. What is the surface area of a cube with an edge length of 12 cm? Write an exponential expression to solve the problem.

   $6(12 \times 12)$ $SA = 864$

   $6(144)$

5. What is the length of the missing leg of the right triangle? Write an exponential expression to solve the problem.

   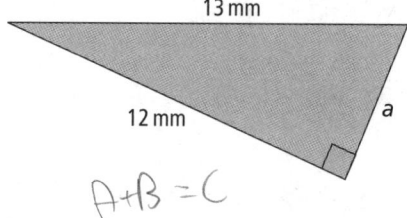

   $A + B = C$

6. Right now there are 100 bacteria in sample P. This population doubles every hour. How many bacteria will there be after each number of hours?

   a) n

   b) 5

   c) 10

7. Due to Earth's curvature, objects, like the setting sun, seem to disappear over the horizon. The taller you are, the farther away the horizon appears to be. The formula $h = \frac{d^2}{12.8}$ is used to determine distance, d, in kilometres, to the horizon based on a person's height, h, in metres, above the ground. How tall is someone to whom the horizon appears to be 5.06 km away? Express your answer to the nearest metre.

8. Write an exponential expression to determine the shaded area inside the square. Then, solve. Express your answer to the nearest tenth.

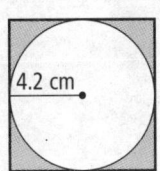

4.2 cm

9. Simplify each formula using exponential notation.

   a) Surface area of a cube: $6 \times s \times s$

   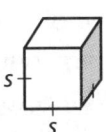

   b) Pythagorean theorem: $h \times h = a \times a + b \times b$

   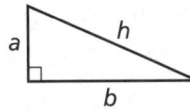

   c) Volume of a cube: $s \times s \times s$

   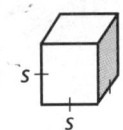

10. Use your answers to #9 to complete the table.

Power(s)	Base(s)	Exponent(s)	Coefficient
a)			
b)			
c)			

11. A large playground cube has sides 1.5 m long.

    a) Calculate the volume of the cube to the nearest hundredth.

    b) Calculate the surface area of the cube that would have to be painted if one end is open and both the inside and outside are painted. Express your answer to the nearest tenth.

3.4 Using Exponents to Solve Problems

Chapter Link

The two bacteria that a microbiologist is studying reproduce at different exponential rates as long as conditions are appropriate. Sample A starts with just 50 bacteria. The population triples every hour. Sample B starts with 600 bacteria and doubles every hour.

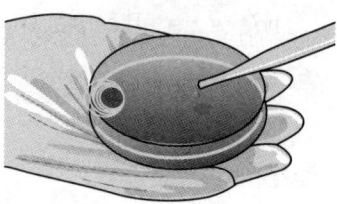

1. Create a chart to show the numbers of bacteria in each sample after 0 to 8 h.

2. Fill in the blanks.

   a) The expression 50 × 3 × 3 × 3 × 3 × 3 × 3 models the number of bacteria in sample _____ after _____ hours.

   b) Write the expression in exponential form.

   c) What number represents the coefficient?

3. What expression models the number of bacteria after a number of hours, n,

   a) in sample A?

   b) in sample B?

4. Use the chart to estimate the time when both samples will have the same number of bacteria. Explain your reasoning.

5. a) Write an exponential expression to determine the difference between the numbers of bacteria in sample A and sample B after 5 h.

   b) Solve the expression. Then, check your answer using values from the chart.

6. What is the sum of the bacteria in both samples after each number of hours?

   a) n

   b) 6

   c) 10

Vocabulary Link

Use the clues to identify the Key Words from Chapter 3. Then, write the Key Words in the crossword puzzle blank.

Across

5. This is one term for a shorter way of writing repeated multiplication, using a base and an exponent.

Down

1. This is another term for repeated multiplication such as $5^3 \times 5^2 = (5 \times 5 \times 5) \times (5 \times 5)$.

2. This is the term for an expression made up of a base and an exponent, such as 6^4.

3. This refers to the number of times you multiply the base in a power. For example, in 6^4, 4 is one of these.

4. This is the number you multiply by itself in a power. For example, in 9^5, 9 is one of these.

Chapters 1–3 Review

1. Write $3^3 \times (3^4)^2 \div 3$ as a single power. Then, evaluate.

2. What type(s) of line symmetry does this gym floor have? Show them.

   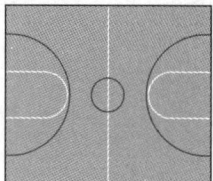

3. Identify three rational numbers between the given endpoints. For each pair of endpoints, sketch a number line to illustrate.

   a) 1.37 and −2.56

   b) −0.6 and −0.61

   c) $\frac{-2}{3}$ and $\frac{1}{6}$

4. Evaluate.

   a) $8^2 + (3^3 - 2^2)^2(4^2 - 2^4)$

   b) $(-1)^3(-60)^0 - \left(\frac{5}{6}\right)^2$

   c) $\dfrac{[-5(-2)]^2 - 9^3 \div 3^2\left(\frac{2}{7}\right)^0}{(-13 + 4^2)^5}$

5. Does this picture have rotational symmetry? If so, state the order and angle of rotation.

6. Evaluate.

   a) $\left(-4\frac{1}{3}\right) + \left(-\frac{1}{2}\right) \times 3\frac{1}{5}$

   b) $1\frac{1}{7} \times \left(-2\frac{5}{6}\right) + \frac{3}{8}$

   c) $-5 \div \left(-\frac{2}{3}\right) + \left(-\frac{5}{9}\right) \times 2\frac{1}{2}$

   d) $3\frac{3}{8} - \left(-2\frac{1}{3} + 4\right)\left(-2\frac{1}{3} + 4\right)$

7. Rewrite each expression using powers. Then, evaluate.

   a) $(-4)(-4)(-4) + (-3)(-3)$

   b) $[5 \times 5 \times 2 \times 2 \times (-1) \times (-1) \times (-1)] [5 \times 5 \times 2 \times 2 \times (-1) \times (-1) \times (-1)] \div (5 \times 5 \times 5)$

8. a) Determine the surface area of the rectangular prism.

   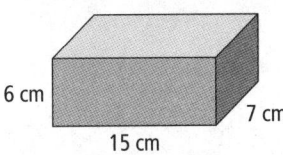

   b) Determine the surface area of the cylinder. Express your answer to the nearest hundredth.

   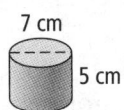

   c) The cylinder is placed on top of the rectangular prism. What is the new surface area? How is it different from when the shapes were separate?

   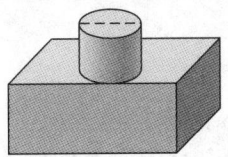

9. A school is having a badminton tournament for all of its grade 9 students. There are 160 students. During each round, r, half the players are eliminated. This situation can be represented by $p = 160(0.5)^r$. How many players, p, remain after five rounds?

10. Evaluate. Express your answer to the nearest hundredth where appropriate.

    a) $1.5 + (-3.6) \div (-1.4) - 7.2$

    b) $(-1.5) \times 0.8 - (-3.2)(-3.2)$

    c) $\dfrac{5.6(-4.5 + 33.4)^3 + 5.6}{(-4.3) \div 0.03 - 0.3}$

11. Mandy wants to wallpaper her room. The dimensions of the floor are 5.2 m by 3.1 m. The walls are 2.5 m high. There is one window that is 1.2 m by 2.5 m. Her closet door and bedroom door are both 2.2 m by 0.75 m in dimension.

    a) What is the total surface area that Mandy will wallpaper? Use a diagram to help you.

    b) One roll of wallpaper covers 5.2 m². How many rolls of wallpaper does Mandy need?

Using Two-Term Ratios

A *part-to-part ratio* compares different parts of a group to each other.
The ratio of white circles to grey circles is 6:3 or 6 to 3.
The ratio in lowest terms is 2:1 or 2 to 1.
A *part-to-whole ratio* compares one part of a group to the whole group.
The ratio of white circles to the total number of circles is 6:9 or 6 to 9.
The ratio in lowest terms is 2:3 or 2 to 3.
A part-to-whole ratio can be written as a fraction, a decimal, and a percent.
The ratio of $\frac{grey}{total}$ is $\frac{3}{9}$ or $\frac{1}{3}$, $0.\overline{3}$, $33.\overline{3}\%$.

1. For each regular polygon, what is the ratio of one side length to the perimeter? Use ratio notation.

   a)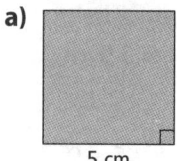
   5 cm

   b)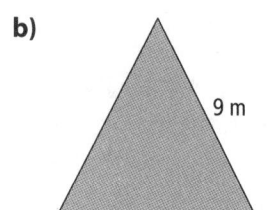
   9 m

   c)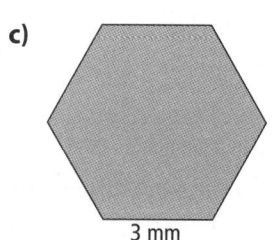
   3 mm

2. Write each ratio in #1 as an equivalent ratio in lowest terms. Show your thinking.

3. Write each ratio in #1 as a decimal and a percent. Show your calculations.

4. Identify the missing value to make an equivalent fraction. Justify your response.

   a) $\frac{3}{4} = \frac{\square}{8}$

   b) $\frac{4}{7} = \frac{12}{\square}$

   c) $\frac{\square}{5} = \frac{3}{15}$

   d) $\frac{7}{\square} = \frac{49}{14}$

Using Proportional Reasoning

A *proportion* is a relationship that says two ratios are equal.
A proportion can be expressed in fraction form.

5. Set up a proportion for each situation.

   a) On a diagram of a machine part, 2 cm represents 200 cm. The actual length of the part is 100 cm. This distance is 1 cm on the diagram.

   b) On a map, 1 cm represents 500 m. Linda wants to ride her bike 3500 m. This distance is 7 cm on the map.

   c) A diagram of a hot tub shows the actual 3-m length of one side of the hot tub as 15 cm. The 8-m length of the square deck around the hot tub is shown as 40 cm.

   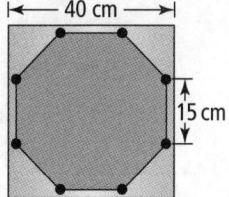

6. A telephone pole that is 12 m tall casts a shadow that is 2 m long. What is the length of the shadow cast by a student who is 1.5 m tall?

   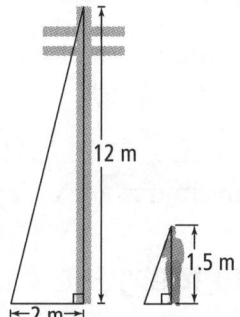

7. The distance between Town B and Town C is 56 km. The distance shown on the map is 7 cm in length. What is the actual distance between Town A and Town C if it is represented on the same map by a length of 12.5 cm?

   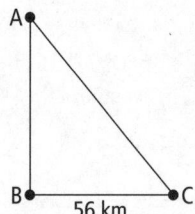

4.1 Enlargements and Reductions

MathLinks 9, pages 130–138

Key Ideas Review

Choose from the following terms to complete #1.

| constant | enlargement | larger | reduction | scale factor | smaller |

1. a) A scale factor greater than 1 indicates a(n) __enlargement__, which results in an image that is the same shape but proportionally __longer__ than the original.

   b) A scale factor less than 1 indicates a(n) __Reduction__, which results in an image that is the same shape but proportionally __smaller__ than the original.

   c) The __scale factor__ is the __constant__ amount by which all dimensions of an object are enlarged or reduced in a scale drawing.

Check Your Understanding

2. Draw an enlargement of each figure using a scale factor of 2.

   a)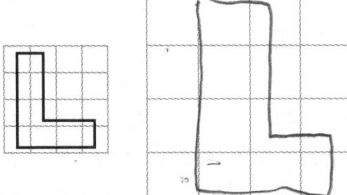

   b)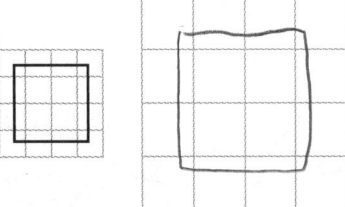

3. Draw a reduction of each letter using a scale factor of 0.5.

   a)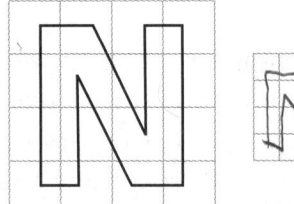

   b)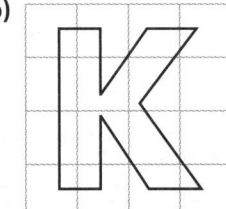

Date: _____

4. For each image in column A, state whether the image in column B has a scale factor
   - greater than 1
   - less than 1
   - equal to 1

	A	B
a) equal		
b) less		
c) Greater		

5. a) Draw an enlargement of the butterfly using a scale factor of 4.

   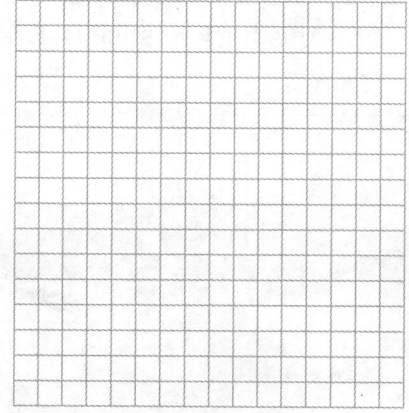

   b) Explain how you know that your drawing is correct.

6. Draw an image of the flag of Greece using a scale factor of $\frac{1}{4}$.

7. Alicia copied a headline from the school newspaper and included it on her election poster.

   a) Is the headline on the poster an enlargement or a reduction of the headline in the newspaper?

   b) What is the scale factor? How do you know?

4.1 Enlargements and Reductions • MHR 45

4.2 Scale Diagrams

MathLinks 9, pages 139–145

Key Ideas Review

Match the term in column A with the correct description in column B.

A	B
1. scale diagram	a) $\frac{1}{120000} = \frac{4}{?}$
2. scale	b) 3 cm × 1 200 000 = ?
3. solve using a scale	c) 1:1 200 000
4. solve using a proportion representation	d) a proportionally smaller or larger object

Check Your Understanding

5. State which numbers you multiply or divide to find the missing value.

   a) $\frac{1}{5} = \frac{?}{85}$ $5 = 85 = 17$ ft

   b) $\frac{1}{?} \stackrel{×6}{=} \frac{6}{132}$ $132 = 6$

6. Determine the missing value. Show your thinking. $9 × 13.5$

   a) $\frac{1}{9} = \frac{13.5}{\boxed{119}}$

   b) $\frac{1}{\boxed{4}} = \frac{12.5}{50}$

7. Use the scale factor to calculate the actual length of each object.

   a) The scale factor for the image of this hockey stick is 1:42.

   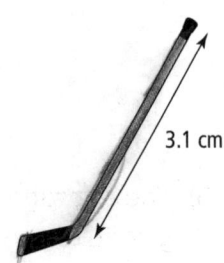

   3.1 cm

   b) The Euvira Micmac beetle below is enlarged using a scale factor of 1:0.05.

   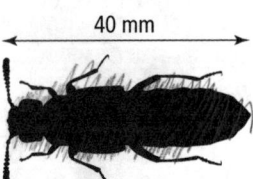

   40 mm

8. Determine the scale factor for each question below. Show your thinking.

a) $\dfrac{1}{2.5} = \dfrac{30}{225}$

b) $\dfrac{1}{4} = \dfrac{3.8}{15.2}$

9. What scale factor is used to create each image below?

a) The actual size of this award is 34.3 cm.

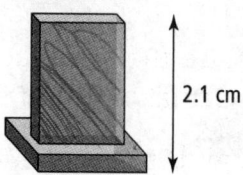
2.1 cm

b) The average height of a male giraffe is 6 m.

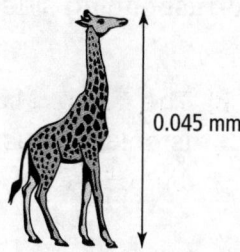
0.045 mm

10. A blueprint is used to show all the measurements needed to build rooms in a house and the house itself.

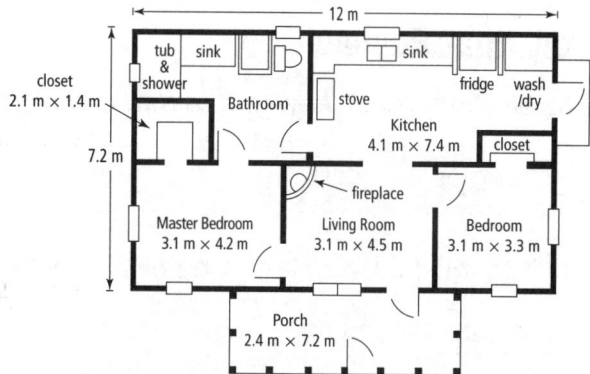

a) What is the scale factor used to draw the blueprint? Express the denominator of the scale factor to the nearest whole number.

b) Draw the master bedroom using a scale factor of 1:290. Express the calculations for the width and length of your drawing to the nearest tenth.

c) What is the area of your drawing in part b)? Express your answer to the nearest hundredth.

4.3 Similar Triangles

MathLinks 9, pages 146–153

Key Ideas Review

Choose from the following terms to complete #1 to 2.

> angles   both   not   proportion   scale factor   sides   similar

1. Triangles are similar if one of the following conditions is true:

    a) Corresponding ___angles___ are equal in measure.

    b) Corresponding ___sides___ are proportional in length.

2. You can solve problems for similar triangles using a ___scale___ ___factor___ or a ___proportion___.

3.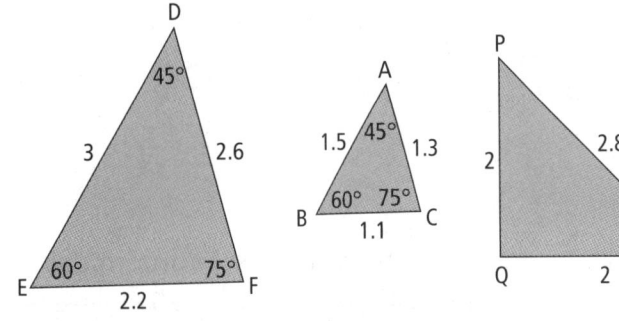

    a) Is △DEF similar to △ABC? (YES) NO Explain. all 3 angle are same

    b) Is △DEF similar to △PQR? YES NO Explain.

Check Your Understanding

4. What are the corresponding angles and the corresponding sides for the following pairs of similar triangles?

   a)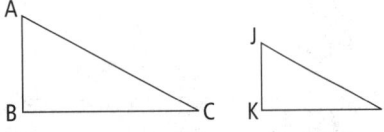

   b)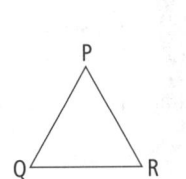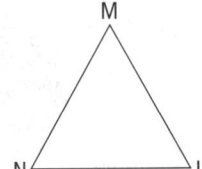

48 MHR • Chapter 4   978-007-097344-2

5. Determine which pair of triangles is similar. Explain how you know.

Triangle	Angles	Sides
△PQR	∠P = 90° ∠Q = 45° ∠R = 45°	PQ = 3 QR = 4.2 PR = 3
△STU	∠S = 90° ∠T = 60° ∠U = 30°	ST = 9.2 TU = 18.4 SV = 15.9
△VWX	∠V = 45° ∠W = 90° ∠X = 45°	VW = 11.3 WX = 11.3 VX = 16

b)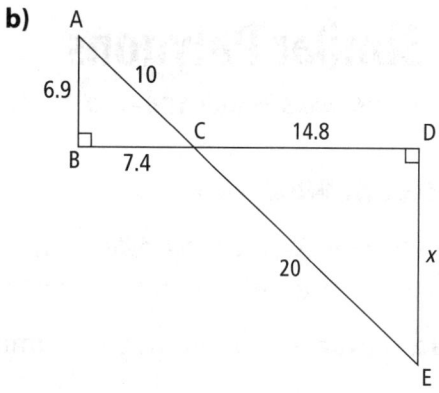

6. Are these triangles similar? Explain how you know.

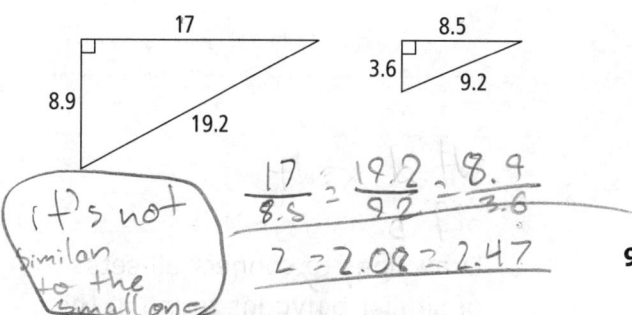

it's not similar to the small one

$\frac{17}{8.5} = \frac{19.2}{9.2} = \frac{8.9}{3.6}$

$2 = 2.08 = 2.47$

7. Determine the missing side lengths of the triangles below. Show your calculations.

a)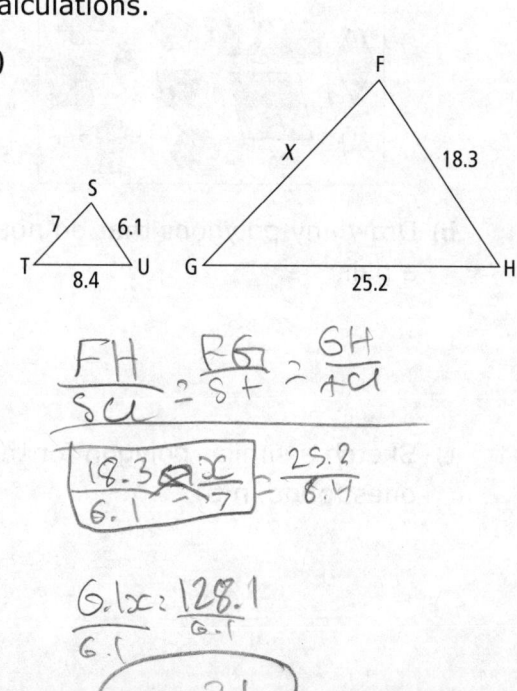

$\frac{FH}{SU} = \frac{FG}{ST} = \frac{GH}{TU}$

$\frac{18.3}{6.1} = \frac{x}{7} = \frac{25.2}{8.4}$

$\frac{6.1x}{6.1} = \frac{128.1}{6.1}$

$x = 21$

8. Draw a triangle that is similar to the one shown. Label the measurements for the angles and sides on your triangle.

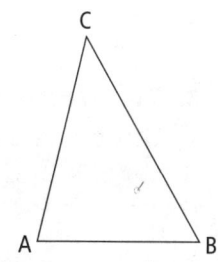

9. Kaylee is 100 cm tall and is standing so that her mother's shadow covers her shadow. She is 90 cm from her mother and her mother's shadow is 225 cm long. How tall is her mother? Express your answer to the nearest centimetre.

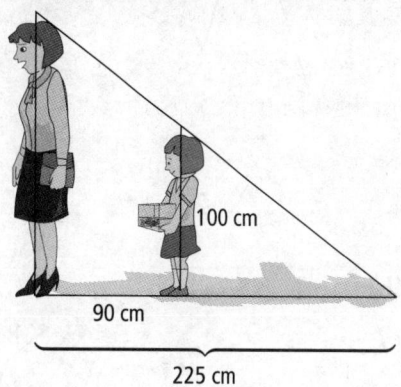

4.3 Similar Triangles • MHR 49

4.4 Similar Polygons

MathLinks 9, pages 154–159

Key Ideas Review

Decide whether each of the following statements is true or false. Circle the word True or False. If the statement is false, rewrite it to make it true.

1. **True/False** Polygons that are similar have some angles that are equal in measure.

   _____

   _____

2. **True/False** You can use polygons that are not similar to determine unknown side lengths.

   _____

   _____

3. **True/False** A polygon is a three-dimensional closed figure made of more than three line segments.

   _____

   _____

Check Your Understanding

4. Is each pair of polygons similar? How do you know?

   a)

   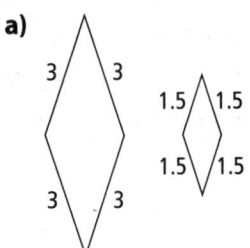

5. a) Draw lines to connect all sets of similar polygons found in the space below.

   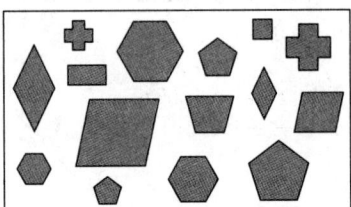

   b) Draw any polygons that do not have a pair.

   b)

   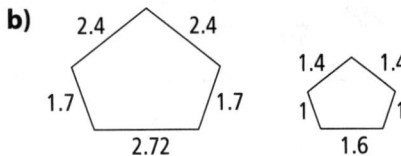

   c) Sketch a similar polygon for the ones found in b).

6. Use each pair of similar polygons to determine each unknown side length.

a)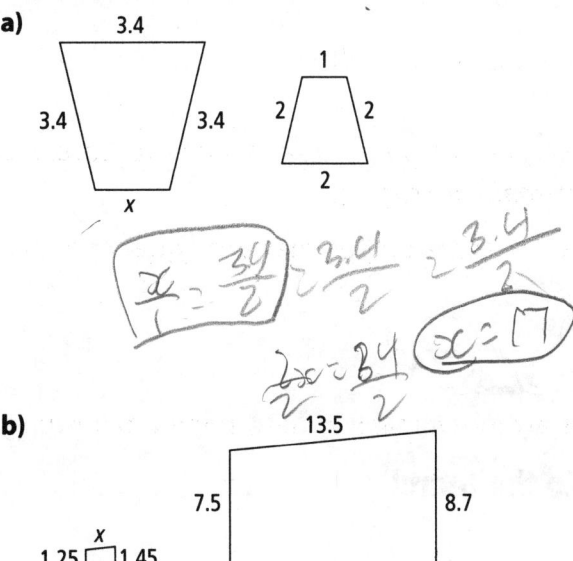

b)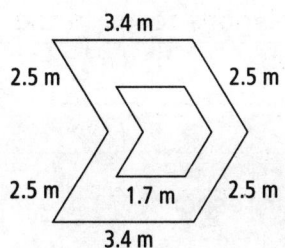

7. As part of an art project, Jamal made an outline of a shape with string. He wanted to create another shape inside the first one.

[Shape with sides: 3.4 m (top), 2.5 m, 2.5 m (left sides), 2.5 m, 2.5 m (right sides), 1.7 m, 3.4 m (bottom)]

a) Calculate the unknown side lengths of the inside shape if it is similar to the outside shape.

b) What is the total length of string Jamal used for his art project?

8. Determine the value of the missing values to the nearest tenth. Show your thinking.

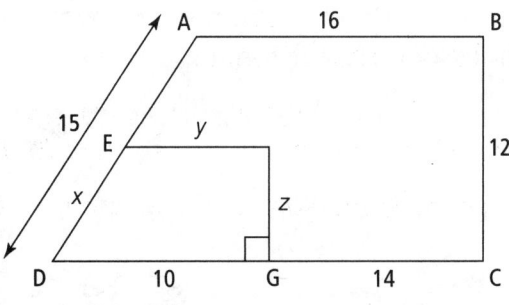

9. A pattern is cut showing the dimensions of a pair of similar trays. How much trim will you need to cover the outside edge of the larger tray? Justify your response.

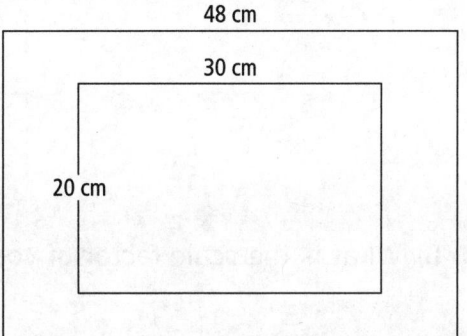

4.4 Similar Polygons • MHR 51

Chapter Link

Date: _____

Keisha was doodling on her notebook and created a design that she thought would be a perfect logo for her team motto.

1. a) Draw an enlargement of the logo, without the text, to put on a T-shirt.

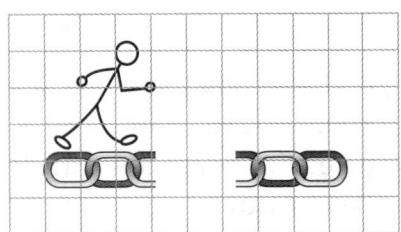

b) What is the scale factor of your enlarged logo? Justify your response.

2. One team member suggested having an arrow go through the logo instead. The text would be included below. Using a scale factor of 3, what are the measurements of an enlarged arrow?

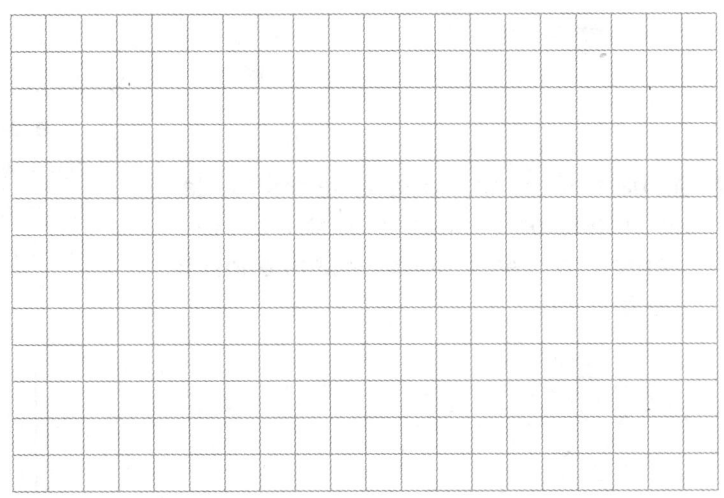

52 MHR • Chapter 4   978-007-097344-2

Vocabulary Link

Draw a line from the description in column A to the correct term in column B. Then, find each term in the word search.

A	B
1. compares quantities measured in the same units	a) corresponding
2. a two-dimensional, closed figure made of three or more line segments	b) enlargement
3. a decrease in the dimensions of an object by a constant factor	c) polygon
4. an adjective for figures that have the same shape but different sizes	d) proportion
5. a comparison between the actual size of an object and the size of its diagram	e) ratio
6. an angle or side with the same relative position in a geometric figure	f) reduction
7. an increase in the dimensions of an object by a constant factor	g) scale
8. the constant factor by which all dimensions of an object are enlarged or reduced in a scale drawing	h) scale diagram
9. a type of drawing that is similar to the actual figure or object	i) scale factor
10. a relationship that shows two ratios are equal	j) similar

```
H U H P G B T Q G G I J S E Z D S D F Q
I A L S S F Z G B W R D K C O H H E B G
Q T M F C H S I M I L A R L A X Z D J S
R B L F A U J R M V X W E X W K D J J W
O U C T L C B Z U M V M S B C P M U F A
Q C M N E V Q S U E N L A R G E M E N T
N C D R F S G Q C R L U X C S C P D C P
P E O N A D J Q Z A A M K Z X S U H E D
R E D U C T I O N T L R P Q S V F W Q C
O V Q T T S I B P I Y E W O V Y C Q B F
P B D R O T U N K O A B D K L L E F O W
O K R E R X B A N Y Q L Z I F Y N C L N
R C O R R E S P O N D I N G A H G L W G
T L C T O P J S I W P U E K J G T O G K
I M D Y O F E C K K L J C B C A R A N I
O K L F U J T A M U J U U K U M M A D L
N P Z Y C G J L O E M U Y K O B E S M P
B F T R V Z P E D N B H B K Q Q X U Q Z
```

Chapters 1–4 Review

1. Explain the difference between 4^7 and 7^4.

2. Identify the types of symmetry in this Celtic knot.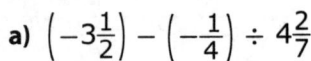

3. Draw a reduction of the figure using the scale factor of 0.5.

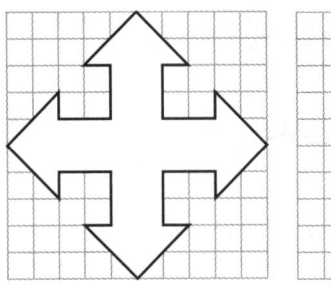

4. Evaluate.

   a) $5^3 + (2^4 - 3^0)^2(3^3 - 9^2)$

   b) $(-2)^3(-1)^4 - \left(\frac{2}{3}\right)^3$

5. a) The tessellation here has rotational symmetry. List all the shapes that you can see with rotational symmetry.

   b) What is the order and angle of rotation of each shape? Give the angle of rotation in both degrees and fractions of a revolution.

6. Evaluate. Show fractions in lowest terms.

   a) $\left(-3\frac{1}{2}\right) - \left(-\frac{1}{4}\right) \div 4\frac{2}{7}$

   b) $7 \div \left(-\frac{1}{3}\right) - \left(\frac{-2}{9}\right) \times \left(3\frac{1}{4}\right)$

   c) $\left(2\frac{1}{5}\right) - \left(-4\frac{2}{5} - (-2)\right)\left(-4\frac{2}{5} - (-2)\right)$

7. The height of the Eiffel Tower in Paris is 300 m. What scale factor would you use if you wanted to draw the tower 10 cm high?

8. Write each expression as the division of two powers.

   a) $\left(\frac{2}{5}\right)^3$ b) $\left(\frac{4}{9}\right)^4$

Date: _____

9. Determine the surface area of the composite shape. Express your answer to the nearest hundredth.

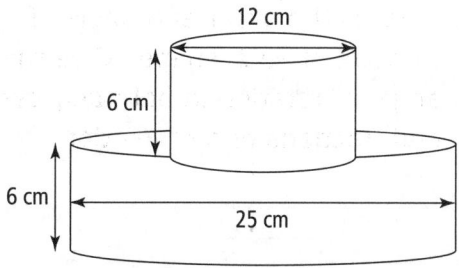

10. You bought some new bedroom furniture (f) for $1500, including tax. The shop owner gave you the option of making no payments for 18 months from the date that you bought the furniture.

   a) If you are charged 16% interest, what would you owe at the end of the 18 months? The formula that represents this relationship is $P = f\left(1 + \frac{0.08}{9}\right)^{18}$.

   b) How much extra would you end up paying if you chose this option? Show your thinking.

11. In the following diagram, △ABC is similar to △DEF. What is the length of BC?

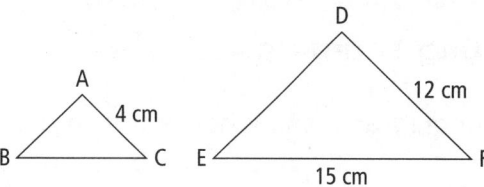

12. Chloe is going to paint a bird house with the measurements shown. The cylindrical perch has a diameter of 1 cm.

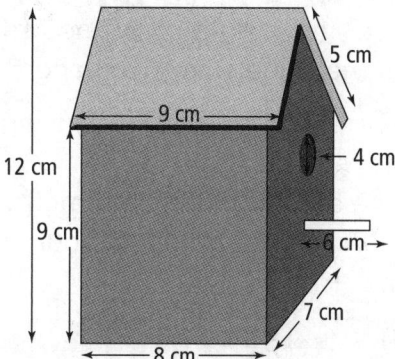

How might you use symmetry to help Chloe determine the outside surface area of the bird house?

13. The label on a 1-L can of paint states that the paint will cover an area of 6 m².

   a) What is the side length of the largest square area that the paint will cover? Express your answer to the nearest hundredth.

   b) If you have 4.75 L of the same paint, what is the side length of the largest square area that you could now cover?

Chapters 1–4 Review • MHR 55

Get Ready

Adding Integers

The diagrams show how you can model the addition of integers.

(+2) + (+1)

(+2) + (−5)

Begin at 0 and move right (positive) or left (negative) according to the first integer. From there, move right or left according to the value of the second integer. The answer is the value where you end on the number line.

(+2) + (+1) = +3   (+2) + (−5) = −3

1. Complete each addition statement. Use a number line to justify your answer.

   a) (+5) + (−2) = (+3)
      5 − 2 —

   b) (+1) + (+4) (+5)
      1 + 4 —

   c) (−3) + (−2) (−5)
      3 + 2 = (−5)

2. What addition statement does each number line model?

   a) (−2) + (+5)

   b) (−1) + (−2)

   c) (−3) + (+7)

Subtracting Integers

You can subtract integers by adding the opposite.
The opposite of 2 is −2.
The opposite of +1 is −1.
(+5) − (−2) = (+5) + (+2) = +7 or 7
(−3) − (+1) = (−3) + (−1) = −4

You can also model these using materials or a diagram.

3. What is the opposite of each integer?

   a) −5   +5

   b) +4   −4

   c) 13   −13

   d) −2   +2

4. Solve.

   a) (+3) − (−1)
      (+4)

   b) (−3) − (+2)
      (−5)

   c) 5 − (+2)
      5 − 2
      (+3)

   d) 2 − (−8)
      2 + 10
      (+10)

Using Expressions

The expression $3w + 2$ consists of:
- a numerical coefficient, 3
- a variable, w
- a constant, $+2$

An expression can be thought of as a shorthand way of writing a word statement. For example, consider the word statement, "The length of a particular rectangle is two units more than triple its width." You could represent the rectangle's length with the expression $3w + 2$, where the variable w is its width.

5. For each expression, identify the numerical coefficient (NC), the variable (V), and the constant (C).

   a) $\underset{NC\ V}{2x} - \underset{C}{7}$

   b) $\underset{NC\ V}{-3b} + \underset{C}{5}$

   c) $\underset{V}{t} - \underset{C}{4}$

   d) $\underset{C}{3} - \underset{NC\ V}{6r}$

6. Write an expression for each phrase. State what each variable represents.

   a) Sarah is 5 years younger than her sister.

   $t = S - 5$

   b) The width of the rectangle is 3 cm less than twice its length.

   $L \times 2 = w - 3$

   c) The perimeter of a triangle is increased by 14 cm.

   $P\triangle + 14$

   d) The school sold half of the concert tickets it expected to sell.

   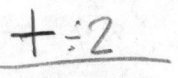
   $t \div 2$

7. Use the information on each diagram to answer the questions below.

   a) What is the perimeter of the square?

   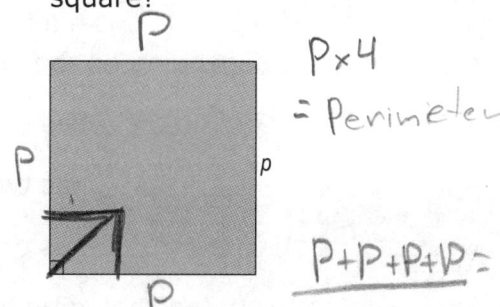

   $P \times 4 = \text{Perimeter}$

   $P + P + P + P =$ _____

   b) Write a word statement describing the length of the rectangle in terms of its width?

   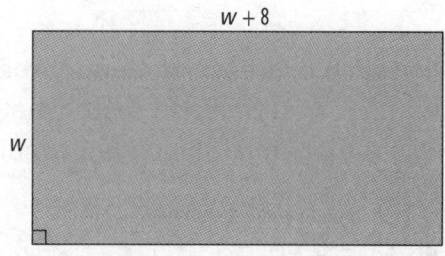

   length of Rectangle is 8 larger then the width.

5.1 The Language of Mathematics
MathLinks 9, pages 174–182

Key Ideas Review

Choose from the following terms to complete the statements in #1 to 3.

> binomial exponents ~~highest~~ ~~monomial~~ ~~polynomial~~
> symbols trinomial variables

1. Algebra uses ~~polynomial~~, often letters, to represent unknown numbers or quantities. These unknown values are called __variable__.

2. A __polynomial__ is made up of terms. Some of these expressions have special names, depending on the number of terms they have.
   - A __monomial__ has one term.
   - A __binomial__ has two terms.
   - A __trinomial__ has three terms.

3. Each algebraic term has a degree, which you can find by adding the __highest__ of the variables in the term. A polynomial has the same degree as its __exponents__-degree term.

Check Your Understanding

4. For each expression, identify the number of terms and state whether it is a monomial, binomial, trinomial, or polynomial.
   a) $2x^2 - 5$ — 2, Binomial
   b) 10 — 1, monomial
   c) $3z^2 - 6z + 7$ — 3, trinomial
   d) $b^2 - ab - 4d + e^2$ — 4, Polynomial

5. For each expression, state the number of terms and the expression's degree.
   a) $ef + gh$ — 2, degree 2
   b) $g^2 - 3g$ — 2, degree 2
   c) 10 — 1, degree 0
   d) $3s^2t - 2$ — 2, degree 3

Date: _____

6. Refer to the following polynomials to answer the questions below.

   $4c^2 - 3c + 2$ $4ab$
   $2f - 4$ -12
   $5p^2 - r$ $g + h + j$

   Which of the above polynomials

   a) are trinomials?
   $4c^2 - 3c + 2$
   $g + h + j$

   b) have a degree of 2?
   $4c^2 - 3c + 2$
   $5p^2 - r$

   c) have a degree of 0?
   -12
   $2f - 4$ $g+h+j$

   d) are monomials?
   $-12, 4ab$

   e) have a coefficient of 4?
   $4ab, 4c^2 - 3c + 2$

7. Write the expression represented by each set of algebra tiles. Shaded tiles are positive and white tiles are negative.

   a)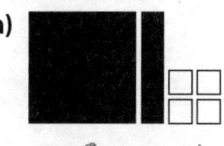
   $x^2 + x - 4$

   b)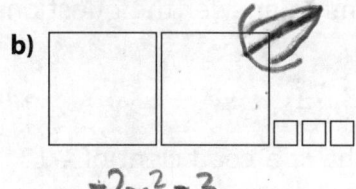
   $-2x^2 - 3$

   c)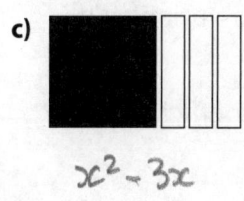
   $x^2 - 3x$

8. Sketch a model that represents the polynomial.

   a) $x^2 + 3x - 2$

   b) $-x^2 - 2x + 1$
   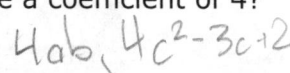

9. Write an algebraic expression for each of the following:

   a) the sum of 7 and x^2

   $x^2 + 7$

   b) the difference of $3x$ and 9

   $3x - 9$

   c) the product of x and 4

   $x \times 4$

10. Use the given variables to write each statement as an algebraic expression.

    a) If n is a number, the product of the number and 5

    b) If w is the width of a rectangle and its length is 5 cm more than its width, the area of rectangle

    c) If x is the number of kilometres, the cost of renting a car, in dollars, if the charge is $40 plus $0.80 per kilometre

5.2 Equivalent Expressions
MathLinks 9, pages 183–189

Key Ideas Review

1. Complete the following statements.

   a) In the monomial 6*ab*, the variables are __a__ and __b__.

   b) In the monomial −7*wx*², the coefficient is __−7__. The variables are *w* and *x*. The exponent for *w* is __1__ and the exponent of *x* is __2__.

   c) For the monomial 18, is there a coefficient or variable?   YES   NO

2. In the three *like* terms below, circle what is *alike* among them. Then, combine the terms.

   $3x^2$ $-4x^2$ $-x^2$ Combined term: _____

3. Are the terms below like terms?   YES   NO   Explain.

   $5x$ $5x^2$ $5y$

Check Your Understanding

4. For each of the following, state the value of the coefficient. Then, state the number of variables for each term.

   a) *y*

   b) $-3b^2$

   c) 6*st*

   d) −15

   e) −*dh*

   f) *bc*

5. Use the following monomial expressions to answer the questions below.

   −*cd*   9*r*   4*x* k^2 −*xy*   −3*jk*

   a) Which have a coefficient of −1?

   b) Which have two variables?

   c) Which have a coefficient of 1?

   d) Which have only one variable, with an exponent of 1?

60 MHR • Chapter 5   978-007-097344-2

6. Circle the like terms in each group.

   a) 14   3r $-r^2$ $-r$ 3s

   b) $-4y$ $8xy$ $2x$ $0.3y$ $\dfrac{y}{2}$

   c) $12c$ cd $1.2d$ $6cd$ cd^2

7. Rearrange the polynomial by grouping like terms.

   a) $9 - 5c - 8 + 5c^2 + c - c^2$

   b) $8m - 9 + 2m^2 + 6 + 3m^2 - 6m$

   c) $-5d^2 + 3d - 2 + 6d^2 - 8d + 7$

8. Rearrange each polynomial by grouping like terms. Then, simplify by adding or subtracting.

   a) $-b^2 + 6 + 5b^2 - 8 + 9$

   b) $7t + 14 + 6t - 5 - 3t^2 + 4t^2$

   c) $5n - 3n^2 - 7 + 9n + 3 - 2n^2$

   d) $3y^2 + 4 - 6y^2 - 6 + 3y - 5 + 2y$

9. Write and simplify an expression for the perimeter of the triangle by combining like terms.

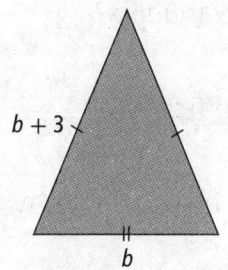

10. a) Draw a figure with a perimeter that is represented by
    $(s) + (2s) + (s + 5) + (3s)$,
    where each value in parentheses represents the length of one side. Label each side length. Explain why you made each side the length that you did.

    b) Simplify the expression for the perimeter by combining like terms.

11. A mechanic charges $70 an hour plus the cost of parts to repair a vehicle. The parts cost $215 for the repair on Tamara's car.

    a) Write an expression for the total cost, C, of repairing Tamara's car for any number of hours, n.

    b) Use the expression you created in part a) to calculate the cost of repairs that take $3\frac{1}{2}$ h.

5.3 Adding and Subtracting Polynomials

MathLinks 9, pages 190–199

Key Ideas Review

1. Which equation does the algebra tile model represent?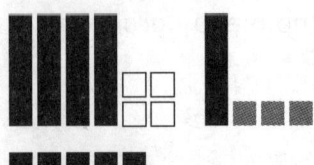

   A $(4x - 4) + (x + 3) = 5x - 1$

   B $(4x + 4) - (-x + 3) = 5x + 1$

   C $(2x - 2) + (3x + 1) = 5x - 1$

   D $(2x - 2) - (-3x - 3) = 5x + 1$

2. One word can replace the question marks in the following sentences: The __?__ of a polynomial is found by taking the __?__ of each of the terms. To subtract polynomials, you can add the __?__.

   The word is _____.

Check Your Understanding

3. Add the polynomials.

   a) $(6y - 4) + (2y + 2)$

   $2y+2$ $8y-2$

   b) $(b^2 + 5) + (-2b^2 - 3)$

   $-2b^2 - 3$ $-b^2 + 2$

   c) $(-3s^2 + 7s) + (-s^2 - 6)$

   $-6 - s^2 - 6$ $-6 - 4s^2 + 7s$

4. Perform the indicated operation. Then, simplify by combining like terms.

   a) $(8 + 5d) + (-d - 9)$

   $-9 - d$ $-1 + 4d$

   b) $(-4m^2 - 4) + (-2m^2 - 1)$

   $-2m^2 - 1$ $-6m^2 - 5$

   c) $(-6r^2 + 3r - 7) + (5r^2 - 2r - 2)$

   $5r^2 - 2r - 2$

   $-r^2 + r - 9$

5. Which of the statements do the algebra tiles represent? __B__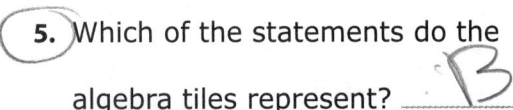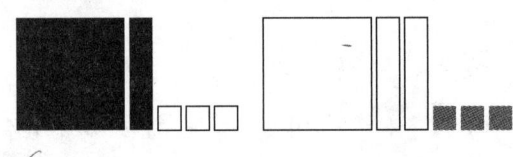

   A $(x^2 + x - 3) + (x^2 - 2x + 3)$

   B $(x^2 + x - 3) + (-x^2 - 2x + 3)$

   C $(x^2 - x - 3) + (-x^2 - 2x + 3)$

   D $(x^2 + x + 3) + (-x^2 - 2x + 3)$

6. Give the opposite of the expression. Express your answer using both diagrams and symbols.

a)

$-x^2 + 2x$

b)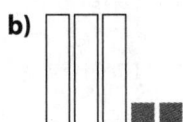

$3x - 2$

7. What is the opposite of each expression?

a) $-3y^2$ = $3y^2$

b) $6g - 3$ = $-6g + 3$

c) $2b^2 - 4b + 7$
$-2b^2 + 4b - 7$

d) $-4d^2 - 3d - 6$
$4d^2 + 3d + 6$

e) $-k^2 - 8k + \frac{1}{2}$
$k^2 + 8k - \frac{1}{2}$

8. Change the subtraction operation to adding the opposite. Then, combine like terms.

a) $(3r - 5) + (5r + 2)$
$-5r - 2$
$-2r - 7$

b) $(6 - 3f) + (4 - 5f)$
$-4 + 5f$
$2 + 2f$

c) $(-4n^2 + 5) - (-n^2 - 9)$
$n^2 + 9$
$-3n^2 + 14$

d) $(6a^2 + 2a - 5) - (4a^2 + 5a + 7)$
$-4a^2 - 5a - 7$
$2a^2 - 3a - 12$

9. Consider the triangle below.

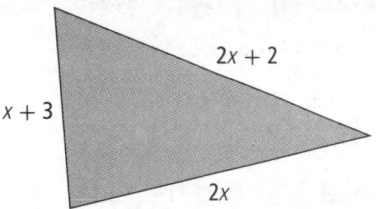

a) Write the unsimplified expression for the perimeter.
$(x+3) + (2x+2) + (2x)$

b) Simplify the expression from part a) by combining like terms.
$(x+3)$
$(2x+2)$
$(2x)$
$5x+5$

c) If the perimeter of the triangle is 25 cm, calculate the value of x. Verify that your answer is correct.
$x = 4$
$5 \times 4 = 20 + 5 = 25$

10. José, Tyler, and Mike split some money they made working on the weekend. They each worked a different number of hours, so they have to split the money fairly. José receives twice the amount that Tyler receives, and Mike receives $10 less than Tyler. Let x represent the amount that Tyler receives.

a) Write the expression that represents the total amount that they receive.

b) Simplify the expression in part a) by combining like terms.

Chapter Link

1. Use the clues to determine the polynomial.

   a) Clues:
      - It is a trinomial.
      - The degree is 2.
      - The middle term is the opposite of 3x.
      - The lowest common multiple of the coefficient of the first term and the constant is 10.
      - The constant is double the coefficient of the first term.

   The polynomial is

   _____.

   b) Clues:
      - It is a binomial.
      - The degree is 2.
      - The model for the first term is:

      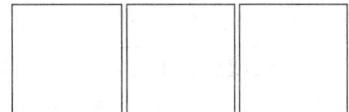

      - The second term has two variables. The second variable follows the other variable in the alphabet.
      - The coefficient of the second term is positive and not written.

   The polynomial is

   _____.

2. Fill in the missing polynomial. Show your work.

   a) $(4d - 7) - (2d + 2) =$ _____

   b) $(-4a^2 - 5a - 2) - \boxed{?} = (-6a^2 - 6a - 5)$

   c) _____ $- (r^2 + 3) = r^2 + r$

3. Cindy wants to rent a truck and trailer to move her household goods from one city to another. The rental company charges $35 per day plus $0.20 per kilometre for the truck and $15 per day for the trailer. The company estimates that the fuel costs will be $200 for the distance Cindy is moving.

   a) Write an expression that represents the truck and trailer rental charge, including the fuel charge. State what your variables represent.

   b) If the distance Cindy is moving is 800 km and the trip takes two days, what will be the total cost for Cindy to rent the truck and trailer? Show your work.

Vocabulary Link

Unscramble the letters of each term in column B. Use the clues in column A to help you. Each term is one to four words long.

A	B
1. an algebraic expression made up of terms connected by the operations of addition or subtraction; for example, $3x^2 - 4$	LYPNAOOIML
2. terms that differ only by their numerical coefficients, such as $3x$ and $-2x$	STEMILKER
3. an expression formed from the product of numbers and/or variables, such as $9x$	MRTE
4. a polynomial with three terms	LIOITRMNA
5. a polynomial with two terms	OMLNIAIB
6. in algebra, terms are often arranged in this order	GDCSDENINE
7. a polynomial with one term	IALNOOMM
8. branch of mathematics that uses symbols to represent unknown numbers or operations	EABLGRA
9. the sum of the exponents on the variables in a single term; for example, for $3xz$, it is 2	EMARDGETEORFE
10. the degree of the highest degree term in a polynomial; for example, for $8b^2 - 7b$, it is 2	LYPNAOOIMLEEEFOAGRD

Chapters 1–5 Review

1. Simplify. Then, for each simplified expression identify:
   - the number of terms
   - the degree
   - the type of expression it is: monomial, binomial, trinomial, or polynomial

   a) $x - 3x + x^2 + 7 + 2x^2$

   b) $(-p + 6) - (-p + 3)$

   c) $(3x^2 + 6xy + 5y^2) + (6x^2 + 6x + 5y)$

2. For each expression, identify the coefficient, variables, and exponent for each variable.

   a) $-3xy^2$

   b) $-a^3$

   c) 5

3. Arrange the following numbers in ascending order:

   $(-4)^3 \quad 5^2 \quad 7 \quad 2^5 \quad (-2)^4$

4. Estimate and calculate the number that has the given square root.

   a) 6.2 b) 13.5

   c) 0.23 d) 0.57

5. Figure ABCDE is rotated counterclockwise 180° about the origin. After the transformation:
   - identify the coordinates of the image
   - state whether the transformation shows symmetry
   - describe the symmetry

   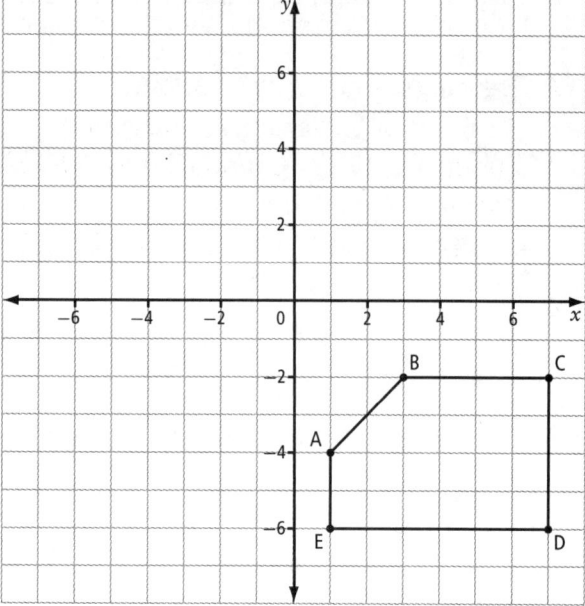

6. Replace each ☐ with >, <, or = to make each statement true.

   a) $\frac{-6}{4}$ ☐ $\frac{3}{-2}$ b) $\frac{-1}{3}$ ☐ -0.3

   c) $-3\frac{5}{8}$ ☐ $-3\frac{7}{9}$ d) $\frac{-4}{12}$ ☐ $\frac{-3}{13}$

7. The formula for the volume of a cylinder is $V = \pi r^2 h$. Determine the volume, V, of a cylinder with a radius of 4 cm and a height of 9.2 cm. Express your answer to the nearest tenth.

Date: _____

8. What is the order and angle of rotation symmetry for this picture? Express the angle in degrees and in fractions of a turn.

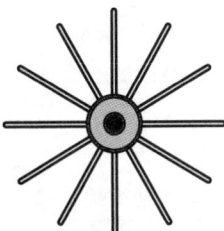

9. Canada's population is about 33 640 000. The United States has about $9\frac{1}{10}$ times Canada's population. Belgium's population is about $\frac{1}{3}$ of Canada's. Justify your answer for each of the following.

   a) How many people live in the United States?

   b) How many people live in Belgium?

   c) How many times greater is the population of the United States than the population of Belgium? Express your answer as a fraction.

10. Evaluate. For part a), keep your answer in fraction form. For part b), express your answer to the nearest thousandth.

    a) $\left(\frac{2}{3}\right)^2 \times \left(\frac{-2}{-3}\right)^3 + \frac{1}{3} \div \frac{2}{5}$

    b) $\dfrac{(-3)^0 \,(2.5)^2 - (1.1)^3 \,(-2)^6}{(-1.2 + 3^3)^2}$

11. Determine the diameter of the Earth. Express your answer to the nearest tenth. The scale factor for the image of the diameter of Earth is 1 cm : 2834.7 km.

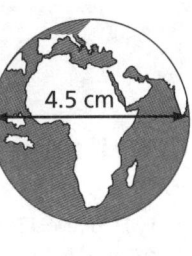

12. A child is playing with five wooden blocks. Each block is a cube with an edge length of 4.5 cm. Express your answers to the nearest tenth.

    a) Calculate the total surface area of the five blocks.

    b) The child builds a tower by stacking five blocks directly on top of each other. What is the surface area of the tower?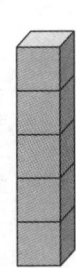

    c) The child knocks the blocks down. All of the blocks become separated. What is the total visible surface area of the separated blocks?

13. Are the following polygons similar? Explain your thinking.

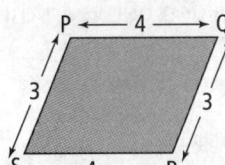 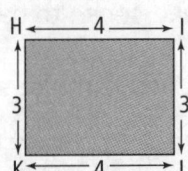

Chapters 1–5 Review • MHR **67**

Get Ready

Date: _____

Creating a Table of Values

You can use the coordinate pairs on the graph to make a **table of values**. Arrange the table of values horizontally or vertically. The first row or column in a table of values has the same title as the horizontal axis on the graph. The second row or column has the same title as the vertical axis.

Number of Shirts, n	1	3	5
Cost, C	15	45	75

Number of Shirts, n	Cost, C
1	15
3	45
5	75

1. Create a table of values from each graph.

a)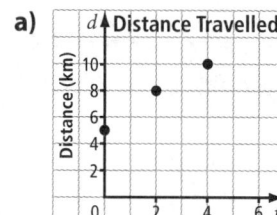

x	y
0	5
2	8
4	10

b)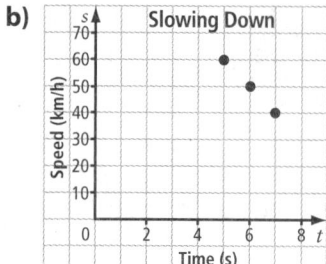

x	y
5	60
6	50
7	40

Analysing Graphs of Linear Relations

A **linear relation** is a pattern made by a set of points that lie in a straight line. Sometimes it is possible to have points between the ones shown on a graph. Ask, "Does it make sense to have values between those on the graph?"

2. Does it make sense to have points between the ones on each graph? Explain.

a)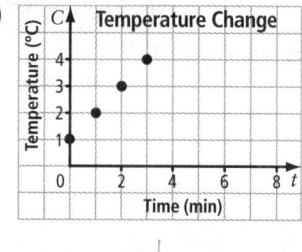

yes because this graph is continuos

b)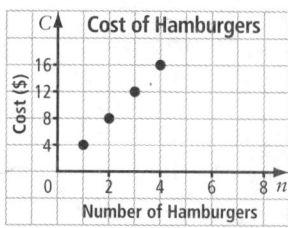

no because you can't cat half a burgers

68 MHR • Chapter 6 978-0-07-097344-2

Patterns in a Table of Values

Linear relations can be represented using a table of values. You can sometimes tell that a relationship in a table is linear if both of the following statements are true.
- Consecutive values in one column change by the same amount.
- Consecutive values in the other column change by the same amount.

s	t
2	6
4	12
6	18
8	24

The difference between consecutive values for s is 2. The difference between consecutive values for t is 6. You can use this information to predict the next values in the table.

For s, the next value could be 10.

For t, the next value could be 30.

3. Determine if each table of values represents a linear relation. Explain how you arrived at your answer.

a)
Distance, d (m)	Speed, s (m/s)
0	2.1
15	4.2
30	6.3
45	8.4

b)
Time, t (s)	Height, h (m)
5	10
10	20
15	40
20	80

4. For each table of values in #3 that represents a linear relation, predict the next ordered pair.

Linear Relationships

Linear relationships represented by formulas or equations can be graphed by
- making a table of values, and
- graphing the ordered pairs from the table of values.

5. For each equation, create a table of values and graph the linear relation.

a) $y = 3x + 2$

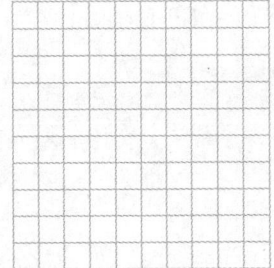

b) $t = -4n + 3$

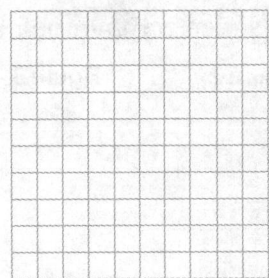

6.1 Representing Patterns

MathLinks 9, pages 210–219

Key Ideas Review

Choose from the following terms to fill in the blanks for #1a) and #2a).

| equation | four | pattern | posts | rails |

1. a) The fence below has a(n) __pattern__. There are __four__ __rails__ between pairs of __posts__.

   b) Complete a table of values for this fence.

   c) Describe the pattern.

2. a) You can use the pattern in the table to develop a(n) __equation__ for the fence.

   b) The equation is _____.

   c) How can you verify what you created in #2b)?

Check Your Understanding

3. a) Create a table of values showing the relationship between the perimeter length of each figure and the figure number.

   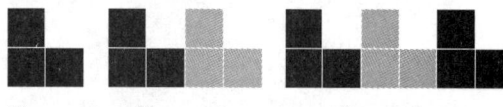
   Figure 1   Figure 2   Figure 3

   b) Write an expression to model the pattern. Explain what each variable represents.

   c) Extend your table of values to the 10th figure.

4. a) Describe the relationship between the figure number and the number of toothpicks needed for each figure.

   Figure 1   Figure 2   Figure 3

   b) Create a table of values to determine an equation for the model. Write the equation.

   $y = x$

   c) Determine if one of the figures could have 2037 toothpicks in it. Show your thinking.

   2037 $y = x$

5. a) Jenny has lost part of her homework. Help her redo it by finishing the table of values for the first seven terms.

x	y
1	−4.5
	−7
	−9.5

   b) Develop an equation that models your table of values.

   c) Use your equation to determine the 67th term.

6. a) A basketball team can buy 12 warm-up jerseys for $179.40. To put a design on any number of jerseys involves a one-time cost of $181.80. If there are 12 people on the basketball team, develop an equation that shows the cost for one player.

   b) Assuming that the team can buy additional jerseys for the same cost per jersey as in a), and that the one-time cost for the design does not change, how much would one player pay if there are 15 people on the team?

   c) Create a table of values to show the cost of a single jersey if 1 to 15 players decide to buy a jersey.

6.2 Interpreting Graphs
MathLinks 9, pages 220–230

Key Ideas Review

For #1, unscramble the letters to form a word that correctly completes the sentence.

1. a) When values are found on a graph within a known range of values, this is called _____ .
    LTNNPTIEOOARI

   b) To find a value on a graph that is beyond the known range of values on a graph is called _____ .
    PNALARXETITOO

   c) On the graph to the right, find the value that corresponds with 3.5 h worked. This practice is called _____ because the values are found
    LTNNPTIEOOARI
    Between known values in a set.
    NETEBEW

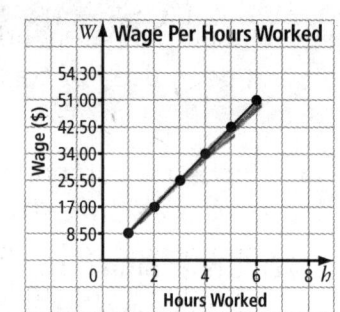

   d) On the same graph, find the value that corresponds with 10 h worked. This practice is called _____ because the values are found
    PNALARXETITOO
    Beyond the known range of values.
    ENDYOB

Check Your Understanding

2. Is it reasonable to interpolate and extrapolate values from the graph? Explain.

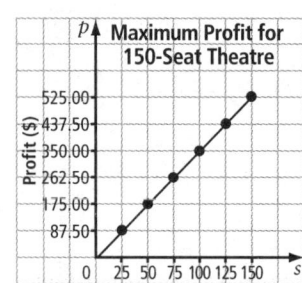

3. The graph shows a relationship between weight and height jumped.

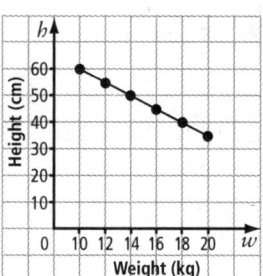

   What is the approximate value of the w-coordinate when $h = 32$ cm? Which method did you use to determine the answer?

72 MHR • Chapter 6 978-007-097344-2

4. The following graph shows fuel consumption over time.

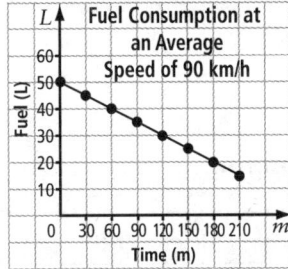

a) Is it reasonable to extrapolate data from this graph? Explain. yes Because you can drive in between Can only Go So far km

b) Approximately how much fuel has been used to travel 225 km?

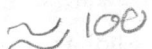
≈ 100

5. A spring is compressed after weights are placed on it. The spring fully compressed is 12 cm long and fully extended is 40 cm long.

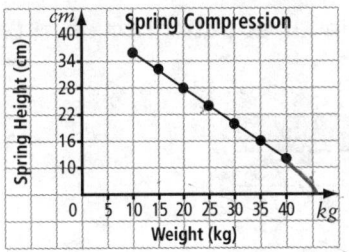

a) Is it reasonable to extrapolate data from this graph? Explain. yes you can go in between those measurement

b) What weight fully compresses the spring?

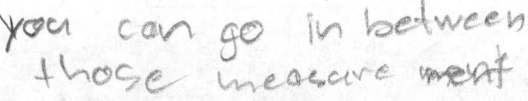
50 kg

c) When a 25-kg weight is placed on the spring, what is the spring's length?

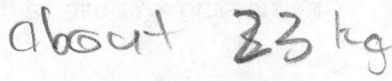
about 23 kg

6. Continental drift occurs at a rate of about 1 cm to 10 cm per year. Assuming an average movement of 5.5 cm per year, use the graph to answer the following questions.

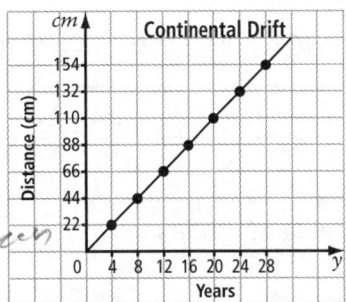

a) Approximately how long will it take the plate to move 2 m?

b) After 17 years, approximately how far will the plate have moved? Which method did you use to determine your answer?

7. The table of values represents the dosage of a medicine needed by body weight.

Weight, kg	18	32	46	60
Dosage, mg	60	75	90	105

a) Plot the linear relation on a graph.

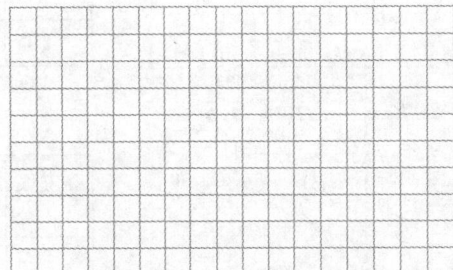

b) From the graph, determine the approximate dosage needed for weights of 40 kg and 100 kg.

c) From the graph, determine the approximate weights needed for dosages of 50 mg and 120 mg.

6.2 Interpreting Graphs • MHR **73**

6.3 Graphing Linear Equations

MathLinks 9, pages 231–243

Key Ideas Review

Select the terms in column B that complete the sentences in column A.

A	B
1. A(n) _____, such as $x = y - 5$, can be used to create a table of values.	a) coordinate
2. You can use _____ pairs developed in a table of values to graph the _____.	b) equation c) extrapolate d) interpolate
3. Graphs can be used to _____ or _____ values when solving problems.	e) linear relation

Check Your Understanding

4. Create a graph and a table of values for each linear equation.

   a) $x = -3$

   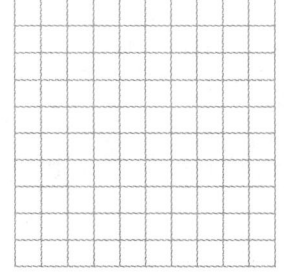

x	y
	-5
	3

   b) $k = -2m + 5.5$

   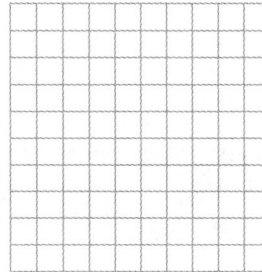

m	k

5. Create a linear equation for each table of values.

   a)
x	y
4	-7.75
3	-5.75
2	-3.75
1	-1.75
0	0.25
-1	2.25

   b)
x	y
15	-7.5
13	-6.5
11	-5.5
9	-4.5
7	-3.5

6. The line *q* passes through the three points G, P, and X.

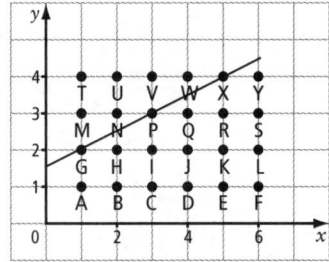

a) What is the linear equation for the line *q*?

b) Write the linear equation of another line that passes through three letters. Identify the line.

c) Write an equation for a line that passes through at least four letters. Identify the line.

7. An aquarium holds 1000 L. The graph shows the relationship between time, *t*, and the number of litres, *L*, of water pumped from the aquarium.

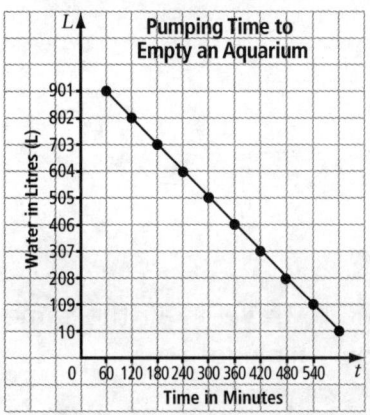

a) What is the linear equation?

b) How long would it take to pump approximately 750 L of water? What method did you use?

c) Jomari states that it would take about 15 h to empty a 1500-L aquarium. Do you agree or disagree with Jomari? Explain.

8. Alex and Zoe live beside each other. Alex leaves home at 9:00 a.m., walking at a steady speed of 1 km per 20 min. Zoe leaves home at 9:30 a.m. and jogs after Alex at a steady speed of 1.25 km per 15 min.

a) Create tables of values for both Alex and Zoe. Include at least five values.

b) Graph the results of both tables. Identify each relation.

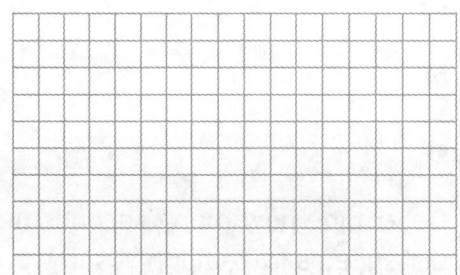

c) At approximately what time will Zoe catch Alex?

d) If they continued at the same pace, how far apart would they be at 10:30 a.m.?

6.3 Graphing Linear Equations • MHR 75

Chapter Link

1. Sound travels at different speeds through different materials.
   - Sound travels through air at 340 m per second.
   - Sound travels through water at 1450 m per second.
   - Sound travels through steel at 5050 m per second.

   a) Create a table of values for the speed of sound in air.

   b) Create a table of values for the speed of sound in water.

   c) Create a table of values for the speed of sound in steel.

2. Create an expression for each table in #1.

   a)

   b)

   c)

3. Determine how many seconds it would take for a sound to travel in air the same distance as it would in 1 s in water and steel. Show your thinking.

   a) water

   b) steel

4. How many seconds would it take for a sound to travel in water the same distance as it would in 1 s in air and steel. Show your thinking.

   a) air

   b) steel

Vocabulary Link

Draw a line from each clue in column A to the correct term in column B. Then, find each term in the word search.

A	B
1. refers to a letter that represents a value	a) coefficient
2. refers to estimating a value that is beyond a given set of values	b) commission
3. name of payment by which a salesperson receives a percentage of the value of sales	c) constant
4. refers to an equation whose graph is a straight line	d) continuous
5. a line on a graph that joins the points	e) extrapolate
6. in the equation $3n - 2$, 3 is a numerical	f) interpolate
7. Example:	g) linear equation
	h) linear relation
	i) variable
8. in the equation $3n - 2$, -2 is a	
9. estimating the value between two given values on a graph	

```
M X S C C V U J A I A O C O N S T A N T
E C A V D Z E T Q N V F Y N N I D Q F V
X S V B E O L I N E A R R E L A T I O N
T K L A M B X E I V C Y V H U C C J F U
R L Q I R I M Z Q C K H F K O P C Y R R
A M H C N I I N C C O N T I N U O U S Z
P B I O H E A N N X R N W D O E G A A
O H N M F S A B T B E F B R B S F B K K
L C W M O K V R L E U B N O P D F Z A D
A P G I Y Z T Z E E R X Y J X P I F O H
T D Z S W M G N P Q D P Z N H W C V V P
E Z A S V O P T N Z U W O O T F I V A V
F M G I T R M F D V R A K L P T E C J M
Q K Z O O U L J S H G E T U A U N A G K
U Q C N B K V G L V Y S A I G T T V D V
I N R O P F M G G R E H U Q O O E V U L
Y K K A Q T D B M A K I D K S N X J E M
F D S L H D M Y M Y J F G L T W F X N H
```

Chapters 1–6 Review

1. Provide an example of each of the following.

   a) binomial of degree 2

   b) polynomial with degree 2

   c) a pair of like terms

2. Determine the linear equation that models each graph

   a)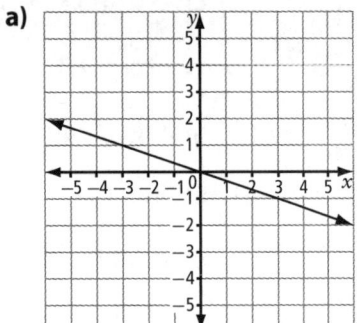

   b)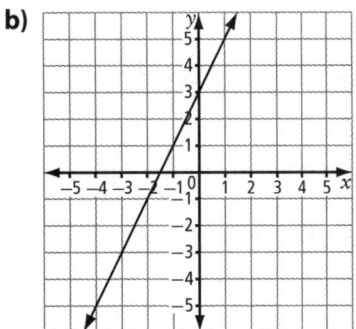

3. Identify a decimal number between each of the following pairs of rational numbers.

   a) $2\frac{1}{3}$, $1\frac{2}{5}$ b) $\frac{-23}{30}$, $-\frac{5}{6}$

4. What is the scale factor on picture 1 versus picture 2? Explain your reasoning.

   Picture 1   Picture 2

5. a) How many lines of symmetry are in this design? Describe and then draw them.

   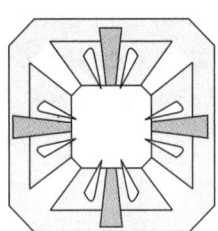

   b) Determine the angle of rotation in both degrees and fractions of a revolution.

6. Estimate and then calculate the following. Express your answer to the nearest hundredth if necessary.

   a) $-2.56 + 6.7 \div 1.3$

   b) $-(-1.4) \times (2.5)^2$

   c) $-(-1.3 - 1.7) \times 4.2$

7. Determine the missing values.

a) $\dfrac{1}{\Box} = \dfrac{5.9}{76.7}$ b) $\dfrac{1}{0.08} = \dfrac{2.7}{\Box}$

8. Chelsea solved the math problem incorrectly. Identify the step where she made her error. Calculate the correct answer.

$16 \div (-2)^2 + 6(5)^2$
$= 16 \div (-4) + 6 \times 25$ Step 1
$= 16 \div -4 + 150$ Step 2
$= -4 + 150$ Step 3
$= 146$ Step 4

9. A large mega block is made of four cylinders that are 2 cm high and have a diameter of 2.5 cm, and one rectangular prism that measures 2.5 cm wide by 12 cm long by 0.5 cm high. Calculate the surface area, to the nearest hundredth.

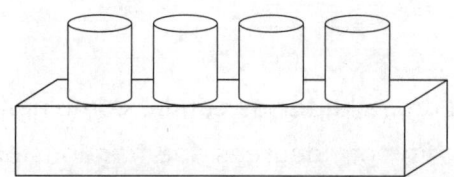

10. Simplify.

a) $(a^2 - 7a - 5) - (2 - 4a^2 + 2a)$

b) $4x^2y - 3xy^2 + 2x^2y - 4xy^2$

11. The surface area of a cube is 127 cm². Determine the side length of the cube, to the nearest tenth.

12. A car rental company charges a flat rate of $30 plus $0.05 per kilometre.

a) Create a table of values for the first 500 km.

b) Graph the linear relation.

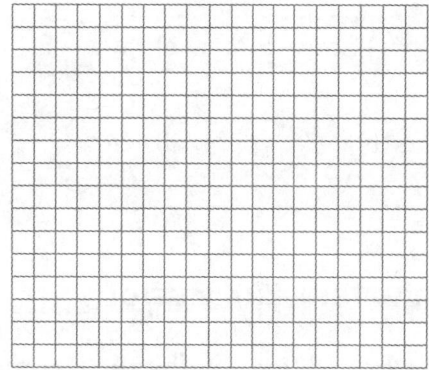

c) Use the graph to approximate how much it would cost to drive the car 250 km.

d) Using the graph, approximate how many kilometres you could drive if you had $52.50.

e) What equation models this situation?

Get Ready

Date: _____

Language of Polynomials

Polynomials are expressions made up of one or more terms. The terms are connected by addition or subtraction. For example, $4x^2 - 8x + 2$ has three terms. Some polynomials have specific names depending on the number of terms that are included:
- A *monomial* has one term.
- A *binomial* has two terms.
- A *trinomial* has three terms.

To find the degree of a term, add the exponents of its variables.

Polynomials have a degree the same as the highest degree term. $7b^2 + 3b - 11$ has degree 2 because the highest degree term, $7b^2$, has degree 2.

1. For each expression, state whether it is a monomial (M), binomial (B), or trinomial (T). Then, identify the polynomial's degree.

   a) $x^2 - 2x + 5$ b) $3y^2 - 9y$
       T   B

   c) $11c + 14$ d) $24d^2$
       B   M

2. Create a polynomial that meets these conditions:
   - contains two variables
   - has three terms
   - is of degree 2

   $2x^2 + 3x - 2$

Equivalent Expressions

Like terms differ only by their numerical coefficients. Like terms can be combined. Unlike terms cannot be combined.

Like terms: $3x$ and $-5x$ can be combined as $-2x$.
                $-4k^2$ and $0.5k^2$ can be combined as $-3.5k^2$.

Unlike terms: $2t$ and t^2 cannot be combined.
                  $-pq$ and $6p$ cannot be combined.

3. Which of the following expressions are equivalent to $3n^2$?

   a) $3n + n$ b) $2n^2 + n^2$

   c) $4n^2 - 1$ d) $-7n^2 + 10n^2$

4. Simplify by collecting like terms.

   a) $x^2 - 6x + 2x^2 + 5$
   $2x^2$ 5
   $3x^2 - 6x + 5$

   b) $4p^2 - 2p + p + 2 - p^2$
   p^2

Using a Model to Add and Subtract Polynomials

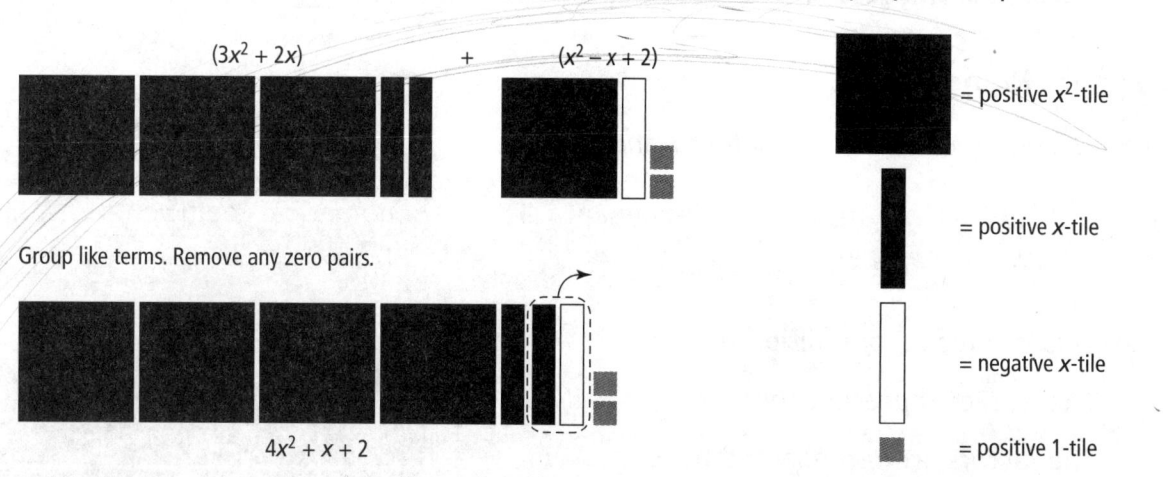

5. Add the polynomials, using models.

   a) $(5x - 7) + (2x - 3)$

   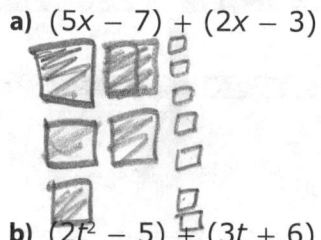

   b) $(2t^2 - 5) + (3t + 6)$

6. Subtract the polynomials, using models.

   a) $(2s - 4) - (2s + 3)$

   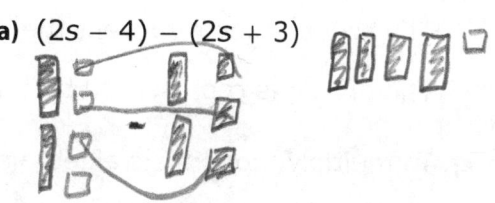

   b) $(-y^2 + 3y - 2) - (-2y^2 - 2y)$

   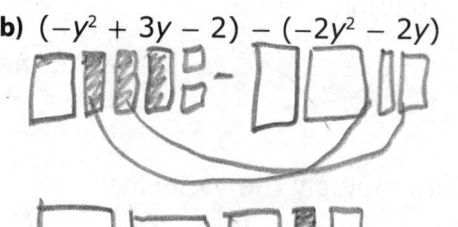

Using Opposites to Subtract Polynomials

To subtract polynomials, you can add the opposite. The opposite of a polynomial is found by taking the opposite of each term. For example, the opposite of $(2x^2 + 3x - 7)$ is $(-2x^2 - 3x + 7)$

$(4x^2 + x + 2) - (2x^2 + 3x - 7) = (4x^2 + x + 2) + (-2x^2 - 3x + 7)$
$= 4x^2 - 2x^2 + x - 3x + 2 + 7$
$= 2x^2 - 2x + 9$

7. Subtract the polynomials.

   a) $(5x^2 + 3x - 7) - (2x^2 - 5x + 3)$

   b) $(2y^2 + 3y - 3) - (2y^2 + 4y + 6)$

7.1 Multiplying and Dividing Monomials

MathLinks 9, pages 254–263

Key Ideas Review

Use the following terms to complete #1 and 2.

| dividend | division | exponent rules | numerical coefficients |
| product | x-tiles | −x-tiles | |

1. a) This is a model of multiplication.

   The x^2-tiles represent the __Product__.

   The factors are represented by __x-tiles__.

   b) This is a model of __division__.

   The six $-x^2$-tiles represent the _____.

   The divisor is represented by three _____.

   c) To multiply monomials algebraically, you can multiply the _____ _____ and then use the _____ _____ to multiply the variables.

2. Rewrite the sentence in #1c) to reflect a similar strategy for dividing monomials.

   _____

   _____

Check Your Understanding

3. Sketch a model of each multiplication statement. What is the product?

   a) $(4x)(-2x)$

   b) $(-4x)(-3x)$

   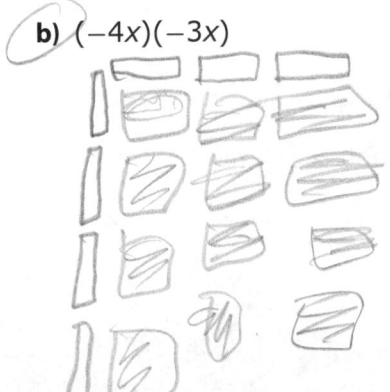

82 MHR • Chapter 7 978-007-097344-2

4. Write a division statement for each model and solve. The grey tiles in b) are *xy*-tiles.

a)

b)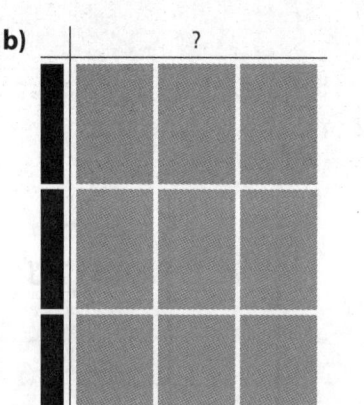

5. Use models to solve the following.
   a) $10xy \div 5y$

   b) $15x^2 \div 5x$

6. Solve. $-6x - 4 = 10$

   a) $(-6a)(-4a)$ b) $(24x)\frac{x}{2}$

   $10a^2$

   c) $\frac{20x^2}{-x}$ d) $-32ac \div -8ac$

7. Write an expression for the area of each shape. What is the simplified expression for the area of each shape?

   a)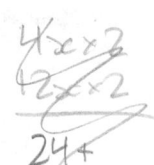
   4x, 12x

   $4x \times 2$
   $12x \times 2$
   24

   $(12x)(4x)$
   $48x$

   b)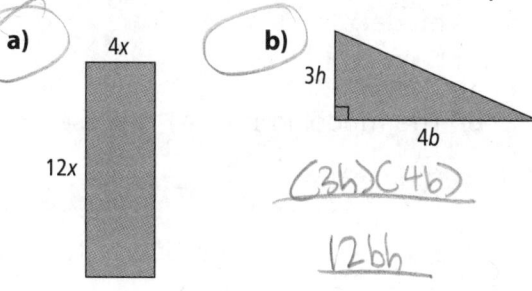
   3h, 4b

   $(3b)(4b)$
   $12bh$

8. A rectangular field is 7 m long and has an area of 84 m². Write an equation you can use to determine the field's width. What is the field's width?

9. Determine the missing dimension in each figure. Show your work.

   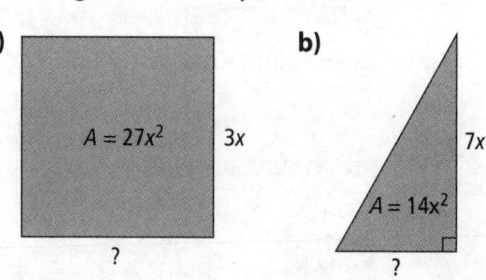

   a) $A = 27x^2$, 3x, ?

   b) 7x, $A = 14x^2$, ?

7.2 Multiplying Polynomials by Monomials

MathLinks 9, pages 264–271

Key Ideas Review

1. Multiplication can be represented using models. Fill in the blanks to complete the statements.

   a) The figure shows an example of a(n) ~~multiplication~~ model.

   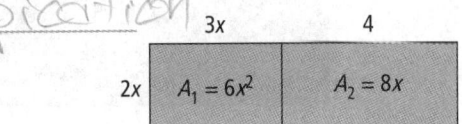

   b) The model in part a) represents the expression

   (_____)(_____ + _____) = _____ + _____.

2. Use the distributive property to multiply the monomial and the polynomial. Then, expand the expression.

   $(-2x)(5x + 6) =$ (_____)(_____) + (_____)(_____)

   = _____ − _____

Check Your Understanding

3. Write the multiplication expression for each model.

   a)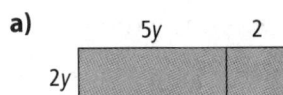

   c)

   b)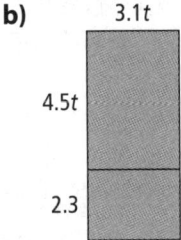

   d)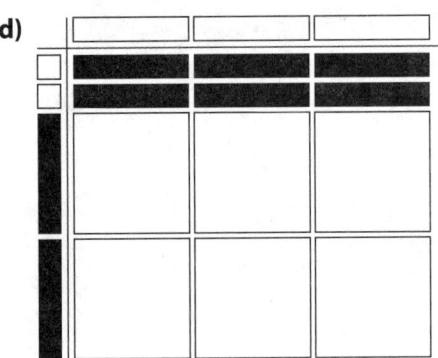

4. Sketch an area model to represent each expression.

   a) $(2.3g)(4.6g + 5)$

   b) $(5 + 7.2f)(2.1f)$

5. Use models to represent each expression.

   a) $(-2d + 3)(-3d)$

   b) $(-s)(-3s - 5)$

6. Use the distributive property to multiply each pair of expressions. Do not simplify.

   a) $(1.2z)(-4z + 2y)$

   b) $(-2e - 3f + 4)(-e)$

7. Multiply. Then, simplify.

   a) $(7v)(-7v - 7x)$

   b) $(-4x)(-7 + 3y)$

c) $(b)(-0.1a + 8b - 0.7c)$

d) $\left(\dfrac{a}{4}\right)(6a - 4)$

8. A rectangular pool has a length 2 m shorter than twice its width.

   a) Write an expression to determine the pool's perimeter. What is its perimeter?

   b) Write an expression to determine the surface area of the pool. What is the surface area?

9. At a restaurant, the menu included the following choices:

Menu	
Coffee	$3.50
Soup of the Day	$5.95
Garden Salad	$6.95
Catch of the Day	Market Value
Cheesecake	$7.75

   a) Sheeyin and Kaitlin each order coffee, soup, a garden salad, the catch of the day, and cheesecake. Write a simplified expression to show the total cost for their meals.

   b) Write an expression to calculate a 15% tip on the total for the meal.

   c) The catch of the day cost $14.95. What was the total bill, including the tip?

7.3 Dividing Polynomials by Monomials

MathLinks 9, pages 272–277

Key Ideas Review

Use the following terms to complete #1 to 3. Terms can be used more than once.

> dividend   divisor   numerical coefficients   product   quotient   variables

1. To divide a polynomial by a monomial algebraically, you can divide the ~~dividend~~ *dividend* and ~~product~~ *divisor* and apply the exponent rules to the *product*. To check your work, multiply the *variable* by the *product*. If the *dividend* equals the *divisor*, your answer is correct.

2. Consider the model. Then, complete the sentences below.

   In the model, the six x^2-tiles and eight x-tiles represent the _____.

   If the divisor is $2x$, the unknown side is the _____. To find the quotient, count the number of tiles along the top row of the _____.

3. The expression represented by the model in #2 is _____. The quotient is _____.

4. In the boxes, write the correct values for the following equation and its check.

   Divide:
   $$\frac{4x^2 - 6x}{2x} = \frac{\boxed{}}{2x} - \frac{\boxed{}}{2x}$$
   $$= 2x - 3$$

   Check by Multiplication:
   $$(2x)(2x - 3) = (2x)\left(\boxed{}\right) - (2x)\left(\boxed{}\right)$$
   $$= 4x^2 - 6x$$

Date: _____

Check Your Understanding

5. Sketch the solution for the unknown value. What is the unknown value?

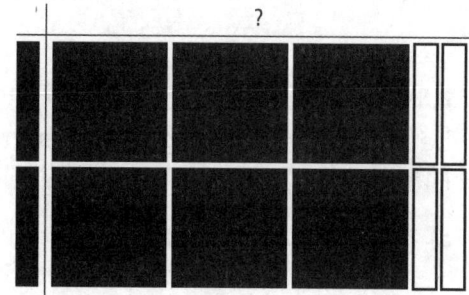

6. Use a model to divide the expression.
   $(-8x^2 + 12x) \div (-4x)$

7. Divide.
   a) $\dfrac{-36y^2 + 10.8y}{6y}$

   b) $\dfrac{4s^2 - 8st + 12s}{-8s}$

   c) $-(8.1d^2 - 7.2d + 3.6) \div (9)$

   d) $(-y^2 - yz - y) \div (-y)$

8. A load of topsoil has a volume of 7.5 m³. You wish to spread the topsoil over an area measuring $(30x + 22.5)$ m². Create an expression for the depth of the topsoil.

9. A triangle has a base of $(3x + 6)$ cm and a height of $24x$ mm. Write an expression you can use to calculate the area of the triangle. What is its area?

10. The formula for the volume of a cylinder is $V = \pi r^2 h$. The volume of a cylinder is $510.5t^2$ cm³, and its height is 6.5 cm. Calculate the approximate radius of the cylinder.

11. The surface area of a cylinder is represented by the formula $SA = A_1 + A_2$, where $A_1 = 2\pi r^2$ and $A_2 = 2\pi rh$. The surface area of a cylinder is 90π m² and $A_1 = 50\pi$ m². Answer the following, showing your work.

   a) What is A_2? Do not change π to an approximate value.

   b) What is the radius of the cylinder?

   c) What is the height of the cylinder?

Chapter Link

Date: _____

Create an expression for each of the following questions. Then, answer the question. Show your work.

1. A homeowner is using square ceramic tiles to tessellate a pathway. The area of the pathway is $(3686.4xy + 1036.8x)$ units².

   a) The width of the path measures $4.8x$ units. How long is the path?

   b) The path is 24 tiles in length. What is the length of one tile?

   c) Each square tile is 0.5 units in height. What is the volume of one tile?

   d) The ceramic tiles are sold in bundles of 5. The bundles cannot be broken apart. Each tile is $1.2x$ units wide. How many bundles of tiles did the homeowner have to buy?

   e) It took the homeowner four trips to the store to bring the tiles home. Her trunk was filled to capacity on each trip. What is the approximate volume of the trunk?

2. A rectangular piece of metal that is to be shaped into piping has a length of $(486d + 162p + 108)$ units.

   a) The metal has a width of $9d$ units. What is the area of the metal?

   b) A model of the pipe is 54 times smaller than the original pipe. What is the area of the model?

3. a) Develop your own question that can be solved by multiplying or dividing polynomials. Solve the question. Check that you have the correct answer.

   b) Exchange questions with another student. Answer each other's questions. Did you need to revise your question or answer? Explain.

88 MHR • Chapter 7   978-007-097344-2

Vocabulary Link

Use the clues to identify Key Words from Chapter 7. Then, write the Key Words in the crossword puzzle blank.

Across

5. This allows you to expand algebraic expressions. For example, $a(b + c) = ab + ac$ and $5(3 + 2) = 5(3) + 5(2)$.

Down

1. This is made up of terms connected by addition or subtraction. Examples include $x + 5$ and $\frac{h^2}{2} - \frac{h}{4}$.

2. This is a type of polynomial that is made up of one term. Examples include $-8cd$ and $3s^2$.

3. This is a type of graphic organizer used to help understand and connect new terms and concepts.

4. This is a type of polynomial that is made up of two terms. Examples include $2x - 5$ and $-8a - 7b$.

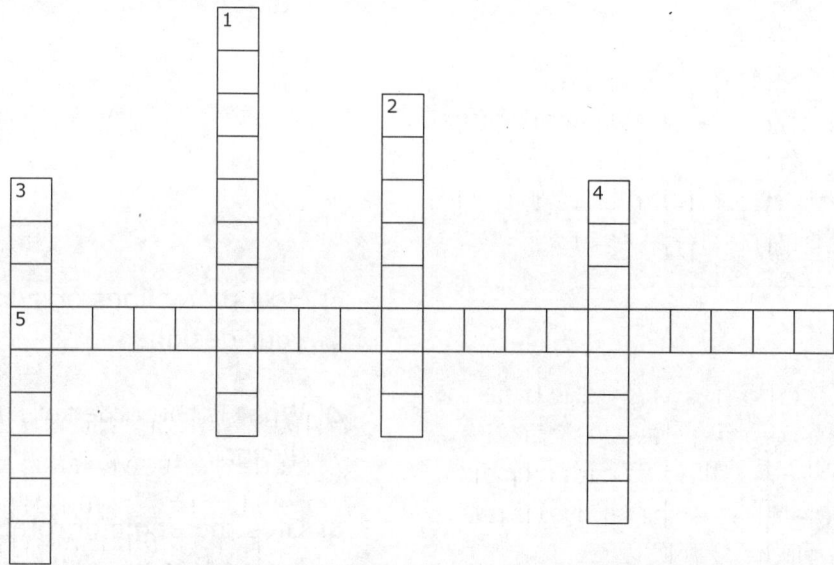

Chapters 1–7 Review

1. Refer to the polynomials below to answer each question.

   > $5x - 20 \quad 5x + y \quad 2x^2 - xy$
   > $5 + c + d \quad 7d^2 - 3cd - 5c + 6$

   a) Write the monomials.

   b) Write the binomials.

   c) Write the polynomials with degree 2.

   d) Identify the variables in the trinomial(s).

   e) Identify the polynomials with a constant.

   f) List the coefficients of the monomials.

2. Determine the linear equation modelled by each graph.

   a)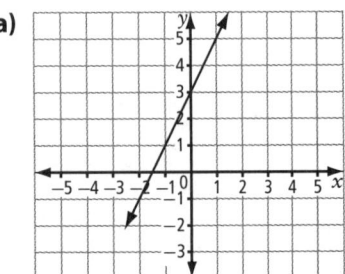

   b)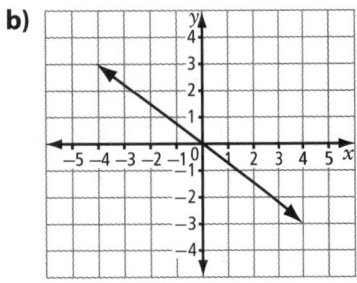

   c)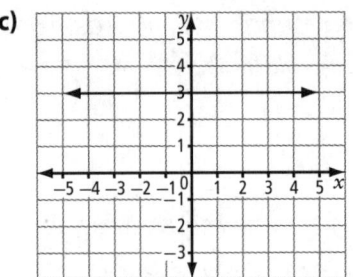

3. Multiply.

   a) $(2.2x^2)(5x)$ b) $(3j)(5j - 6)$

4. Determine the quotient.

   a) $\dfrac{-12x^2 - 8xy}{4x}$

   b) $(16t^2 + 8t) \div (0.5t)$

5. a) Create a design that shows both line and rotation symmetry.

   b) How many lines of symmetry are in your design?

   c) What is the order of rotation in your design?

   d) Give the angle of rotation in both degrees and fractions of a revolution.

90 MHR • Chapter 7 978-007-097344-2

6. Evaluate.

   a) $(-2)^3 + (-4.7)^2 \times 6 \div 2$

   b) $\dfrac{(3^3 - 5) \times 3 \div (-11) + 4}{4^2 - (3^2 \times 6)^0}$

7. A population of bacteria doubles every hour. This relationship is represented by the formula $P = 3(2)^h$ where h is the number of hours. How many bacteria are there after:

   a) 3 h?

   b) 20 h?

   c) 1 day?

8. Complete the subtraction pyramid. Determine the value in any box by subtracting the two expressions in the boxes immediately below it. Subtract in order from left to right.

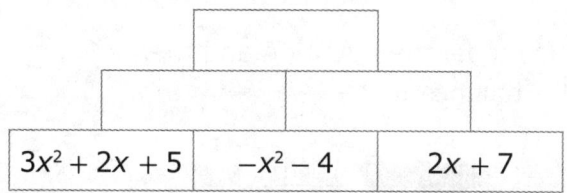

$3x^2 + 2x + 5$ $-x^2 - 4$ $2x + 7$

9. Given the area of each square, determine its side length. Express your answer to the nearest hundredth where appropriate.

   a) 1.69 m²

   b) 74.3 cm²

   c) $\dfrac{1}{9}$ m²

10. Yvonne wants to host a party at a specific hall. This hall charges a flat fee of $100 plus an additional fee of $5 per person.

    a) Create a table of values showing the costs for the first 40 people.

    b) Graph the linear relation.

    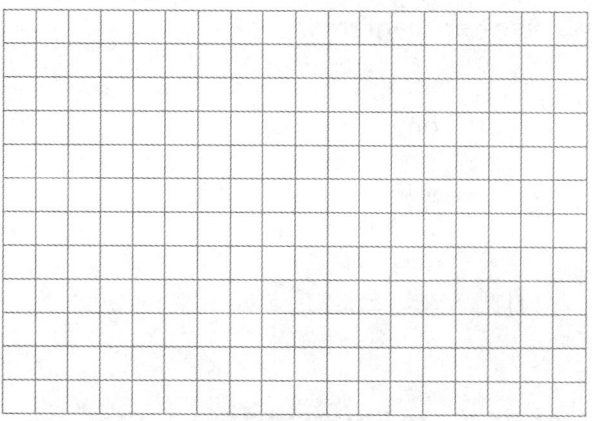

    c) Use the graph to approximate how much it would cost for 25 people to come to the party.

    d) Using the graph, approximate how many people could come for $500.

    e) What equation models this situation?

11. Redraw the star, reducing it by a factor of 0.5.

    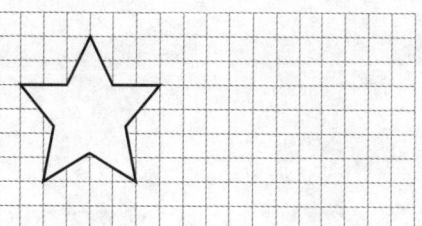

Get Ready

Modelling Equations

You can model an equation using concrete materials, such as algebra tiles. In the figures below, shaded tiles are positive and white tiles are negative.

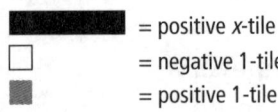

1. Model each equation using algebra tiles or diagrams.

    a) $2x = 8$

    b) $4r - 2 = 10$

2. Write the equation modelled by the algebra tiles.

    a)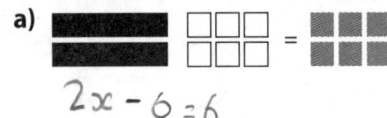

    $2x - 6 = 6$

    b)

    $6 = 3x - 9$

Solving an Equation

Two ways of solving an equation are:
- perform the opposite operation on both sides of the equal sign
- model the equation and then balance it

Solve $3x - 5 = 4$.
$$3x - 5 = 4$$
$$3x - 5 + 5 = 4 + 5$$
$$3x = 9$$
$$\frac{3x}{3} = \frac{9}{3}$$
$$x = 3$$

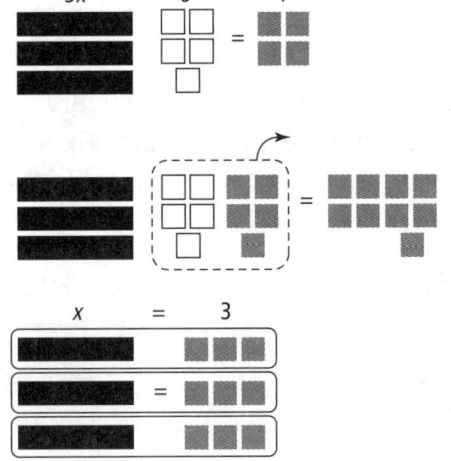

3. Solve each equation modelled by algebra tiles.

a) 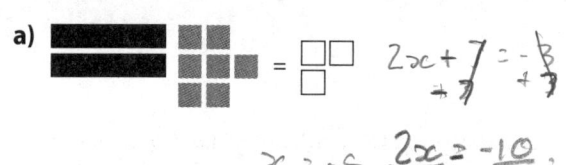 $2x + 7 = -3$
$-7 -7$
$\dfrac{2x}{2} = \dfrac{-10}{2}$ $\underline{x = -5}$

b) $3x - 4 = 5$
$+4 +4$
$\dfrac{3x}{3} = \dfrac{9}{3}$ $\underline{x = 3}$

4. Solve each equation.

a) $\dfrac{s}{2} = 3\ (2)$
$\boxed{s = 6}$

b) $12 - 2x = -4$
$-12 -12$
$\dfrac{-2x}{-2} = \dfrac{-16}{-2}$ $\underline{x = -8}$

Checking an Equation

You can check your solution to an equation by substituting your answer back into the equation. Both sides should have the same value.
Check if $x = 5$ is the solution to $4x + 3 = 23$.

Left Side $= 4x + 3$ Right Side $= 23$
$= 4(5) + 3$
$= 20 + 3$
$= 23$

Left Side $=$ Right Side
The solution, $x = 5$, is correct.

5. Show whether $x = -4$ is a solution to each equation.

a) $5x + 7 = -13$
$- 7 - 7$
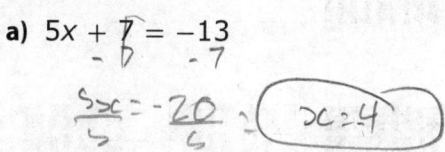

b) $12 - 5x = 8$
$-12 -12$
$\dfrac{-5x}{-5} = \dfrac{-4}{-5}$

6. Solve and check.

a) $x - 2 = 5$
$+2 +2$ $\underline{x = 7}$

b) $3t + 4 = 10$
$-4 -4$
$\dfrac{3t}{3} = \dfrac{6}{3}$ $\boxed{t = 2}$

c) $2g - 7 = -11$
$+7 +7$
$\dfrac{2g}{2} = \dfrac{-4}{2}$ $\boxed{g = -2}$

8.1 Solving Equations: $ax = b$, $\frac{x}{a} = b$, $\frac{a}{x} = b$

MathLinks 9, pages 292–303

Key Ideas Review

Choose from the following terms to complete #1 to 3.

| algebraic | facts | materials | number lines | solution | substitution |

1. You can solve equations using diagrams such as __substitution__, concrete __material__ such as cups, coins, and paper clips, or an __algebraic__ method.

2. You can check solutions by using __substitution__.

3. When checking the solution for a word problem, verify that the __solution__ is consistent with the _____ given in the problem.

Check Your Understanding

4. Each paper clip represents the variable x. Write an equation to represent the model. Then, solve it.

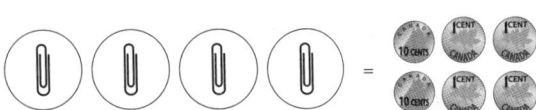

5. Model the solution to the equation $2x = -\frac{5}{2}$ on this number line.

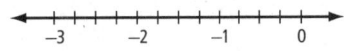

6. Solve. Show your work.

a) $5m = \frac{7}{3}$

b) $\frac{x}{2} = \frac{4}{9}$

c) $-3\frac{3}{4} = \frac{1}{3}x$

d) $-\frac{6}{5}k = -\frac{4}{3}$

7. Solve and check.

   a) $4.8 = \dfrac{w}{3.2}$ b) $-2.8d = 3.15$

   c) $\dfrac{x}{7.5} = -3.1$ d) $-8.2m = -2.091$

8. Solve and check.

   a) $\dfrac{8.4}{r} = 4$ b) $-1.2 = \dfrac{4.2}{x}$

9. Solve. Express each solution to the nearest hundredth.

   a) $\dfrac{8.8}{t} = 3.4$ b) $-0.7 = \dfrac{6.41}{y}$

10. Average speed, s, is related to distance travelled, d, and time of travel, t, by the formula $s = \dfrac{d}{t}$. Write and solve an equation to determine:

    a) how far Marko will ride if he travels at 18.5 km/h for 0.75 h

    b) how much time it will take Sandra to drive 128 km at 90 km/h

11. A new desk is on sale for 35% off. The sale price of the desk is $168.87. Write and solve an equation to determine the regular price.

12. One 250-mL serving of tomato juice contains $\dfrac{2}{5}$ the recommended daily intake of vitamin C. How much tomato juice does a person need to consume to get the full recommended daily intake?

13. Lorena is the goalie for her hockey team. During one game, she stopped approximately 86.1% of the shots she faced. She stopped 31 shots. How many goals were scored?

14. On the school rugby team, the number of 14-year-old players is $\dfrac{2}{3}$ the number of 15-year-old players. If eight players are 14 years old, how many players are on the team in total? Show your thinking.

8.1 Solving Equations: $ax = b$, $\dfrac{x}{a} = b$, $\dfrac{a}{x} = b$ • MHR   95

8.2 Solving Equations: $ax + b = c$, $\frac{x}{a} + b = c$

MathLinks 9, pages 304–313

Key Ideas Review

For #1 to 4, unscramble the letters to form a word that correctly completes the statement.

1. A __Model__ can help determine or check some solutions.
   EDLMO

2. The reverse order of operations can isolate the variable in a two-step equation:
   - First, add or __Subtract__.
     ABCRSTTU
   - Then, __multiply__ or divide.
     ILLMPTUY

3. To solve a two-step equation with fractions, you can first multiply all terms by a common multiple of the __Denominators__ to convert the fractions to integers.
   ADEIMNNOORST

4. You can check the _____ by
   ILNOOSTU
   - using _____
     BIINOSSTTTUU
   - modelling
   - verifying it is consistent with the _____ given
     ACFTS

Check Your Understanding

5. Write an equation that could be modelled by this diagram. Then, solve.

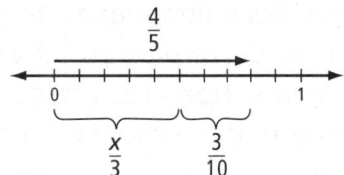

6. Model the equation $4x + 0.24 = 0.72$ using concrete materials. Sketch your model. Then, solve.

Date: _____

7. Jasmine solved the equation 2.5x − 0.62 = 1.2 as shown. Do you agree with her solution? Explain.

$$25x - 62 = 120$$
$$25x - 62 + 62 = 120 + 62$$
$$25x = 182$$
$$\frac{25x}{25} = \frac{182}{25}$$
$$x = 7.28$$

8. Solve.

a) $5x - \frac{3}{2} = \frac{5}{4}$

b) $\frac{x}{3} + \frac{7}{6} = \frac{2}{3}$

c) $1\frac{1}{4} = -2\frac{3}{8} + \frac{3}{5}g$

d) $4 - \frac{2}{3}q = \frac{3}{5}$

9. Solve and check.

a) $0.3x - 1.7 = 0.88$

b) $-1.56 = 3.7f + 5.1$

c) $\frac{b}{-3} + 4.6 = -8.3$

10. A pool contains 300 L of water. It empties at a rate of 6.4 L/min. Write an equation to determine how long it will be until the pool contains only 60 L of water. Then, solve.

11. The area of Banff National Park is 6641.0 km². This is 529.6 km² less than 5.1 times the area of Kootenay National Park. Write and solve an equation to determine the area of Kootenay National Park.

12. An isosceles triangle with a perimeter of 47.4 cm has one short side and two equal longer sides. The short side is 8.6 cm. Write and solve an equation to determine the length of one longer side.

13. Jasmine has a newspaper delivery job. She earns $5.70 plus $0.09 per paper she delivers. How many papers does she need to deliver to earn a total of $12?

8.3 Solving Equations: $a(x + b) = c$

MathLinks 9, pages 314–321

Key Ideas Review

For #1 to 2, choose from the following terms to complete each statement.

| distributive | divide | substitute |

1. The first step in solving $5(x + 2) = 15.25$ is to ___substitute___ both sides or use the ___distributive___ property.

2. To check that $x = 1.05$, you can ___divide___ 1.05 into the equation $5(x + 2) = 15.25$.

3. To avoid fraction operations, rewrite $\frac{1}{3}(x - 4) = 2$ as ___distributive___.

Check Your Understanding

4. Solve and check.

   a) $3(x + 4.2) = 10.5$

   $3x + 12.6 = 10.5$
   $-12.6 -12.6$
   $\dfrac{3x}{3} = \dfrac{-2.1}{3}$

   b) $-2.7 = -5(m - 3.2)$

   $-2.7 = -5m + 15.6$

   c) $-2.7 = 3(a + 3.2)$

   d) $4(2 - x) = 0$

5. Solve. Express your answer to the nearest hundredth.

   a) $-7(2.45 + v) = 12.2$

   $-7.45 + 7v = 12.2$

   b) $-3.56 = 2.7(4 - y)$

   $-3.56 = 2.7(4 - y)$
   $-2.7 - 2.7$
   $4.8 = 4y$

   c) $3(u - 12.75) = -3.41$

   d) $6(0.15 + w) = 10$

Date: _____

6. Solve.

   a) $\dfrac{x+3}{2} = \dfrac{3}{8}$ b) $-\dfrac{6}{5} = \dfrac{2-x}{4}$

   c) $\dfrac{2(p-3)}{3} = \dfrac{1}{4}$ d) $\dfrac{1}{3}(e+3) = \dfrac{1}{5}$

7. Solve and check.

   a) $\dfrac{K-2.1}{7} = 3.4$ b) $2.4 = \dfrac{9.3+j}{-3}$

   c) $\dfrac{y+0.139}{-1} = -4.61$ d) $-2.5 = \dfrac{n+7.34}{-6}$

8. The side length of a small square is s. A larger square has a perimeter of 124.8 cm. Its sides are 3.2 cm longer than those of the small square.

   a) Represent the situation with an equation of the form $a(x + b) = c$. Then, determine the side length of the smaller square.

   $4(x+3.2) = 124.8$

   b) Verify your solution by using a model.

9. Valerie bought five packages of golf balls on sale for $29.50. Each package had a discount of $2.75. Write and solve an equation to determine the regular price of each package.

   $5(9 - \$2.75) = 29.50$

10. Four-fifths of the sum of a number and three is equal to six and a half. What is the number?

    $0.80(x+3) = 6.5$

11. The distance a boat travels upstream can be found using the formula $d = t(b - r)$, where d is the distance travelled, t is the time of travel, b is the speed of the boat in still water, and r is the speed at which the river is flowing.

    a) Determine b when $r = 2.5$ km/h, $d = 2.8$ km, and $t = 0.4$ h

    b) Determine r when $d = 5.95$ km, $t = 0.7$ h, $b = 11.7$ km/h

8.4 Solving Equations: $ax = b + cx$, $ax + b = cx + d$, $a(bx + c) = d(ex + f)$

MathLinks 9, pages 322–329

Key Ideas Review

Decide whether each of the following statements is true or false. Circle the word True or False. If the statement is false, rewrite it to make it true.

1. **True/False** To solve $7x + 5 = 3x - 11$ by the distributive property, first subtract 5 from both sides of the equation.

    to solve 7x+5=3x-11 you have to get like terms

2. (**True**)/False The equation $2(4.5x + 3) = -5(3x - 1.3)$ becomes $9x + 6 = -15x + 6.5$ by using the reverse order of operations.

3. (**True**)/False The solution $x = 0.02$ is correct if the left and right sides of the problem equation are equal when that value is substituted for x.

Check Your Understanding

4. Solve and check.

    a) $3x - 7 = 8x$
    $-3x \quad -3x$
    $\dfrac{-7 = 5x}{5} \quad \dfrac{}{5}$

    b) $4n = -5n + 4.5$
    $+5n \quad +5n$
    $\dfrac{9n = 4.5}{9} \quad \dfrac{}{5}$

    c) $2.6x = 10 - 1.4x$
    $\quad\quad\quad +1.4$
    $\dfrac{4x = 10}{4} \quad \dfrac{}{4}$

    d) $13.8 - 0.6y = -1.1y$
    $+0.6 \quad +0.6$
    $13.8 = 0.5$

5. Solve. Express your answers in fraction form.

    a) $\dfrac{2}{3}(2x - 3) = 4x$

    b) $\dfrac{3}{5}c = \dfrac{1}{4}(2 - 3c)$

    c) $\dfrac{1}{6}(13 + 3x) = \dfrac{4}{3}x$

    d) $-\dfrac{9}{2}w = \dfrac{3}{8}(7 - 4w)$

Date: _____

6. Solve. Express each answer to the nearest hundredth.

   a) $8x + 13 = 15x - 2$

   b) $12p - 0.7 = 5p + 3.2$

   c) $2 - 11m = -2m + 21$

7. Solve.

   a) $6(p - 1.5) = 5(2p + 1.8)$

   b) $\dfrac{2x - 5}{3} = \dfrac{3x + 1}{2}$

   c) $\dfrac{3}{4}(2k - 7) = -\dfrac{1}{8}(5 - 2k)$

8. Brian has $45.25 saved and earns $7.25/week. Dakota has $25.25 saved and earns $9.75/week. In how many weeks will they have the same amount?

9. Determine the value of x so that the square and the rectangle shown have equal perimeters.

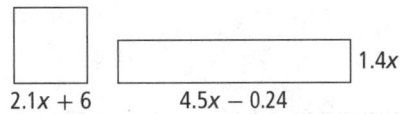

10. Torrin rode his bike to school at 13.5 km/h. He returned home using the same route at 10.5 km/h. Torrin took a total of 36 min to ride to school and back. Express your answer to the nearest hundredth.

    a) How many minutes did Torrin take to ride to school?

    b) How far is it from Torrin's house to school?

11. A local sports centre charges $8 per visit. For an annual membership fee of $45, the cost per visit is only $5.50. What is the least number of visits needed in a year in order for the membership to be a better deal?

8.4 Solving Equations: $ax = b + cx$, $ax + b = cx + d$, $a(bx + c) = d(ex + f)$ • MHR **101**

Chapter Link

Companies that rent cars can charge a fixed rate, a rate per kilometre driven, or a combination of these. Use the information in the chart to answer the following questions.

Company	Fixed Rate	Rate per Kilometre
Fleet Auto Rentals	$22.50	$0.15
Economo Rent-a-Car	none	$0.28
Breeze Rentals	$64.95	none
Alex's Car Rentals	$41.85	$0.06

1. A customer rents a car from Alex's Car Rentals. How many kilometres can she drive for $42? Use a model or diagram to represent this situation. Then, solve.

2. Use an equation to determine how many kilometres a customer would need to drive to make Fleet Auto Rentals cost the same as Breeze Rentals.

3. Mitch has a coupon from Economo Rent-a-Car for 50 free kilometres. He wrote the equation $0.28(d - 50) = c$ to model this situation. How far can he drive for a cost of $30? Express your answer to the nearest kilometre.

4. Fleet Auto Rentals claims to cost as much as Economo Rent-A-Car over a distance of 170 km. Is this true? Use an equation to verify your solution.

5. A group of people is comparing the cost of renting two large cars from Alex's Car Rentals or three small cars from Fleet Auto Rentals. For approximately what distance driven will these two options cost the same? Write an equation to represent this situation. Then, solve to the nearest hundredth.

Vocabulary Link

Draw a line from the example in column A to the related term in column B. Then, find each term in the word search.

A	B
1. a, in the expression $\frac{a-1}{5} = \frac{3}{2}$	a) constant
2. $\frac{T + (-18.1)}{2} = -13.2$ is one example	b) distributive property
3. 2, in the expression $2t = 17$	c) equation
4. $5(b + c) = 5b + 5c$	d) fraction bar
5. acts as a grouping symbol and a division symbol in $\frac{y+5}{2}$	e) numerical coefficient
	f) opposite operations
6. 1.6, in the expression $q + 1.6$	g) variable
7. $+$ and $-$ are one pair, $\div$ and $\times$ are another	

```
G K D Z C D U T D O B I I N N U I E T I
E H S N O I T A R E P O E T I S O P P O
Z I I V L R N D I H S U Z U L P I Q J M
J B W A J K Y S S T J U G M X P A U G K
N U M E R I C A L C O E F F I C I E N T
P B K P L X R Z T F X W A E T O D A C E
O I A I P Z X X R A H I W R K S X T M Q
D V I F A Q N D Z I I N O W I K I N I L
U B L R B V M M R F B B M T P C W T N K
D N O A L A V Z X K U V H F W A Q E O Q
R U W C E R Y E P D T F G X J C L H I D
D I S T R I B U T I V E P R O P E R T Y
Z Q L I B A R T P A I J M N L M C C A P
H F O O M B A X F A V H S Y E K O V U E
I L I N X L K F W N P T K Z U M F V Q A
O E X B I E R I Z V A P F J T R X U E L
L G E A V L B I B N O U T V H I Z I Q A
R Y S R N U R E T C C F K I W N F X J Z
```

Chapters 1–8 Review

1. Simplify each expression. Then, for each one:
   - state the number of terms
   - identify the degree
   - identify the type of expression: monomial, binomial, trinomial, or polynomial

   a) $x(2 - 5x) + 3 - 2x^2$

   Number of Terms: _____

   Degree: _____ Type: _____

   b) $(-p + 8) - (-3p - 7)$

   Number of Terms: _____

   Degree: _____ Type: _____

2. A plumber charges a $30 service fee plus an hourly rate of $50 per hour. The graph shows this linear relationship. Use the graph to answer the following.

   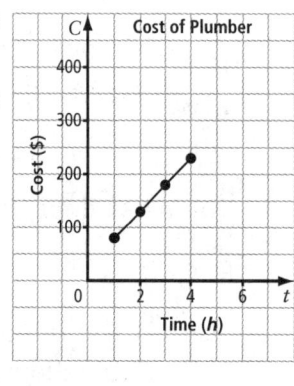

   a) Approximately how much would the plumber charge for 7 h of work?

   b) Approximately how many hours would the plumber work to charge $210?

3. Determine the scale factor of each enlargement or reduction.

   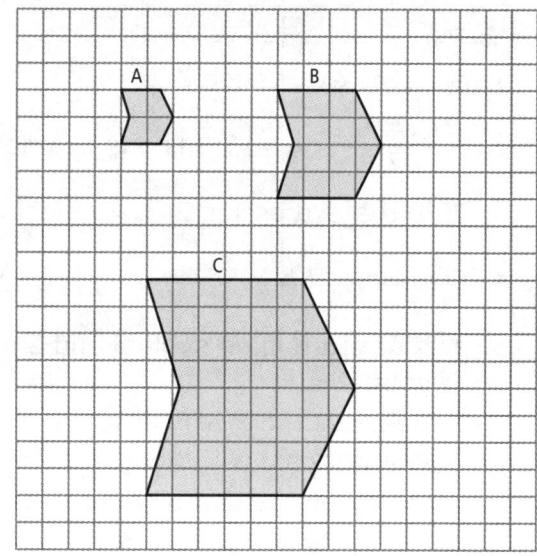

   a) from A to B

   b) from A to C

   c) from B to C

   d) from C to A

   e) from C to B

4. The triangle shown has an area of $6x^2 - 2x$ square units. What is the height, h?

   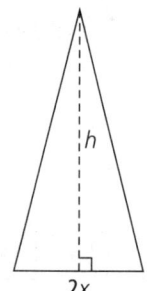

104 MHR • Chapter 8 978-007-097344-2

Date: _____

5. Use line symmetry to make a new diagram.

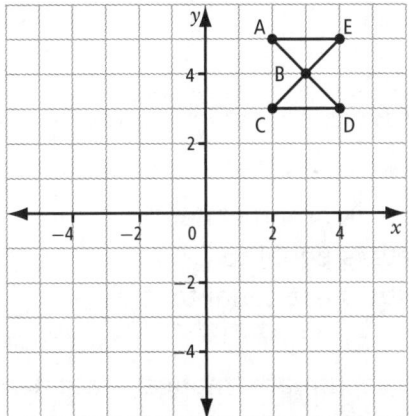

- First, use the y-axis as a line of symmetry.
- Then, use the x-axis as a line of symmetry for both figures.
- Determine the coordinates of each image.

6. Dimitri's Bike Shop sells a tricycle for $40, a two-wheeled children's bike for $90, and an adult mountain bike for $110. One day, the store sold $600 worth of bikes. What number of each item did the store sell? Show that more than one answer is possible.

7. Create a table of values with four values and draw a graph for $y = 3x - 5$.

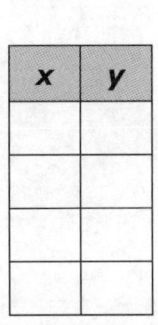
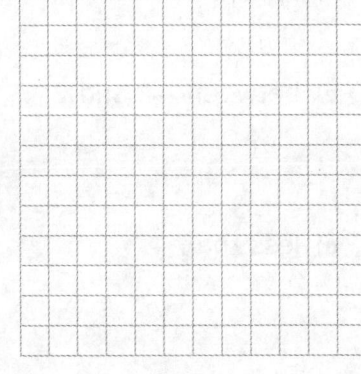

8. Solve and check.

a) $\frac{1}{7}c + \frac{5}{2} = \frac{11}{14}c$

b) $-0.35g = 0.6 - 0.65g$

c) $13.7f + 34.6 = 11.8 - 9.1f$

d) $2(3r + 6) = 3(5r - 3)$

e) $\frac{4b + 6}{5} = \frac{3b - 2}{4}$

9. Write $\frac{(-5)^3(-5)^9}{(-5)^6(-5)}$ as a single power. Then, evaluate.

10. If you flipped a coin three times, there would be 2^3 possible combinations. One possible combination is HTT.

a) What does the exponent, 3, represent?

b) What does the base, 2, represent?

c) List the remaining possible combinations.

d) How many combinations are possible if you flip the coin 10 times? Express as a power. Then, evaluate.

Date: _____

Use Symbols to Describe Relationships

Mathematicians use symbols for operations and to show relationships between quantities. For example,

× represents multiplication
÷ represents division
< represents is less than

> represents is greater than
= represents is equal to
≠ represents is *not* equal to

1. Write each word statement using symbols.
   a) 5 is greater than 2.
   b) 7 is less than 20.
   c) 5 multiplied by 3.
   d) 9 is equal to $\frac{18}{2}$.

2. Write each mathematical statement in words.
   a) 4 < 8
   b) 8 > 2
   c) 14 ÷ 2
   d) 4 ≠ $\frac{8}{3}$

Use *Between*

Between can be used to describe a physical relationship or location. For example, "Paul is *between* Sue and Shasta in line." Similarly, *between* can be used in mathematics. For example, "What are all of the integers *between* −2 and 3?"

The answer is −1, 0, 1, and 2. Note that the word *between* does not include the −2 and 3.

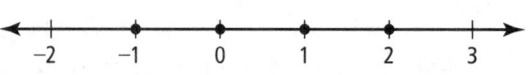

3. List all of the whole numbers that satisfy the following. Use the number line to help you.

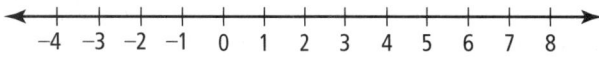

   a) between 6 and 3
   b) between −2 and 2
   c) between 4.6 and 7.1
   d) less than 4

Use Inequality Symbols

An *inequality* expresses a relationship between numbers or quantities. Two inequality symbols are < and >.

5 < 6 means 5 is less than 6. This same information can also be shown as 6 > 5, which means 6 is greater than 5.

4. Use both the less than, <, and greater than, >, symbols to write two expressions showing the relationship between the given numbers.

   a) 1 and 7

   b) 4 and −1

   c) 3 and 3.5

   d) 0 and 1

5. List the whole numbers that satisfy each statement.

   a) $x < 4$

   b) between 4 and 8

   c) $t > 11$

   d) $a < 15$

Solve Equalities

When you are asked to solve an equation, you are being asked to find all values for an unknown that make a true statement.
Solve $2x - 1 = 7$.

Solution
$2x - 1 + 1 = 7 + 1$
$\quad\quad 2x = 8$
$\quad\quad\, x = 4$

Check:
$2(4) - 1 = 7$
$\quad 8 - 1 = 7$
$\quad\quad\, 7 = 7$

6. Solve each equation and then verify your answer.

   a) $x + 4 = 6$

   b) $-2x + 1 = 9$

   c) $-5x - 3 = -8$

   d) $4x + 9 = 21$

9.1 Representing Inequalities
MathLinks 9, pages 340–349

Key Ideas Review

Choose from the following terms to complete the statements in #1 to 6.

> algebraically   boundary   closed   conditions   combination   equal
> graphically   greater   left   less   open   right   verbally

1. Inequalities can be represented __algebraically__, __graphically__, and __verbally__.

2. A(n) __boundary__ point separates values greater than from values less than a specified value.

3. On a number line, the inequality $x \leq -7.2$ has a(n) __closed__ circle at -7.2 and an arrow to the __left__.

4. When shown graphically, the inequality $x > 5$ has a(n) __open__ circle at 5 and an arrow pointing to the __right__.

5. The inequality $13 \geq x$ means that all values of the variable are __less__ than or __equal__ to 13. Values __greater__ than 13 are not possible for x.

6. A(n) __combination__ of inequalities can be used to represent a situation involving two __boundary points__.

Check Your Understanding

7. For each list of numbers, circle the values that are possible for x in the inequality.

   a) (2), (4), (6), 8, 10
      $x \leq 6$

   b) (−17), (−16), −15, −14, −13
      $x > -15$

   c) (−6), (−2), 1, 4, 5
      $3 \geq x$

8. Show each inequality on the number line.

   a) $x \geq 5$

   b) $x < -3.5$

   c) $25 < x$

9. Express each inequality shown on the number line algebraically and verbally.

   a) number line with open circle at 5, marks at 2, 4, 6, 8, 10

   b) number line with closed dot at -10, marks at -40, -20, 0

   c) number line with closed dot at 1.5, marks at 1, 2

10. For each list of numbers, circle the values that are possible for x in the corresponding combination of inequalities.

    a) −9.1, −5.6, 1.7, 3.2, 7.8
       x > −7 and x < 5

    b) −26, −14.5, −12, −4.3, 0
       x ≤ 0 and x > −14

11. Sketch each combination of inequalities.

    a) x < 28 and x ≥ 16
       number line with marks at 10, 20, 30

    b) x > 2.2 and x ≤ 3.6
       number line with marks at 2, 3, 4

12. Write a combination of inequalities for each.

    a) number line with open circle at 3 and open circle at 8, marks at 2, 4, 6, 8, 10

    b) number line with closed dot at -15 and open circle at 15, marks at -20, -10, 0, 10, 20, 30

13. Represent each with an inequality.

    a) The time spent on the activity can be at most 13 min.

    b) The volume of the container must be a minimum of 1.8 L and a maximum of 2.5 L.

14. Label the number line and sketch the inequalities from #13.

    a) blank number line

    b) blank number line

15. In Canada, by law, any product sold as a *nutritional supplement* or *meal replacement* must provide a minimum of 225 kcal of energy per serving.

    a) If c represents the energy content of one serving, write an inequality to represent this regulation.

    b) Use the number line below to show the possible energy content values according to the regulation.

       blank number line

16. Danielle's track coach tells the team that to be considered for the 100-m race, a runner has to be able to run 100 m in less than 13 s. Draw and label a number line to represent this situation.

17. On Saltspring Island in British Columbia, the height of the tide varies one day from a low of 0.8 m to a high of 3.2 m.

    a) What type of inequality do you need to use to show the range of tide heights? Explain.

    b) Express the situation algebraically, and then represent it using a number line.

9.1 Representing Inequalities • MHR 109

9.2 Solving Single-Step Inequalities

MathLinks 9, pages 350–359

Key Ideas Review

Decide whether each of the following statements is true or false. Circle the word True or False. If the statement is false, rewrite it to make it true.

1. **True/False** An inequality can have many specific solutions.

   _____

   _____

2. **True/False** The inequality $10 \geq -2x$ can be solved by dividing by -2.

   _____

   _____

3. **True/False** The inequality $\frac{x}{5} < -10$ can be solved by multiplying by 5 and reversing the inequality sign.

   _____

   _____

4. **True/False** The inequality $-10x < 30$ has the same solution as the inequality $10x < -30$.

   _____

   _____

Check Your Understanding

5. Solve each inequality.

   a) $x + 12 < 20$

   b) $x - 7.5 \geq -12.8$

   c) $160 \geq 200 + x$

6. Solve each inequality.

   a) $-4x \geq 11$

   b) $\frac{x}{3} < 21$

   c) $-3 \leq \frac{1}{5}x$

7. Each of the cards in the following diagram shows an operation. Circle each one for which you need to reverse the inequality symbol when the operation is performed on both sides of an inequality.

   | $-(-3)$ | $\div(-5)$ | $\times 20$ | -154 | $+(-2)$ | $\times(-0.7)$ |

8. For each list, circle the values that are specific solutions of the corresponding inequality.

   a) 6, 7, 8, 9, 10
      $x + 5 < 13$

   b) 1.5, 2, 2.5, 3
      $2x > 5$

   c) −25, −20, −15, −10, −5, 0
      $-5 + x \geq -15$

   d) −8, −4, 0, 4, 8
      $-4x \geq 1$

9. Verify whether the number line below is the correct solution to the inequality $10 > x + 4$.

10. Verify whether $x \leq -5$ is the correct solution to the inequality $-8x \geq 40$. Explain.

11. Lauren works for a bookstore. One of the store's suppliers has a promotion in which any in-stock children's book costs $4, including tax. Lauren has been told that she can spend at most $150 on books for the store. How many books can Lauren buy and stay within the store's spending limit?

    a) Use an inequality to represent the situation.

    b) Determine the solution and use it to solve the problem.

    c) Verify your solution.

12. Customers can use a pottery studio's kiln and equipment. They can pay in two ways for access to the studio. How many uses in a year would make the members' plan the better option?

    Studio Access Rates

    Single Use: $37.50 per session
    Members' Plan: $285 for unlimited use annually

    a) Use an inequality to represent the situation.

    b) Use the inequality to solve the problem.

    c) Is the boundary point itself a reasonable solution to the problem? YES   NO   Explain.

13. Serena can rent a video game for $3.49 per day. She can buy the game for $49.95. After how many days does it become cheaper for Serena to buy the game?

    a) Use an inequality to represent the situation.

    b) Use the inequality to solve the problem.

    c) If the game takes Serena 25 h to solve and she plays 1.5 h a day, should she rent or buy the game? Verify your solution.

9.2 Solving Single-Step Inequalities • MHR **111**

9.3 Solving Multi-Step Inequalities

MathLinks 9, pages 360–367

Key Ideas Review

For #1 to 3, unscramble the letters to form a word that correctly completes the statement.

1. To solve a multi-step inequality, _____ (OTIAELS) the variable in the same way that could be used to solve a(n) _____ (TNQAEIOU). Remember to _____ (EEESVRR) the inequality sign when _____ (IIUYPLGLMNT) or _____ (NDDVGIII) by a _____ (AVEETING) number.

2. There are often several possible methods for solving a _____ (ILUMT) – _____ (ETSP) inequality. The variable can be isolated on the _____ (FLET) or the _____ (GTRIH), depending on which is more convenient.

3. Problems that involve _____ (GOMACRNPI) different options can often be modelled and solved using _____ (QETEANIIILUS).

Check Your Understanding

4. Solve each inequality.

   a) $3x + 7 < 34$

   b) $\frac{x}{3} - 4 \geq -10$

   c) $30 - 5x > 42$

   d) $-22 \leq -10 + 8x$

5. Solve.

   a) $3x \geq 5x + 24$

   b) $3x - 7 < 8x + 3$

   c) $2.5(4 + 7x) + 3 \leq 5.5x - 17$

   d) $3(8 - 3x) < 11 - 4(2x - 3)$

Date: _____

6. a) Verify whether $x \leq 3$ is the solution to the inequality $7x \geq 20x - 39$. Show your work.

   b) Verify if $x > 1$ is the solution to the inequality $7 - 4x > -2(3x - 5)$. Show your work.

   c) Verify whether $x \leq 3\frac{2}{5}$ is the solution to the inequality $9x - 13\frac{3}{5} < 5x$. Show your work.

   d) Verify whether $x < -4.7$ is the solution to the inequality $2x > 5x + 14.1$. Show your work.

7. Ethan can download music from Site A for a flat rate of $29 per month plus $0.80 per download. He can download music from Site B for $17 per month plus $1.19 per download. How many downloads make Site A the better deal?

   a) Choose a variable and identify what it represents.

   b) Write an inequality to represent the situation.

   c) Solve the inequality and answer the question.

8. Trailways Bike Shop offers two options for renting bikes. How many hours would make the all-day plan the better deal?

   Hourly: $25 plus $8 per hour
   All Day: $55

   a) Choose a variable and identify what it represents.

   b) Write an inequality to represent the problem.

   c) Determine the solution and use it to solve the problem.

9. Sheila, Melanie, and Claudette live in different towns, as shown on the map. Whenever they visit Melanie, Sheila and Claudette leave their houses at exactly the same time. Claudette always travels at 75 km/h.

   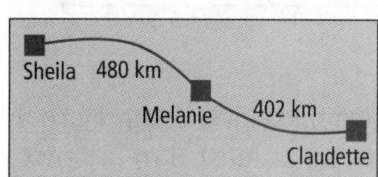

   a) If Sheila travels at 105 km/h, use an inequality to determine after what amount of time she is closer to Melanie's house than Claudette is.

   b) How fast does Sheila have to travel so that she never arrives at Melanie's later than Claudette? Express your answer to the nearest tenth.

Chapter Link

Michele and Hani have teamed up to paint a fence. Each paints one side. Hani is just starting on his side and paints at 3.5 m per hour. Michele paints at 3 m per hour, but starts 5 m along her side because she painted the first part yesterday.

1. Hani wants to spend more than 6 h painting today. Represent this situation algebraically and graphically.

    <---|---|---|---|---|---|---|--->

2. Michele plans on painting at most 20 m of fence today, in addition to what she painted yesterday.

    a) Write an inequality to show the total length of fence that might be painted on Michele's side at the end of the day.

    b) Express your inequality graphically.

    <---|---|---|---|---|---|---|--->

3. Hani plans on taking a short break when he has at least 5 m of fence painted. How long must Hani paint before taking a break?

    a) Write an inequality to represent the situation.

    b) Use the inequality to solve the problem.

4. If Michele and Hani both paint non-stop for t hours, when will Hani have painted farther along the fence than Michele?

    a) Write an inequality and use it to solve the problem.

    b) Verify the solution. Show your thinking.

Vocabulary Link

Unscramble the letters of each term. The terms are one to four words long. Use the clues to help you solve the puzzles.

A	B
1. can be written using the symbols >, <, ≥, ≤, or ≠	IAUINYLEQT
2. shows that the number is not part of the boundary point	EOCINREPCL
3. this is an example	NBCEUISELIQINTAFMNOOAITIO
4. shows that the number is part of the boundary point	LODERILCECSC
5. showing an inequality, using visuals such as diagrams and graphs. Example:	LAHIYRGPACL
6. showing an inequality using words. Example: all numbers greater than 5.5	LRALYBEV
7. showing an inequality using mathematical symbols such as numbers, variables, and operations	LIEYAALGRCABL
8. value or set of values that satisfies an inequality	IAUINYLEQTFOSNOLUAIONT
9. separates the values less than from the values greater than a specified value. Example:	DUNATOBPROINY

Chapters 1–9 Review

1. Create a single polynomial with three terms, two variables, degree 2, a constant term, and at least one coefficient of −4.

2. The graph shows a linear relation.

   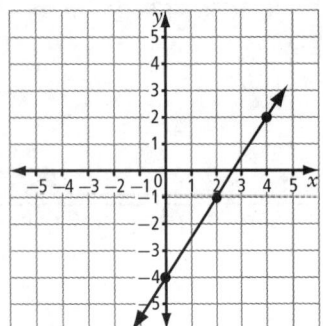

   a) What is the approximate value of the y-coordinate when $x = 1.5$?

   b) What is the approximate value of the x-coordinate when $y = 0.5$?

   c) Determine the equation that represents this graph.

3. Simplify by combining like terms.

   a) $(5x - 4) + (2x - 3) + (x - 7)$

   b) $(5a^2 - 2a) + (5a - 4) - (a^2 - 3)$

   c) $(7t^2 - t + 2) - (t^2 + 5t - 3) + (4t^2 - 6t - 1)$

   d) $(3x - 2.7) - (4.5x - 2.7) - (0.8x - 0.2)$

4. The height of an adult Triceratops was about 240 cm.

   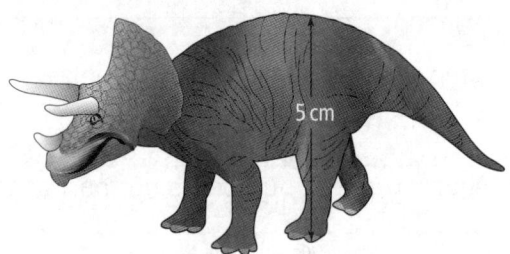

   a) What is the scale factor of this drawing?

   b) If the length of this Triceratops drawing were 12.6 cm, what is the length of the actual reptile? Show how you know.

5. Determine each product or quotient.

   a) $12k \div (-6k)$ b) $7n(-2m + 6n)$

   c) $\dfrac{-27pq + 3q - 9q^2}{-3q}$ d) $\left(\dfrac{2}{5}s\right)\left(s - \dfrac{2}{3}\right)$

6. Given that △ABC is similar to △ADE, what is the length of side BC?

   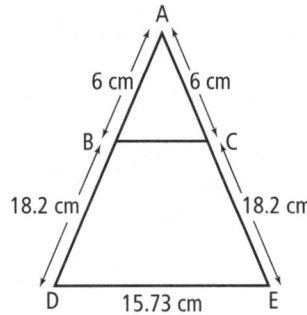

7. For this design, answer the questions below.

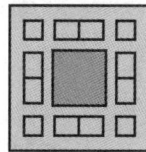

a) Does the design have rotation symmetry? If so, what is the order and angle of rotation? Express the angle in degrees and in fractions of a turn.

b) Does the design have line symmetry? If so, draw the lines of symmetry. Describe each line of symmetry using the terms *vertical*, *horizontal*, and *oblique*.

8. Explain the errors in the following solutions. Determine the correct answers.

a) $(-4)^3 + 5 \times 3^4 = -64 + 5 \times 81$
$ = -59 \times 81$
$ = -4779$

b) $(6 \div 2)^4 + (4 + 3)^2 = (3)^4 + 4^2 + 3^2$
$ = 81 + 16 + 9$
$ = 97 + 9$
$ = 106$

9. Two blocks are placed one on top of the other.

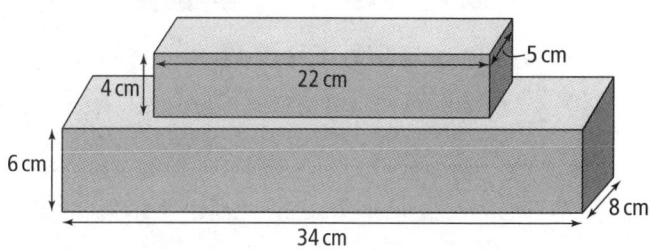

a) What is the total surface area for each of the blocks when separated?

b) What is the exposed surface area of the stacked blocks?

10. Solve and check.

a) $-\dfrac{a}{54} = -1.5$

b) $7.6(3 - p) = -2.4(p + 10)$

11. a) Determine the number with a square root of 3.9.

b) Determine $\sqrt{0.4761}$.

c) Estimate $\sqrt{10}$.

d) Calculate $\sqrt{10}$ to the nearest hundredth.

12. Solve and verify.

$3(2x + 3) > 2(7x + 6)$

Working With Circles

The *diameter* is the distance across a circle through its centre. The diameter of a circle is twice the length of the circle's *radius*. The *circumference* is the distance around a circle.

$d = 2r$ or $r = \frac{d}{2}$, where r = radius and d = diameter

$C = \pi d$ or $C = 2\pi r$, where C = circumference, r = radius, and d = diameter of a circle.

The radius of a circle is 2.4 cm.

The diameter is $d = 2r$.   The circumference
2(2.4) = 4.8   is $C = \pi d$.
The diameter is 4.8 cm. $= \pi (4.8)$
                            $\approx 3.14(4.8)$
                            ≈ 15.07

The circumference is about 15.07 cm.

> The value of π is approximately 3.14. You can estimate the circumference to be about three times the length of the diameter.

1. Measure the diameter of each circle.

   a)    b)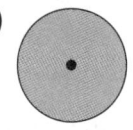

2. a) Estimate the circumference of each circle in #1.

   b) Calculate the length of the circumference for each circle in #1. Use 3.14 as an approximate value for π.

Working With Angles

You can estimate the size of an angle in relation to 90° or a quarter turn.

The angle 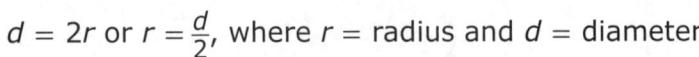 is less than 90°. You could refine your estimate by considering its size compared to  or 90° and or 45°.

You might conclude that the angle is between 45° and 90°, but closer to 45°. The actual measure of the angle is 60°.

Date: _____

3. Estimate the size of each angle.

   a) 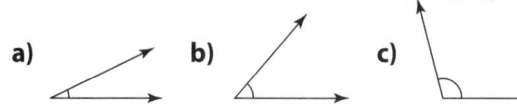 b) c)

5. Sketch an angle that you estimate has a measure of 55°. Then, use a protractor to draw an angle that measures 55°. How close was your estimate to the actual angle measure?

4. Measure each angle in #3.

   a)   b)   c)

Bisecting Angles

An *angle bisector* divides an angle into two equal parts.
OB bisects ∠AOC, making ∠AOB = ∠BOC.
You can bisect an angle by:
- using paper folding
- using a ruler and a protractor

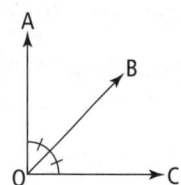

6. Bisect each angle.

   a) 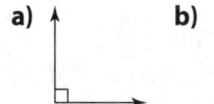 b) 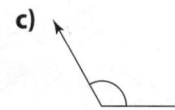 c)

7. What is the measure of the angle created by the bisector in #6a)? How do you know?

Perpendicular Bisectors

A *perpendicular bisector* is a line that divides a line segment in half and is at right angles (90°) to the line segment. DC is the perpendicular bisector of AB.

You can make a perpendicular bisector using:
- paper folding
- a ruler and a right triangle
- a compass

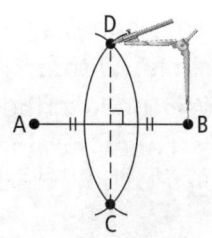
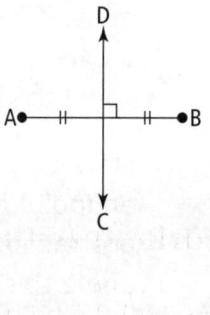

8. Draw the perpendicular bisector for each line segment.

   a) 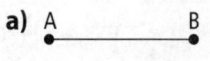 b)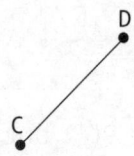

9. Draw the perpendicular bisector for diameter AB. What information do you know for sure about AB or its perpendicular bisector?

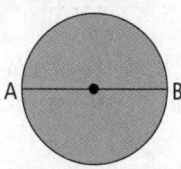

Get Ready • MHR **119**

10.1 Exploring Angles in a Circle

MathLinks 9, pages 378–385

Key Ideas Review

1. Choose from the following terms to complete each sentence.

   arc   inscribed angle   subtended

   a) Inscribed angles are equal when subtended by the same _____.

   b) When subtended by the same arc, a central angle is twice the measure of a(n) _____.

   c) An inscribed angle is equal to 90° when _____ by the diameter of the circle.

Check Your Understanding

2. a) On a sheet of paper or inside the back cover of this Practice and Homework Book, use a compass to draw a circle 10 cm across.

   b) Create two radius lines (radii) and mark the central angle these radii create. Measure the central angle. Label the angle measurement.

   c) Mark two chords that share one endpoint on the circle. With a protractor, measure the inscribed angle this creates. Label the angle measurement.

   d) Use a coloured pencil or pen to mark the portions of the circle that form the arc(s) across the endpoints of your central and inscribed angles.

3.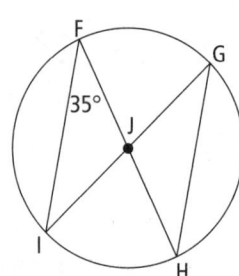

   a) What is the measure of ∠FHG? Explain your reasoning.

   35 it's the same as other inscribed angle

   b) What kind of angle is ∠FJG? How do you know?

   inscribed it doesn't have two Radii.

c) What is the measure of ∠FJG? Explain your reasoning.

70° because it's a central angle (×2 of inscribed)

4. Point O is the centre of this circle.
   diameter LN = 5 cm
   chord LM = 3 cm

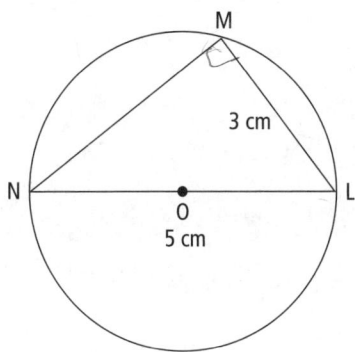

a) What is the measure of angle ∠LMN?

90 Half of 180

b) How long is chord NM?

$3^2 + 5^2 = b^2$
$9 - 25 = \sqrt{16} = 4$

5. a) Label the measure of the angle between the hands of this clock.

b) The angle made by the hands is bisected. The bisector is drawn so that it extends across the diameter of the clock. What numbers does the bisector touch on the clock?

6. Point P is the centre of the circle.
   diameter MO = 19 cm
   chord MN = 17 cm

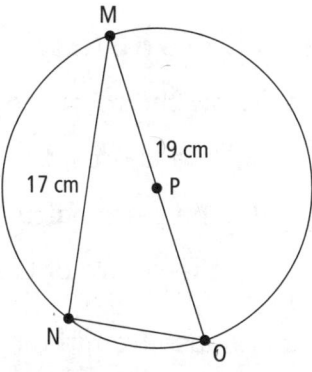

a) How long is the radius?

9.5cm (Half of diameter)

b) What is the measure of ∠MNO?

90° Half of 180°

c) What is the length of chord NO, to the nearest tenth?

7. Point T is at the centre of this circle. ∠TSR = 37°. Justify your answer to each of the following questions.

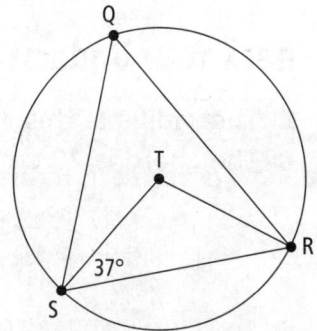

a) What is the measure of ∠RTS?

b) What is the measure of ∠RQS?

10.1 Exploring Angles in a Circle • MHR **121**

10.2 Exploring Chord Properties
MathLinks 9, pages 386–393

Key Ideas Review

1. Draw the following features on this circle.
   a) two chords, BD and EF
   b) the perpendicular bisector of each chord
   c) the centre of the circle

2. Choose from the following terms to complete each sentence.

bisector(s)	centre	chord(s)

   a) The __centre__ of a circle can be found where the perpendicular __bisector__ of two __chords__ meet.

   b) A __chord__ is perpendicular to a __bisector__ if it passes through the circle's __centre__.

   c) A line through the __centre__ of a circle that intersects a chord at right angles is a __bisector__ of the __chord__.

   d) The shortest path between the __centre__ of a circle and a __chord__ is the perpendicular __bisector__ of the chord.

Check Your Understanding

3. The radius of this circle is 15 cm. The chord is 20 cm long.

   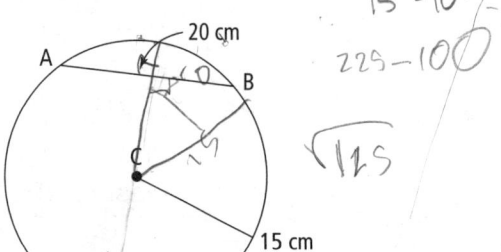

   $15^2 - 10^2 =$
   $225 - 100$
   $\sqrt{125}$

   a) Draw the perpendicular bisector of the chord.

   b) How long is the bisector from the centre to the chord, to the nearest tenth?

   Guessing 12 cm

   11.2 cm

Date _____

4. An archer wants to draw a target in the centre of a 60-cm circle for bow-and-arrow practice. Draw and label a diagram to show him how to find the centre.

6. When an engineer inspects a pipeline, she notices a high water mark. How much space is there between the high water level and the top of the pipe, to the nearest hundredth?

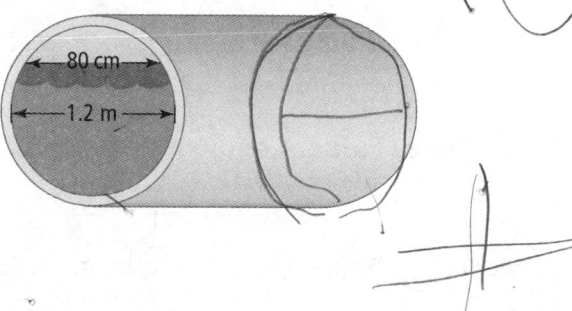

5. This clock face has a diameter of 40 cm. The chord shown is 28 cm long.

a) How long is the hour hand, to the nearest hundredth?

14 cm

b) How far is it from the midpoint of the chord to the outside of the clock face?

5.92 cm

c) Estimate the height of the number 5. Show your thinking.

2.86 cm

7. An archaeologist has found the border of a tipi ring. Some of the stones have been moved.

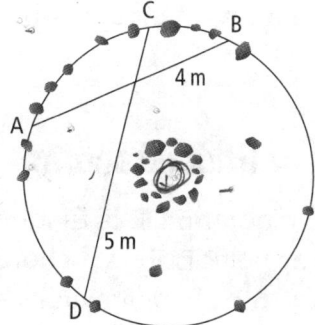

a) Explain or show how four ropes can be used to find the centre of the circle.

b) What is the diameter of the tipi ring, to the nearest tenth of a metre?

10.2 Exploring Chord Properties • MHR **123**

10.3 Tangents to a Circle

MathLinks 9, pages 394–403

Key Ideas Review

Decide whether each of the following statements is true or false. Circle the word True or False. If the statement is false, rewrite it to make it true.

1. **True/False** A tangent never touches a circle.

   _____

2. **True/False** The place a tangent touches a circle is called the perpendicular.

   _____

3. **True/False** A chord perpendicular to a tangent is the diameter of the circle.

   _____

4. **True/False** A tangent is perpendicular to the radius of a circle.

   _____

Check Your Understanding

5. In the diagram, DE is tangent to the circle at point F, FI is a chord, and ∠FDG = 60°. Explain your reasoning when answering each of the following questions.

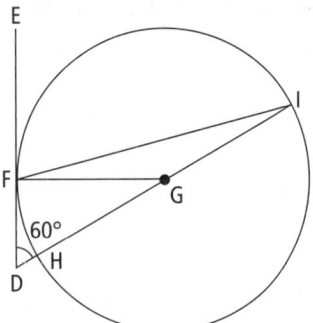

   a) What is the measure of ∠DFG?

   b) What is the measure of central angle ∠FGD?

   c) What is the measure of ∠FHG?

124 MHR • Chapter 10 978-007-097344-2

6. A rod is connected through the centre of these two pulleys. Calculate the length of the rod between the two centre points. Show your work. Express your answer to the nearest tenth.

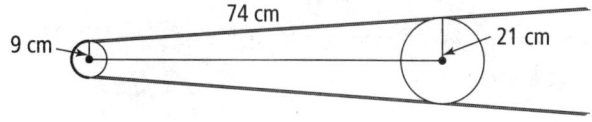

8. a) Darcy threw a discus 12 m. His hand is 90 cm from the centre of his body. How far did the discus actually travel from the spot on which Darcy was standing? Express your answer to the nearest hundredth.

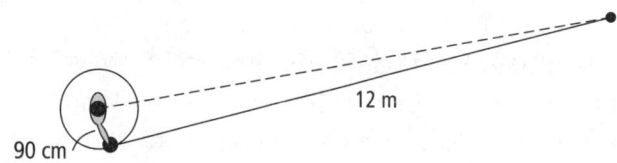

7. A car wheel is frozen in ice. The rim of the wheel has a radius of 19 cm. The chord formed by the ice is 46 cm.

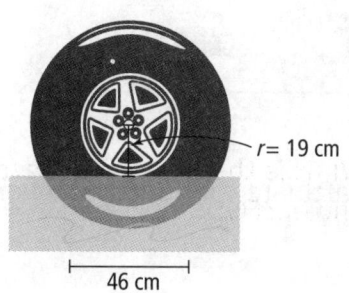

a) How deep is the tire stuck in the ice to the nearest tenth? Show your thinking.

b) What angle is formed between the ice and the radius at the right edge of the tire? Explain your thinking.

b) Explain the relationship of radius, diameter, and tangent using the situation above.

9. In the diagram, $\angle DEF = 75°$ and $\angle DCF = 150°$. Determine the measure of $\angle CFE$.

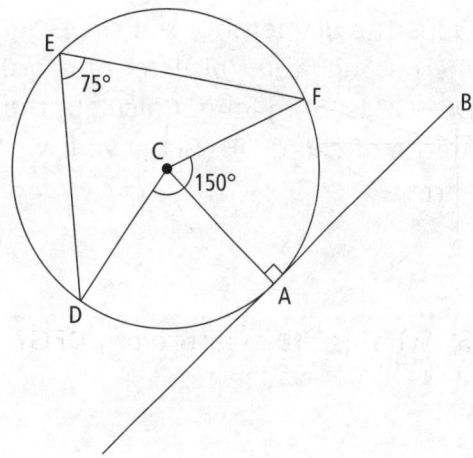

Chapter Link

Triangular supports provide strength inside circular structures such as bicycle tires and this amusement park ride. A Ferris wheel needs to support passengers as it rotates. Use your knowledge of circle geometry to answer the questions below. Show your thinking. Express all linear measurements to the nearest hundredth.

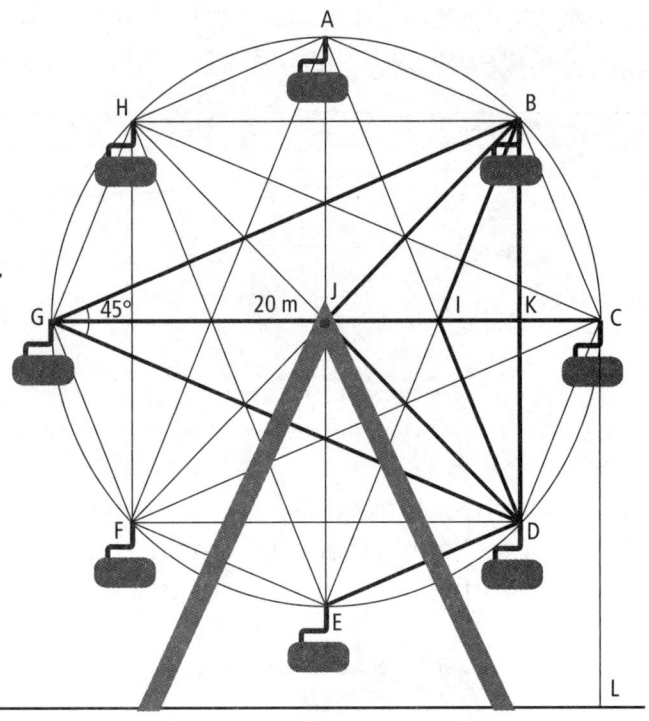

1. a) What is the measure of angle ∠DJB?

   b) Is this an inscribed or a central angle?

2. Calculate the measure of angle ∠JDB.

3. Is ∠HED a right angle? Explain.

   b) Calculate the length of chord DG.

   c) What is the length of chord DE?

4. GC is the diameter of the circle and the perpendicular bisector of chord DB. GC is 20 m long. Calculate the length of chord DB. Show your work.

6. A passenger's hat fell off at point C, falling along tangent CL. What is the measure of ∠DCL?

5. a) What is the distance from point K to point C?

Vocabulary Link

Write the letter of the term in column B that best matches each item in column A. Then, find each term in the word search.

A	B
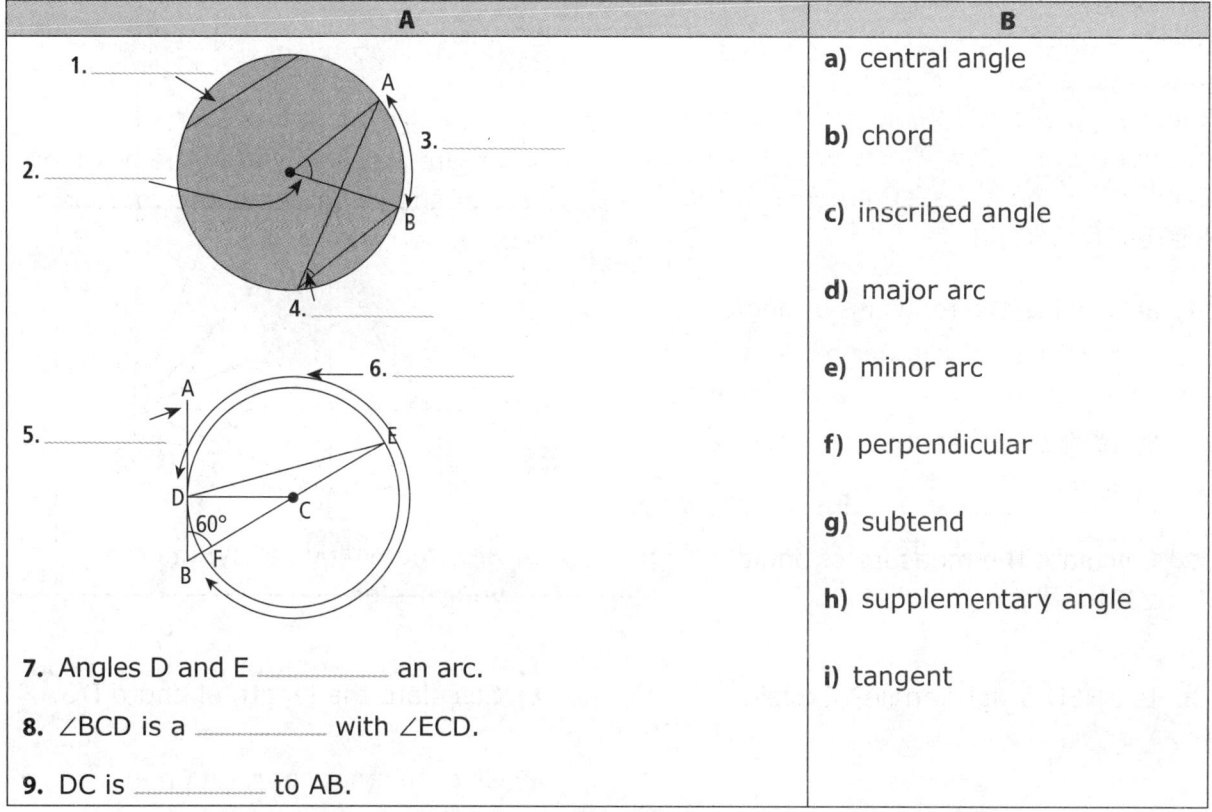 7. Angles D and E _____ an arc. 8. ∠BCD is a _____ with ∠ECD. 9. DC is _____ to AB.	a) central angle b) chord c) inscribed angle d) major arc e) minor arc f) perpendicular g) subtend h) supplementary angle i) tangent

```
T A N G E N T C G S W Q S O F S S A R C
J P E R P E N D I C U L A R V C U T C H
C I C H C V O D C H V B U T N Q P Z A Z
E X L O W M R H R U L M T U H X P A R A
N N F X X O J Y V D W V O E C Q L W P R
T S Q W H R P H Y I D J O Y N O E I E C
R A I C J T K C J B D V V M U D M C N O
A T J T G K B U O I B F G J R M E N T F
L F J X R X Q M F L H H G E A X N T E A
A E B W J N R O P U W R Y J D C T V R C
N R M E O A J Z F H K V O G O L A B S I
G C I C A W M Z M X C R D B P D R X S R
L I N S C R I B E D A N G L E R Y O Q C
E B O S S S A Z H R P U I G U M A S U L
C B R C I T O V C E M G C D A S N T A E
W J A K C V O H Y T A N Q S T V G H R R
E S R D O P L B S F R G P S M I L N E G
R X C T K C J V E R Q F C L U B E N A I
```

Chapter 10: Vocabulary Link • MHR 127

Chapters 1–10 Review

1. Write each statement as an algebraic expression. Tell what your variables represent.

   a) Five and a number are added together.

   b) Steven sells bikes. How many bikes does he have after he sold six of them?

2. Hyun Ji has $27 in her bank account. She plans to deposit $20 every week for a year.

   a) Create a table of values to show her total savings after each of the first five deposits.

   b) What equation models this situation?

   c) How much money will Hyun Ji have in her account after 32 weeks?

3. Is figure ABCD proportional to figure EFGH? Explain how you know. If it is proportional, state the scale factor.

   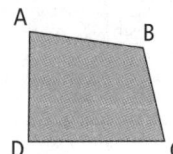 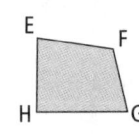

4. Complete each statement.

   a) $-3\frac{5}{6} \times \boxed{} = -5\frac{1}{8}$

   b) $\boxed{} \div \left(-\frac{2}{3}\right) = 1\frac{1}{4}$

5. a) Create a design within the hexagon that shows both line and rotation symmetry.

   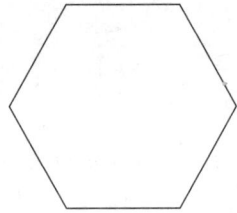

   b) How many lines of symmetry are in your design?

   c) What is the order of rotation in your design?

   d) Give the angle of rotation in both degrees and fractions of a revolution.

6. Evaluate.

   $$\frac{[-8(-3)]^2 + 8^3 \div 4^2 \times \left(\frac{3}{5}\right)^0}{(-14 + 4^2)^5}$$

7. Solve and check.

   a) $-\frac{27}{a} = -2.25$

   b) $3.7(3 - p) = -7.4(p - 5)$

Date: _____

8. The following object has been drawn on isometric dot paper. The distance between the dots is 2 cm. Determine the surface area of the object.

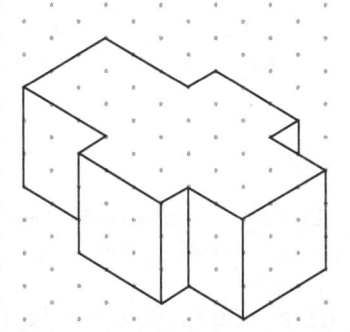

9. Determine the measurements of angles a, b, c, and p if the two lines outside the circle are tangent to it.

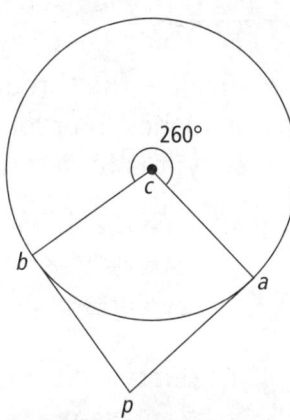

10. Solve each inequality. Verify each solution.

a) $\frac{x}{3} - 7 < 12$

b) $2x \leq 3x + 5$

c) $5(2x + 4) > 2(7x + 4)$

11. The graph represents the relationship between the cost of electricity and the amount used in a house. The electricity is measured in kilowatt hours (kWh).

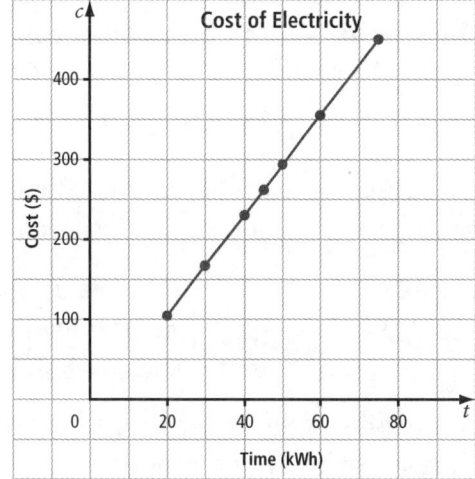

a) Is it reasonable to interpolate or extrapolate values on this graph? Explain.

b) Approximately how much does it cost to use 45 kWh of electricity?

c) Approximately how many kilowatt hours of electricity could you use for $450?

12. In this circle, the chord AE = 6 cm and BC = 4 cm. Determine the size of ∠AED and the length of the radius of this circle.

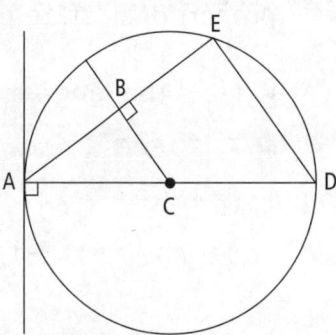

Chapters 1–10 Review • MHR **129**

Measures of Central Tendency

Measures of central tendency are sometimes called averages.
- The **mean** is commonly called the average. It is the sum of a set of values divided by the number of values in the set.

$$\frac{1+1+2+3+4+4+4+5}{8} = \frac{24}{8} = 3. \text{ The mean is 3.}$$

- The **median** is the middle number in a set of data after the data have been arranged in ascending or descending order.

  1, 1, 2, 3, 4, 4, 4, 5 There is an even number of data values. The median is the value halfway between the two middle numbers 3 and 4. The median is 3.5.

- The **mode** is the most frequently occurring number in a set of data. A data set can have more than one mode.

  1, 1, 2, 3, 4, 4, 4, 5 The mode is 4.

Give all answers to the nearest hundredth where necessary.

1. What are the mean, median, and mode for each data set?

   a) 1, 2, 3, 5, 8, 8, 8, 15, 15

   b) 4.2, 4.3, 4.3, 5, 5.1, 6.1, 7

2. Arrange the three measures of central tendency in order according to how easy it is to determine each one. Use the data set 3, 5, 7, 3, 5, 2, 7, 3.

Calculating the Range

The **range** provides information about the spread of the data.
Range = highest value − lowest value
1, 1, 2, 3, 4, 4, 4, 5 The range is 5 − 1 = 4.

3. What is the range of each set of data?

   a) 9, 8, 8, 3, 7

   b) 16, 11, 7, 29, 31, 24, 18, 18, 18

4. If the lowest value in a set of data is 10 and the range is 7, what is the highest value in the set? Explain.

Date: _____

Representing Data

Data can be presented using graphs. Different graphs may display certain types of data better.

Bar graphs are best for comparing data across categories.

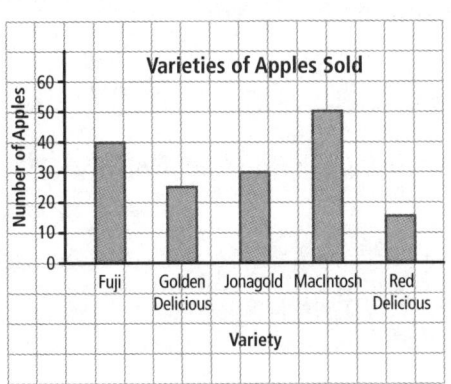

Line graphs are best for showing changes in data over time.

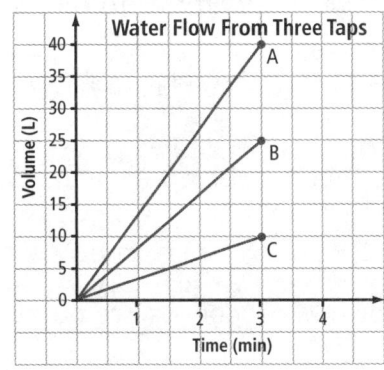

Circle graphs are best for comparing parts of a whole using percents.

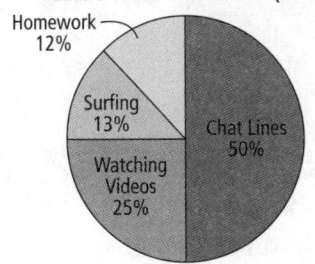

Pictographs are best for comparing data that can be counted easily.

5. The school web site posted the results of a survey about the television viewing habits of grade 9 students.

   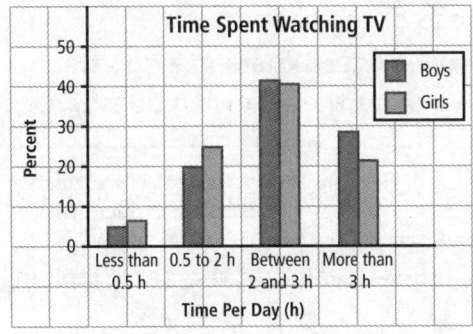

a) What percent of boys watch more than 3 h of TV per day?

b) What percent of girls watch 2 to 3 h of TV per day?

c) If the data in this graph are accurate, how many boys in a population of 500 boys would you expect to watch up to 2 h of TV per day?

11.1 Factors Affecting Data Collection
MathLinks 9, pages 414–421

Key Ideas Review

Choose from the following terms to complete the statements in #1 to 4.

| bias | ethics | influencing factors | survey |

1. A _____ can be used to collect opinions and/or information about a topic.

2. Several _____ _____ affect how data are collected or how responses are obtained.

3. An influencing factor that shows a preference for a specific product is an example of _____.

4. An influencing factor that involves judgments of right and wrong is an example of _____.

Check Your Understanding

5. In each case, identify and describe any factors that may affect the collection of data.

   a) Survey teachers about the new menu in the student cafeteria.
   Influencing factor(s):

   b) Ask customers at a sporting goods store about what brand of snowboard they prefer.
   Influencing factor(s):

   c) Survey students about the timetable in September. Students who respond will be entered in a draw for a digital audio player.
   Influencing factor(s):

   d) Ask grade 9 students if they would use a cell phone in class, even though it is not allowed.
   Influencing factor(s):

6. For each situation, identify whether there is bias. If so, highlight the parts that show bias. Then, rewrite to correct the bias.

   a) Ask customers in a sporting goods store the following question.

   > Titanium Skateboards are the fastest and smoothest skateboards in this store. What brand will you buy?

   Bias: YES   NO
   Rewrite:

b) A sales representative in a grocery store asks customers the following question.

> Which drink do you prefer?
> A Cola
> B Coffee
> C Root beer

Bias: YES   NO

Rewrite:

7. In each case, describe the effect of any influencing factors on the collection of data. Then, write an improved survey question.

a) A government party member asks the following question.

> Is the current premier not the best premier in Canadian history?
> YES   NO

Influencing factor(s):

Rewrite:

b) A small electronics company asks the following question.

> Do you know about the RC Games Company that supplies the excellent games and systems that you and your friends need?
> YES   NO

Influencing factor(s):

Rewrite:

8. For each situation, write two different survey questions that may have resulted in each conclusion.

a) Blue is the most popular car colour.

Question 1:

Question 2:

b) Four out of five mechanics surveyed recommend regular oil changes for family vehicles.

Question 1:

Question 2:

9. Write a survey question for each situation. Identify whom you would ask to participate in the survey.

a) You want to find out which music group teens like best.

Question:

Whom to ask:

b) You want to find out if brand or options is more important when buying a digital music player.

Question:

Whom to ask:

10. Rewrite the survey question so that it collects more helpful data.

> Is lacrosse your favourite sport?
> YES   NO

Question:

11.2 Collecting Data

MathLinks 9, pages 422–429

Key Ideas Review

1. Identify the difference between a population and a sample. Give an example of each.

_____

_____

_____

Connect each statement in column A with the related type of sample in column B.

A	B
2. All of the people leaving a concert are handed a card and asked to mail in their response.	a) convenience sample
3. A food services company surveys 10% of the students at each of four high schools in the district.	b) random sample
4. Every tenth person on a voters' list is polled about whom they will vote for in the next election.	c) stratified sample
5. Franco surveyed all of his friends about their favourite pastime.	d) systematic sample
6. At the mall, a marketing representative asks customers chosen at random about which grocery store they prefer.	e) voluntary response sample

Check Your Understanding

7. Identify the population for each survey question. Indicate whether the population or a sample should be used for the survey. Justify your choice.

   a) Who will be next year's student council president?

   Population:

   Survey ☐ the population ☐ a sample

   Justify:

   b) What colour do you prefer for the lacrosse team shirt?

   Population:

   Survey ☐ the population ☐ a sample

   Justify:

Date: _____

8. For each context, identify and describe the sample you would select for a survey.

   a) The mayor of a city wants to know what people think about the recreational programs offered to residents.

   b) A school librarian wants to know which fiction books to order for the library.

9. For each context, would you recommend surveying the population or a sample? Justify your choice.

   a) You want to determine the water quality in Shuswap Lake, BC.

   b) You want to test the quality of jet engines.

10. A member of the city council plans to ask every person visiting a local park the following questions.

    Do the park rules need better signs?
    YES   NO
    Should the city allow concerts in the park?
    YES   NO

    a) Identify the sample.

    b) Identify the population.

    c) Will the results of the survey accurately represent the population? Explain.

    d) Should the same sample be used for both questions? Explain your thinking.

11. a) Anya, Dhara, and Ian plan to ask students the following question: "What mascot would best represent our new school?" How might you improve the survey question? Explain your reasoning.

    b) There are 1400 students enrolled at the school. Anya suggests using a random sample of 30 students. Dhara suggests using a stratified sample to get input from each grade. Ian wants to survey the whole student population. Whose sampling method is better? Explain your reasoning.

11.2 Collecting Data • MHR   135

11.3 Probability in Society

MathLinks 9, pages 430–439

Key Ideas Review

Unscramble the words to complete each of the following sentences.

1. A _____ _____ can make survey results inaccurate.
   DESBIA   PELSMA

2. If a sample represents the population, you can _____ the results to the population.
   ELIZERAENG

3. You can use _____ probability and _____ probability to help make decisions based on probability.
   LATPEREXINEM   CALORETTHEI

Check Your Understanding

4. A computer chip factory samples chips as they come off the assembly line. A random sample shows that 1 chip out of every 40 is defective. In a run of 3200 chips, the quality manager predicts that 80 chips will be defective.

   a) What assumptions did the quality manager make in her prediction?

   b) Is her prediction reasonable? Justify your answer.

5. A playing card factory samples every 200th deck of cards for damage. The sample shows a 0.20% probability of damage. How many decks of cards would you expect to be damaged in the daily production of 100 000 decks of cards? Include any assumptions you made in your prediction.

6. A manufacturer makes the following claim about the lifetime of its batteries.

   > Each battery has a lifetime of 100 h.

   Carla and Pedro tested 20 batteries to check the claim. Five batteries lasted less than 100 h and two batteries lasted exactly 100 h. The rest lasted longer than 100 h. The students predicted that 25% of the batteries made by the company would not meet the claim.

   a) Did the sample lead the students to make a false prediction? Explain.

   b) If the prediction is false, explain what you would change to make the prediction more accurate.

7. A school with 5400 students is electing a student council president. A reporter for the student newspaper polled 100 people. The table shows that 45% chose candidate A, 15% chose candidate B, and the rest chose candidate C.

   a) According to the poll, how many students will choose each candidate?

Candidate A	Candidate B	Candidate C	Total
45%	15%		100%
			5400

   b) What is the experimental probability for candidate C? What is the theoretical probability that a voter will choose candidate C? What assumptions did you make?

   Experimental probability:

   Theoretical probability:

   Assumptions:

   c) The reporter predicts that candidate C will win the election. Do you agree with her prediction? Explain your reasoning.

8. Cody records the scores from his ten most recent golf games.

Game	Score
1	70
2	69
3	71
4	73
5	74
6	72
7	73
8	75
9	78
10	74

   a) Calculate Cody's mean score based on all ten games.

   b) Use the first three game scores as a sample. Calculate the mean.

   c) Use the last three game scores as a sample. Calculate the mean to the nearest hundredth.

   d) Compare the mean from each sample to the mean for all games. Are the samples a good predictor for Cody's overall score? Explain.

9. Karen read an article claiming that 1 out of every 6 people is born with blue eyes. She predicts that 10 people in a sample of 100 people will have blue eyes. She tested the prediction by rolling a die 100 times for each of 8 trials. Here are the results.

Trial	Blue Eye Colour	Other Eye Colour
1	17	83
2	13	87
3	15	85
4	10	90
5	10	90
6	18	82
7	17	83
8	18	82

   Do these experimental results confirm Karen's prediction or the article's claim? Show your thinking.

Date: _____

11.4 Developing and Implementing a Project Plan
MathLinks 9, pages 440–443

Step 1: Develop the project plan.

You may wish to refer to your work on **BLM 11–9 Section 11.2 Math Link**.

a) Write the research question. Check that your question is clearly written and free of influencing factors.

b) Write the hypothesis. Be specific and limit your hypothesis to one sentence.

c) Identify and describe the population.

d) Describe how you will collect data from studies and surveys that have already been done. Where will you look?

e) List at least three studies related to your research question. Include complete source information. Record your notes for the studies on **BLM 11–11 Section 11.3 Math Link**, on index cards, or on a separate sheet of paper.

Date: _____

Step 2: Create a rubric to assess your project.

Use **BLM 11–12 Research Project Rubric** to create your rubric.

Step 3: Continue to develop the project plan.

a) Describe how you will organize and display the data.

_____
_____
_____

b) Describe your method for analysing the data from the studies you find. Consider the following ideas.

- Describe any assumptions that were made. Explain the limitations of each assumption.
- Discuss the accuracy of any predictions made about the population.

_____
_____
_____
_____
_____
_____
_____

c) Describe how you will present your findings. You might choose a written or oral report, use technology, or use a combination of formats.

_____
_____
_____

Step 4: Complete the project according to your plan.

a) Display and analyse the data on separate sheets of paper.

b) Draw a conclusion or a prediction you can make from the data.

_____
_____
_____

Date: _____

c) Evaluate the research results. Consider using the following questions.
- Do the data answer your question or do you need to do further research?
- Do the data support your hypothesis? Explain.
- Are the data biased? Explain.
- What questions could you ask as a result of your research?
- What other sampling methods could have been considered?
- Troubleshoot any problems you had, such as the following:
  - Was your research question too broad?
  - How well were the data collected?
  - Were there influencing factors on the collection of data? If so, what were the influencing factors?

_____
_____
_____
_____
_____
_____

Step 5: Present your findings.

Present your findings in a format of your choice. Check off each item as you include it.

☐ a title indicating the purpose of your project
☐ a research question and a hypothesis
☐ a description of the population
☐ for the studies researched,
   ____ the sampling methods used
   ____ the methods used to collect data
   ____ the results and conclusions
☐ your display of the data and data sources
☐ your conclusion to answer the research question
☐ your evaluation of the research results
☐ a bibliography of all sources

Date: _____

Step 6: Self-assess your project.

Use the rubric you developed to assess your research project.

a) For which criteria was your project strong? Explain.

_____
_____
_____

b) For which criteria was your project weak? Explain.

_____
_____
_____

c) Did the project meet the requirements you set?   YES   NO   Explain.

_____
_____
_____
_____

d) Identify two things you liked about your project.

_____
_____
_____

e) Identify one thing you would do differently next time.

_____
_____
_____

f) Have a classmate who read or watched your presentation assess your project using the rubric. Ask for constructive feedback on how to improve the project.

g) List the most useful feedback you received. Use the list to improve your project.

_____
_____
_____
_____
_____

Chapter Link

Pam found a study about the Internet browsers that grade 9 students prefer. The survey was conducted on 5000 students, using a stratified sample of Canadian provinces.

Internet Browser	Percent
Internet Explorer	52%
Firefox	27%
Safari	16%
Other	____%

1. a) How many students polled chose "Other"?

   b) What is the experimental probability that a student prefers a browser different from "Other"?

   c) What is the theoretical probability that a grade 9 student will choose Firefox? What assumptions did you make?

   d) Compare the experimental and theoretical probabilities of choosing Firefox.

   e) Pam predicts that Internet Explorer is the preferred browser of grade 9 students in Canada. In your opinion, is the prediction accurate? Explain your reasoning.

2. Emil plans to survey grade 9 students about their preferred online activity.

   a) Identify the population.

   b) Advise Emil on whether he should survey the population or a sample. Give a reason.

   c) Recommend two different types of samples he could use. Describe how to use each one.

   d) Write a survey question that is free from influencing factors.

Vocabulary Link

Unscramble the letters of each term in column B. Use the clues in column A to help you. Each term is one to three words long.

A	B
1. affect how data are collected or how responses are obtained	CUEININFLNGTROSCAF
2. sample created by dividing the population into groups, and then choosing the same fraction of members from each group	DIFESRAITTMASPEL
3. sample created by selecting individuals from the population who are easy to reach	VENONENICCEPLEMSA
4. sample in which each individual has an equal chance of being chosen	DNMOARMPLEAS
5. all of the individuals in a group being studied	NOTPIOLAPU
6. used to collect opinions	VURYSE
7. sample that does not represent the population	SEDAIBSPLEAM
8. sample created by selecting individuals at fixed intervals from an ordered list of the population	TAMICSTEYSPLEASM
9. sample created by inviting the population to respond to a survey	RYLTAOVUNPONRESSELEPMAS
10. any group selected from the population	PELSAM
11. make a broad statement from facts	ZEGENALIER

Date: _____

MathLinks 9 Practice Final Exam

For each multiple choice question, circle the correct letter. For each numerical response question, record your answer in the space provided.

Shopping Malls
Some large shopping malls have amusement parks and/or movie theatres, as well as stores, restaurants, and offices. Use your math skills to solve questions related to shopping malls.

Use this information to answer #1 to 2.

This is part of a game at an amusement park.

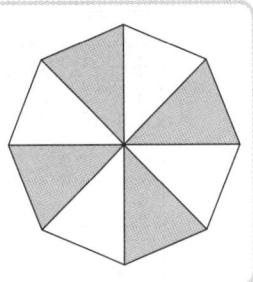

1. What is the order of rotational symmetry?

   A 8   **B** 6   **C** 4   **D** 2

2. What is the angle of rotation?

   A 45°   **B** 90°   **C** 120°   **D** 180°

Use this information to answer #3.

A Ferris wheel has braces AB, AC, DC, and DB.

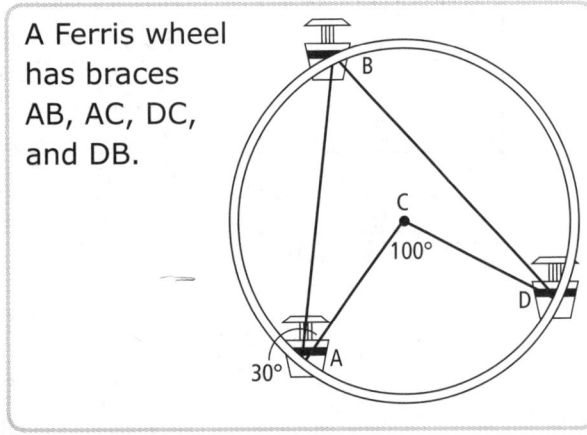

3. What is the measure of the inscribed angle?

   A 30°   **B** 50°   **C** 100°   **D** 200°

Use this information to answer #4.

This vest is in a clothing store window.

Numerical Response

4. How many lines of symmetry are there in the front of this vest?

   _____

Use this information to answer #5.

The skill-testing question on a ballot for a free shopping spree is $(6 - 1)^3 + 64 \div (-2)^3$.

5. What is the answer to the skill-testing question?

   A −9   **B** 7   **C** 117   **D** 133

Use this information to answer #6.

> A clothing store made a profit of $1.3 million in its first year, lost $400 000 in the second year, and lost $300 000 in the third year.

6. What was the average profit (+) or loss (−) over the three years?

   A +$200 000   B +$600 000

   C −$200 000   D −$600 000

Use this information to answer #7.

> This tiered stand is covered with velvet to display jewellery.
>
>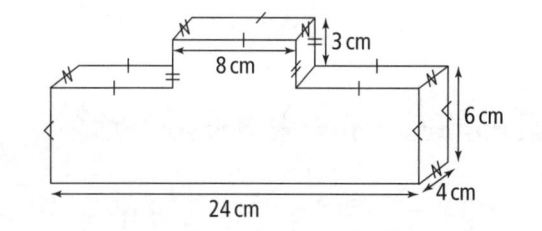

7. What is the surface area of velvet on the exposed faces (all except the base)?

   A 348 cm²   B 444 cm²

   C 504 cm²   D 800 cm²

Use this information to answer #8 to 10.

> Waiters at a restaurant are paid $8.00 per shift and $11.25 per hour.

8. Which table of values represents the total wages a waiter is paid in the first 5 h of a shift?

A.

Hours Worked, h	Total Wages, w ($)
1	11.25
2	19.75
3	30.50
4	41.75
5	53.00

B.

Hours Worked, h	Total Wages, w ($)
1	19.25
2	38.50
3	57.75
4	77.00
5	96.25

C.

Hours Worked, h	Total Wages, w ($)
1	19.25
2	22.50
3	33.75
4	45.00
5	56.25

D.

Hours Worked, h	Total Wages, w ($)
1	19.25
2	30.50
3	41.75
4	53.00
5	64.25

Practice Final Exam • MHR

Date: _____

9. Which of the following would be used to determine the total wages for 3.5 h of work?

   A interpolation	B extrapolation
   C simulation	D assumption

10. An equation is written for the total wages for any number of hours within one shift. Which of the following represents the amount paid per shift?

    A constant
    B variable
    C numerical coefficient
    D linear equation

Use this information to answer #11 to 12.

A poster displaying a pair of shoes uses a scale of 1:4. The length of a shoe on the poster is 6.5 cm.

11. What is the actual length of the shoe?

    A 32.5 cm	B 26.0 cm
    C 24.0 cm	D 10.5 cm

Numerical Response

12. What is the scale factor of the reduction?

Use this information to answer #13.

Every tenth person who makes a purchase at a store is asked a survey question.

13. The type of sampling used is best described as

    A random	B convenience
    C systematic	D stratified

Use this information to answer #14.

A shoe salesperson who earns $2.50 per pair of shoes sold needs to earn at least $45.00 per shift.

Numerical Response

14. What is the least number of pairs of shoes that the salesperson needs to sell?

Use this information to answer #15.

A longer ladder is needed to hang decorations from the top of the wall in the mall. The length of the ladder needed is x.

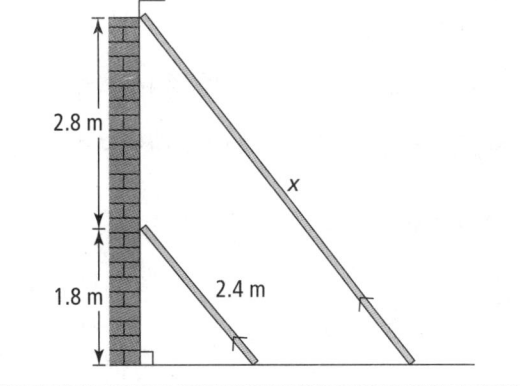

15. Which length of ladder to the nearest metre is needed?

    A 4 m B 5 m C 6 m D 7 m

Use this information to answer #16.

A membership at a movie rental store costs $35.00/year. Movie rentals are $4.00 with a membership and $6.95 without a membership.

Numerical Response

16. What is the least number of movies that would need to be rented in a year to make buying a membership worthwhile?

_____

Use this information to answer #17.

A square in the mall has side lengths $2.8x$. An equilateral triangle-shaped water feature with an area of $2.2x^2$ is being cut out of the centre of the square.

17. Which is the remaining area of the square?

   A $0.6x$ B $0.6x^2$

   C $5.64x$ D $5.64x^2$

Use this information to answer #18.

The diameter of the stained-glass hanging for sale is 60 cm. A chain is attached at A and B so that AD and BD are tangent to the circle.

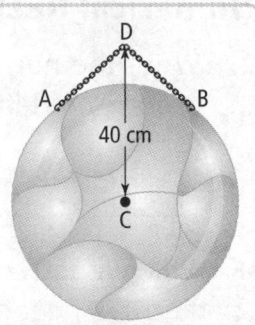

18. Which is the total length of the chain, to the nearest centimetre?

   A 27 cm   B 32 cm

   C 53 cm   D 64 cm

Connections

Many concepts that you study in mathematics are related and can help you solve a variety of problems. Connect the skills and concepts you have learned to solve the following problems.

Use this information to answer #19 to 20.

These algebra tiles model polynomial multiplication and division. Shaded tiles are positive and white tiles are negative.

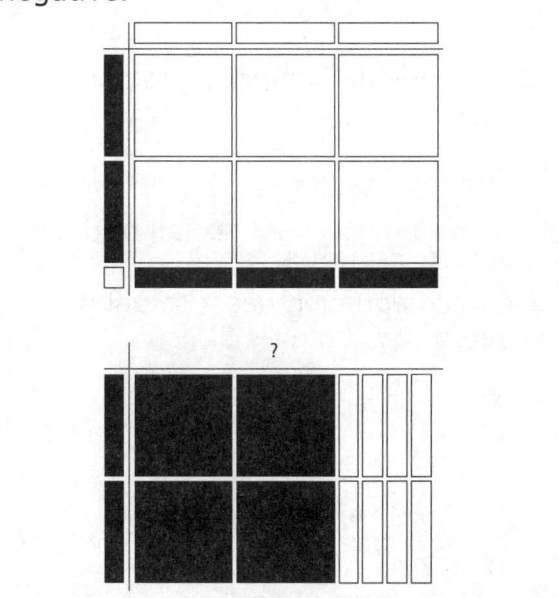

19. Which multiplication statement is modelled by the top tile arrangement?

   A $(3x)(-2x + 1) = -6x^2 + 3x$

   B $(-3x)(2x - 1) = -6x^2 + 3x$

   C $(-3x)(2x + 1) = -6x^2 - 3x$

   D $(3x)(-2x - 1) = -6x^2 - 3x$

20. Which is the quotient of the division modelled by the bottom tile arrangement?

   A $-2x - 4$ B $-2x + 4$

   C $2x + 4$ D $2x - 4$

Date: _____

Use this information to answer #21

This number line is a solution to an inequality.

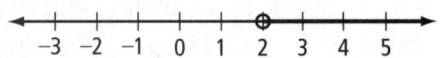

21. For which inequality is the number line the solution?

   A $2x + 5 \geq 9$
   B $-2(x - 7) < 10$
   C $\frac{x}{3} + 6 < 4$
   D $6x + 8 < 4x + 12$

22. Which is an influencing factor when collecting data?

   A ethics
   B bias
   C cost
   D all of them

23. Which equation has a solution of $x = 4$?

   A $\frac{x}{2} + 1 = \frac{3}{4}$
   B $\frac{-5.2}{x} = -1.3$
   C $\frac{2x - 1}{4} = \frac{5x - 6}{4}$
   D $1.2(4x + 6) = 8.4$

Use this information to answer #24.

A square has side length $4a + 0.2$. An equilateral triangle has side length $3a + 2.6$. They have the same perimeter.

24. The value for a is

   A 1.0   B 2.0   C 2.4   D 3.4

Use this information to answer #25

These algebra tiles model two polynomials that are to be added

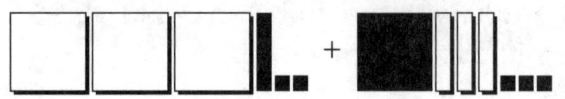

25. What is the sum?

   A $4x^2 - 4x + 5$
   B $-2x^2 - 2x + 5$
   C $-4x^2 + 4x - 5$
   D $2x^2 + 2x - 5$

26. Which polynomial is not of degree 2?

   A $4 + 2x$
   B $xy - 2$
   C $x^2 + 3$
   D $x^2 + xy - 1$

Use this information to answer #27

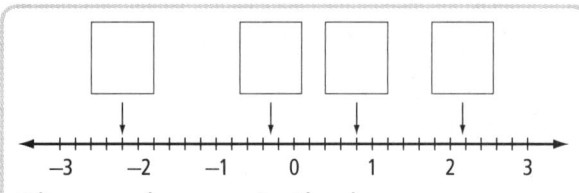

These values go in the boxes:
$\frac{3}{4}$, -0.3, $-2\frac{1}{4}$, $2\frac{1}{8}$

Numerical Response

27. Write the numbers in the correct order from left to right.

_____

Use this information to answer #28

$x + y + 5$	$x^2 + 2$
$3x^2 - 4x + 1$	$xy + x + 2$

28. Except $x^2 + 2$, all of the expressions are best described as

   A polynomials   **B** monomials

   C binomials   **D** trinomials

29. A bacterium triples every 20 min. If there are 35 bacteria present to start, how many will be present in 3 h?

   A 945   **B** 2835

   C 25 515   **D** 688 905

30. What is the value of $2 \times \left(\frac{3}{4}\right)^3$?

   A $\frac{18}{12}$ **B** $\frac{27}{32}$ **C** $\frac{27}{64}$ **D** $\frac{18}{128}$

31. Which value is the best estimate for the side length of a square with an area of 6.4 cm²?

   A 0.8 cm   **B** 2.5 cm

   C 3.2 cm   **D** 12.8 cm

Show your work for #32 to 36 on a separate paper. You will also need one sheet of grid paper.

Use this information to answer #32.

A store carries just one brand of jeans. Due to poor sales, the owner is going to switch to a brand that better appeals to 15- to 30-year-olds.

32. How can the owner collect data to decide what brand to switch to? Explain fully, including who and what to ask.

Use this information to answer #33 to 36.

The store switches to a brand that sells for $89.99 before tax. The revenue from jean sales should be at least $1000.00 per day.

33. Define variables and write an equation to model the sale of jeans. Do not include tax.

34. Create a table of values for the equation for at least five pairs of jeans. Graph the results.

35. Write an inequality that represents the required sales for the day.

36. How many pairs of jeans must be sold in the day to reach the minimum sales? Justify your answer mathematically.

0.5 Centimetre Grid Paper

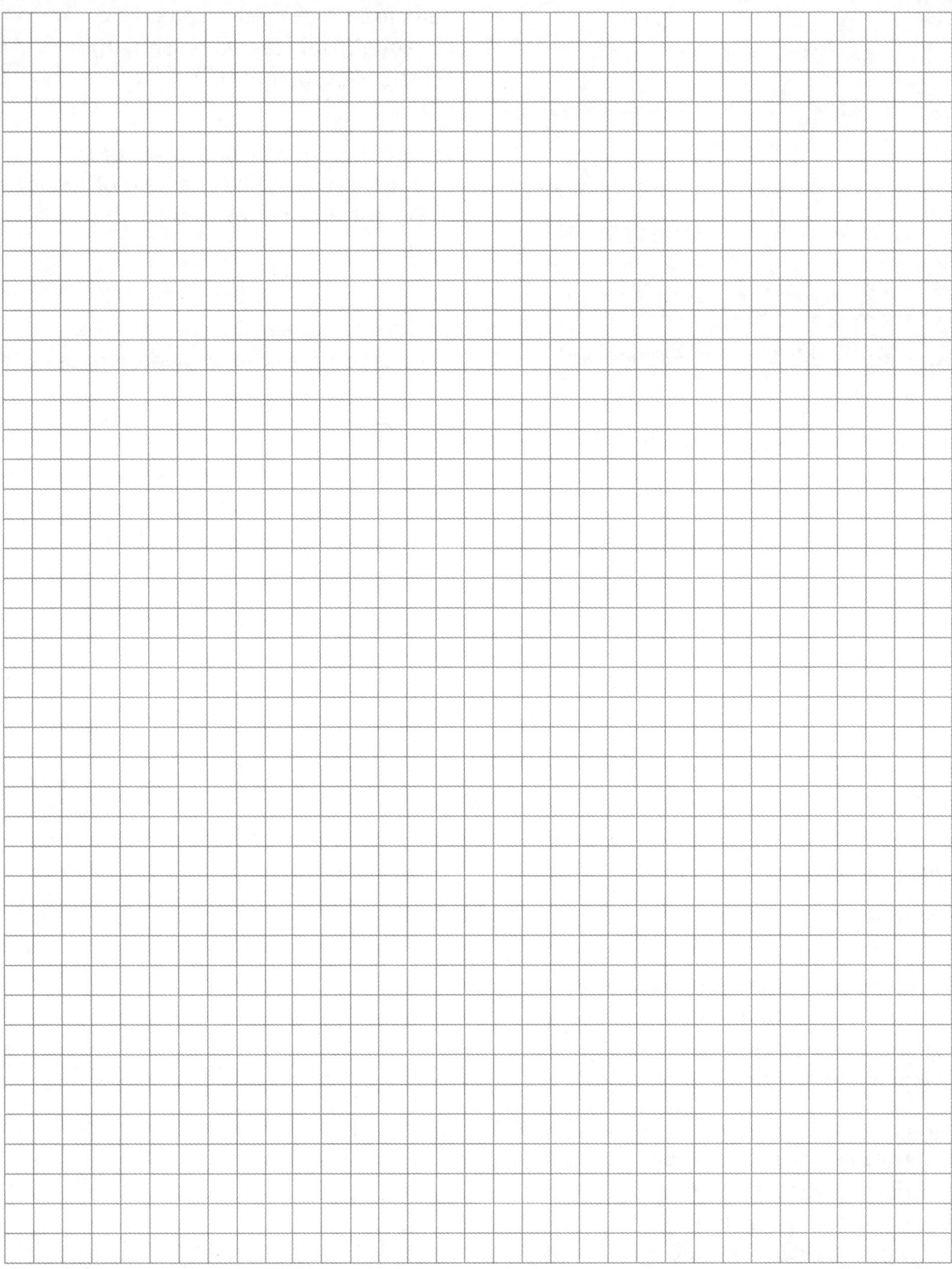

0.5 Centimetre Grid Paper

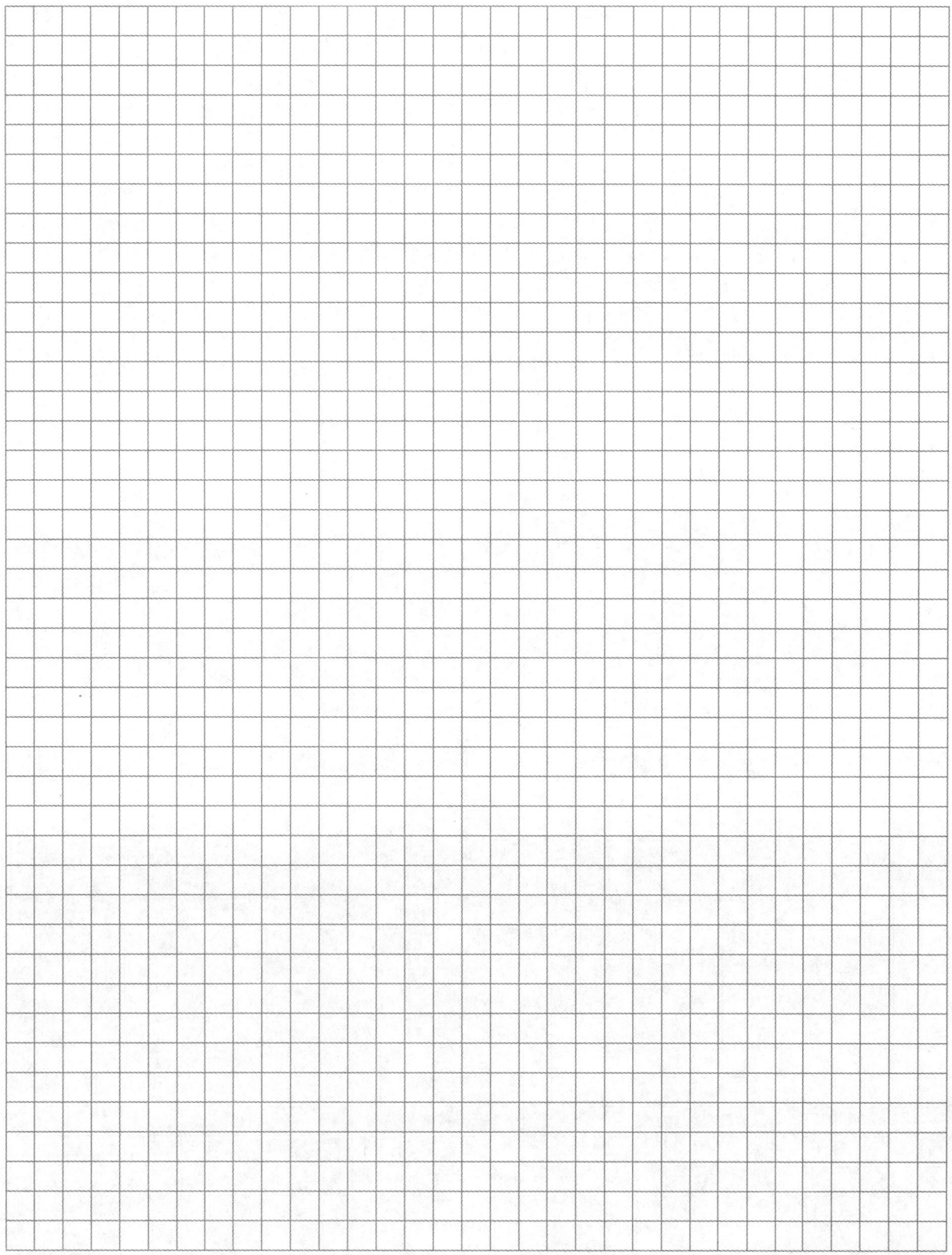

0.5 Centimetre Grid Paper

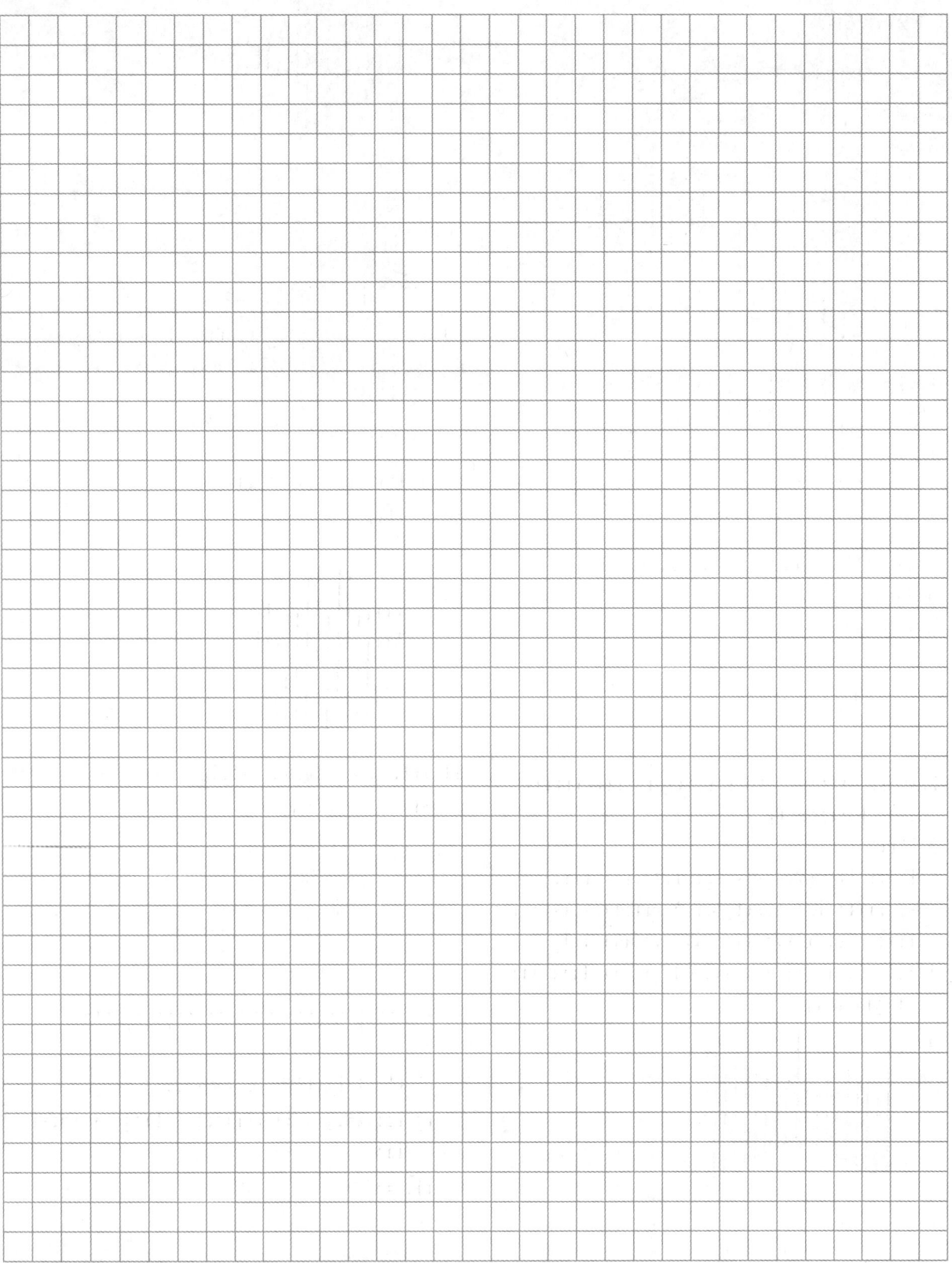

Workbook Answers

1 Get Ready

1. Triangle ABC is translated 4 units up.
2. P'(3, 3)
3. a) 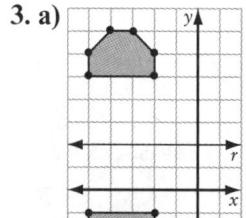 b)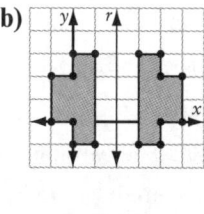
4. a)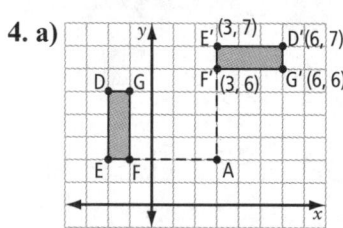

   b) a 270° counter-clockwise rotation
5. 286 cm²
6. a) 5 b) 3

1.1 Line Symmetry

1. True
2. False. Example: An isosceles triangle has one line of symmetry.
3. True
4. False. Examples: A shape that has a line of symmetry is symmetrical. A shape that does not have a line of symmetry is asymmetrical.
5. False. Example: A curved shape may have lines of symmetry.
6.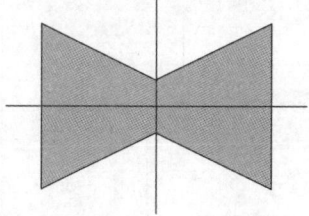

7. Example:

   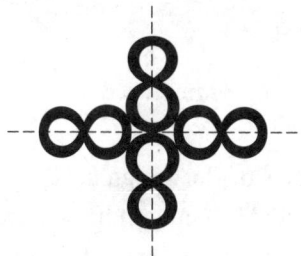

8. Three lines of symmetry

   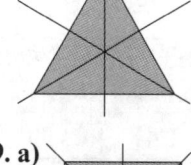

9. a) Four lines of symmetry

   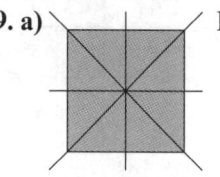

   b) Two lines are oblique.
10. a) There are none.

    b) One line

    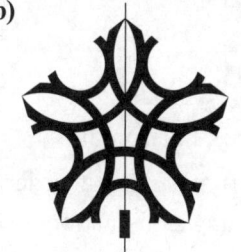

11. a) K(2, 8), L(8, 8), M(5, 2)

    b)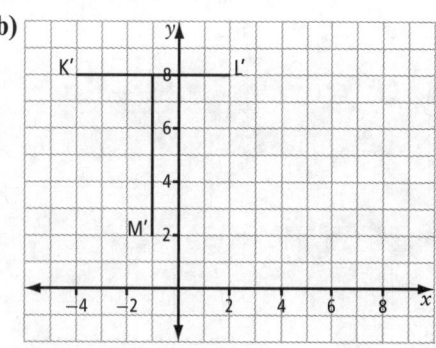

    c) K'(−4, 8), L'(2, 8), M'(−1, 2)
    d) Yes. They show symmetry along a vertical line.
    e) $x = 2$

Answers • MHR **153**

1.2 Rotation Symmetry and Transformations

1. a) rotation b) order c) symmetry d) centre
   e) circle
2. Both. Example: Parts of the design have rotational symmetry. The octagon has an order of 8 and the square has an order of 4. There is line symmetry because there is a reflection along any side of any figure.
3.

Shape	Lines of Symmetry	Order of Rotation	Angle of Rotation
Small square	4	4	90°
Octagon	8	8	45°

4. a) Example:

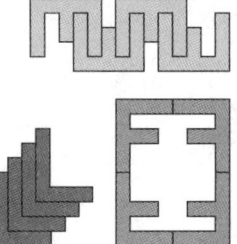

   b) Example: The letter E; horizontal
   c) Example: The design with F has an order of rotation of 2 and an angle of rotation of 180°.
5. a) Example:

   b) Example: 180°
6. a) Four
   b) Example: Yes. Susan could repeat the pattern using rotational symmetry, or line symmetry, or both.
7. a) 2 b) 2 c) 2
   d) 2. Note that if the letter is perfectly square, there may be four lines of symmetry.

e) Examples: I, O
f) Examples: A, B, C, D, E, I, K, M, O, T, U, V, W, Y

1.3 Surface Area

1. a) 675 cm² b) 706.9 cm² c) 1488 cm²
   d) 477.5 cm² e) 1.5 m²
2. Example: The total area of all of the surfaces of a shape.
3. Example: The can has the greater surface area of approximately 596.9 cm². The surface area of the tetra box is 444 cm². The difference between the objects is approximately 152.9 cm².
4. a) 280 cm² b) 460 cm²
5. a) 30 240 cm² b) 22 680 cm² c) 52 920 cm²
6. a) 53 176.4 m².
   b) Each side is 21 513.6 m². The total surface area of the four triangular sides is 86 054.3 m².
   c) The total area of the pyramid is 139 230.7 m².
7. 1738.2 cm²
8. a) 72 cm² b) 108 cm²

1 Chapter Link

Answers will vary.

1 Vocabulary Link

1. line of symmetry
2. line symmetry
3. rotation symmetry
4. symmetry
5. centre of rotation
6. translation
7. angle of rotation
8. surface area
9. symmetrical

Chapter 1 Review

1. a) rotational symmetry
   b) horizontal, vertical, and rotational symmetry

2.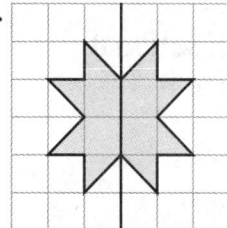

3. a) Example: A type of symmetry where an image can be divided into two identical reflected halves by a vertical line of symmetry.

   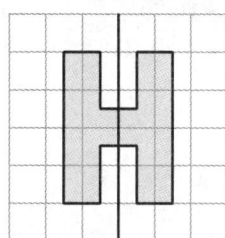

   b) Example: A type of symmetry where an image can be divided into two identical reflected halves by a horizontal line of symmetry.

   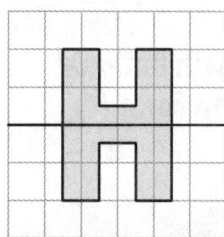

   c) Example: A type of symmetry where an image can be divided into two identical reflected halves by a diagonal line of symmetry.

   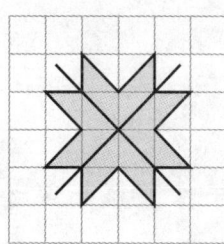

   d) Example: A type of symmetry where an image can be turned about its centre of rotation so that it fits onto its outline more than once in a complete turn.

   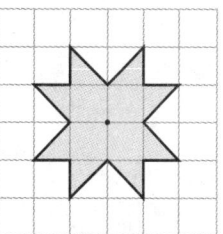

4. a) rotation symmetry

   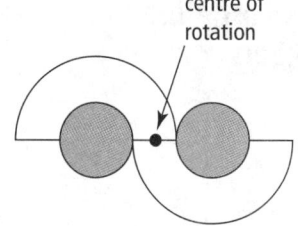

   b) This design is not symmetrical. Example: To give the design symmetry, reflect a row of cats. The two rows of cats would then have symmetry along the line of reflection.

5. a)–b)

   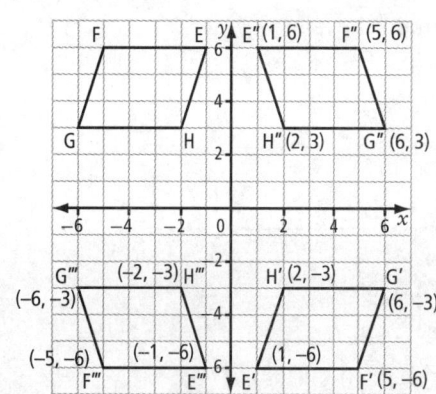

6. a) 167.5 m² b) 277.7 m²
7. a) 128.425 m² b) 1285

2 Get Ready

1. a) 152.85714 **b)** 272.430 **c)** 390.166 00

2. It is less than 349 since we are multiplying by a number less than 1.

3. a) $\frac{3}{4}$, 0.75 **b)** $\frac{4}{10}$, 0.4

4. a) $\frac{7}{10}, \frac{3}{4}$ **b)** $\frac{2}{7}, \frac{1}{3}, \frac{3}{8}$

5. a) $\frac{1}{5} + \frac{3}{10}$ **b)** $\frac{2}{3} - \frac{3}{5}$ **6. a)** $\frac{7}{8}$ **b)** $\frac{1}{12}$

7. a) $\frac{5}{8}$ **b)** $\frac{33}{8}$ or $4\frac{1}{8}$ **8. a)** 10 **b)** $\frac{10}{3}$ or $3\frac{1}{3}$

2.1 Comparing and Ordering Rational Numbers

1. a) 2.1, $-\frac{3}{2}$, 3, -55

b) 3.0, $\sqrt{9}$, $\frac{-21}{-7}$, $\frac{3}{1}$

2. a) $-\frac{14}{5}$, -2.1, $-\frac{3}{4}$, $\frac{0}{3}$, $\frac{3}{4}$, $\frac{5}{4}$, $\frac{6}{4}$, 1.8

b) $-\frac{3}{4}, \frac{3}{4}$ **c)** $\frac{3}{4}$

3. a) C **b)** B **c)** A **d)** E **e)** D

f) Example: I estimated where the rational number would go on the number line, then identified the related letter.

4. a)–b)

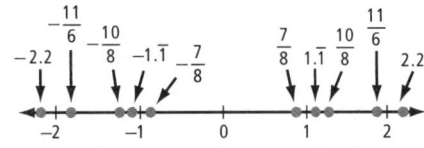

5. a) $-\frac{3}{2}$ **b)** $6.\overline{8}$ **c)** $2\frac{1}{5}$

6. a) 1.125, $-1.\overline{6}$, $0.\overline{54}$

b) -1.7, $-1\frac{2}{3}$, 0.511, $\frac{6}{11}$, $\frac{9}{8}$

7. a) $0.8\overline{3}$, -2.4, -1.75

b) $\frac{5}{6}$, 0.7, $-1\frac{3}{4}$, -2.1. $-\frac{12}{5}$

8. Examples: **a)** $\frac{-6}{8}$ **b)** $-\frac{2}{3}$ **c)** $\frac{3}{2}$ **d)** $-\frac{10}{6}$

9. Examples: **a)** $-\frac{5}{8}$ **b)** $\frac{7}{9}$ **c)** $-\frac{1}{4}$ **d)** $-\frac{8}{7}$

10. a) $\frac{1}{3}$ **b)** $\frac{3}{5}$ **c)** $-1\frac{1}{6}$ **d)** $-\frac{3}{4}$

11. a) $\frac{2}{3}$ **b)** $-\frac{11}{12}$ **c)** $-\frac{7}{4}$ **d)** $-2\frac{5}{6}$

12. a) 0.25, 0.125; Example: 0.13

b) $-0.\overline{6}$, -0.8; Example: -0.7

13. a) 6.5 °C, 0.1 °C, -15.7 °C, -17.0 °C, -22.1 °C, -23.2 °C, -23.6 °C, -32.2 °C

b) -22.2 °C

14. a) > **b)** > **c)** < **d)** =

2.2 Problem Solving With Rational Numbers in Decimal Form

1. adding **2.** negative **3.** positive

4. a) first **b)** multiply **c)** subtract

5. a) 3, 2.5 **b)** -18, -17.87 **c)** -14, -13.84
d) 7, 6.79

6. a) 24, 26.66 **b)** -5, -5.2 **c)** -36, -34.71

7. a) -24.96 **b)** 5.154 **c)** -16.765

8. a) 11.2 **b)** -14.4 **c)** -14.3 **d)** 10.8
e) -85.548 **f)** 64.49

9. 0

10. a) -6.9 **b)** -9.8 **c)** -2.2 **d)** -7.5

11. a) -0.73 **b)** 0.25

12. a) Example: $-12.7 - 6.9$ **b)** 19.6 °C

13. a) Example:
$[-0.5(3 \times 60)] + 0.7[(1 \times 60) + 15]$
b) -37.5 m

2.3 Problem Solving With Rational Numbers in Fraction Form

1. e) number line

2. a) adding the opposite

3. b) improper fractions

4. d) positive fractions

5. c) multiplication and division

6. a) $-1\frac{1}{2}$, -1 **b)** 1, $1\frac{1}{6}$
c) 1, $1\frac{3}{4}$ **d)** $7\frac{1}{2}$, $7\frac{2}{3}$

7. a) -1, $-\frac{2}{5}$ **b)** $\frac{1}{4}$, $\frac{1}{6}$
c) $\frac{1}{2}$, $\frac{5}{14}$ **d)** -2, $-1\frac{7}{8}$

8. a) 1, $1\frac{1}{6}$
b) -1, $-1\frac{1}{11}$
c) 4, $3\frac{1}{7}$ **d)** $\frac{1}{2}$, $\frac{4}{9}$

9. Examples:
$1 - \frac{2}{5} - \frac{1}{3} = \frac{4}{15}$ h,
$60 - \left(\frac{2}{5} \times 60\right) - \left(\frac{1}{3} \times 60\right) = 16$ min
10. $495 **11.** 9.6 m

2.4 Determining Square Roots of Rational Numbers

1. d) **2.** e) **3.** b) **4.** c) **5.** a)

6. a) Any rational number between 25 and 36 is correct. Example: 26

b) Any rational number between 9 and 16 is correct. Example: 12

7. a) 4, 4.84 **b)** 81, 75.69
c) 121, 127.69 **d)** 1, 0.8464

8. a) 196 cm², 216.09 cm² **b)** 4 km², 5.29 km²

9. a) Yes, both 4 and 9 are perfect squares.
b) $0.4 = \frac{4}{10}$. No, 10 is not a perfect square.
c) $0.81 = \frac{81}{100}$. Yes, both 81 and 100 are perfect squares.
d) No, 2 is not a perfect square.

10. a) $0.16 = \frac{16}{100}$. Yes, both 16 and 100 are perfect squares.
b) No, 90 is not a perfect square.
c) $0.001 = \frac{1}{1000}$. No, 1000 is not a perfect square.
d) $\frac{8}{18} = \frac{4}{9}$. Yes, both 4 and 9 are perfect squares.

11. a) 17 **b)** 0.19 **c)** 35 **d)** 2.3

12. a) 1.5 cm **b)** 19 m

13. a) 5, 6 **b)** 7, 8 **c)** 0.4, 0.5 **d)** 0.8, 0.9

14. a) 5.5 **b)** 7.2 **c)** 0.42 **d)** 0.88

15. 2.3 m **16.** 7.5 cm

17. No, the sides of the room are $\sqrt{15}$ m or approximately 3.87 m, which is larger than the width of the carpet roll.

2 Chapter Link

1. 9 h

2. a) $\frac{9}{10}$, 7.5, $\frac{3}{4}$, 6 h 30 min, $\frac{2}{3}$, $4\frac{2}{8}$, $\frac{4}{9}$ **b)** Saturday

3. a) Example: Estimated bed area of 4 m² is less than the area of the room, so it will fit. Room sides are about 1.45 m longer than the bed, so it will fit.

b) Both the flower rug and the geometric rug have sides longer than the bed but shorter than the room.

4. 1 h 25 min

2 Vocabulary Link

Across
6. non-perfect square

Down
1. equivalent numbers
2. parentheses
3. quotient
4. rational number
5. perfect square

Chapters 1–2 Review

1. $3\frac{2}{5}$, -2, $\frac{7}{4}$, -0.7, $1\frac{1}{3}$, 2.5

2. Vertical, horizontal, and rotational symmetry of order 2 with an angle of rotation measuring 180°

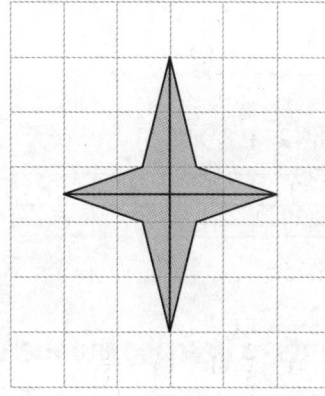

3. a) < **b)** = **c)** > **d)** > **e)** =

4. a) A(1, 1), B(3, 3), C(11, 2), and D(10, 0)

b)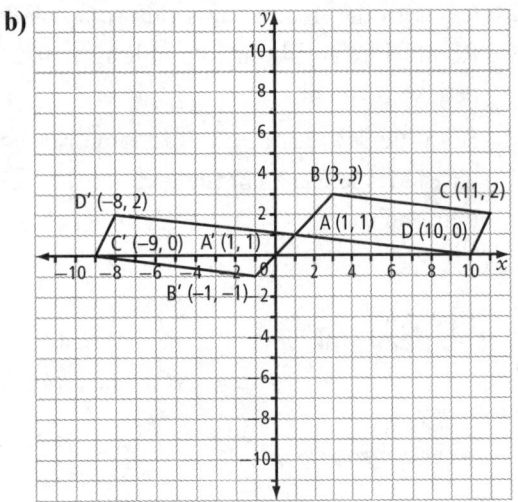

c) A′(1, 1), B′(−1, −1), C′(−9, 0), and D′(−8, 2)

5. 57 °C

6. Estimates are first, then calculations.
   a) −17.5, −17.12   **b)** 2, 1.7787

7. a) 1   **b)** 1   **c)** $-1\frac{1}{2}$ **d)** $-\frac{1}{2}$

8. a) $\frac{32}{49}$ **b)** $3\frac{11}{15}$ **c)** $-\frac{2}{5}$ **d)** $\frac{3}{10}$

9. approximately 25.24 cm²   **10.** 40

11. a) Yes, $\frac{1}{5}$ **b)** No   **c)** Yes, 0.01   **d)** Yes, 0.7

12. a) 7.1, 7.2   **b)** 0.801, 0.819

13. a) approximately $1275

   b) This is not possible because a square gives the maximum area with the minimum perimeter.

3 Get Ready

1. a) 25 cm²   **b)** 81 m²   **2. a)** 8 mm   **b)** 6 cm

3.

m (kg)	0	3	5	6	9
t (°C)	24	48	64	72	96

4. 120 cm³   **5.** 18 cm³

3.1 Using Exponents to Describe Numbers

1. a) power, multiplication   **b)** exponent, base

2. a) $3^4 = 81$ **b)** $(-5)^3 = -125$ **c)** $2^9 = 512$

3. a) $4^3 = 64$ **b)** $(-7)^4 = 2401$ **c)** $8^3 = 512$

4. a) $6 \times 6 \times 6 = 216$

   b) $(-10) \times (-10) \times (-10) \times (-10) \times (-10)$
   $= -100\,000$

   c) $-(4 \times 4 \times 4 \times 4) = -256$

5–6. Look for one of the following answers for each part.
   a) 9×9, 9^2; $(-9) \times (-9)$, $(-9)^2$; $3 \times 3 \times 3 \times 3$, 3^4; $(-3) \times (-3) \times (-3) \times (-3)$, $(-3)^4$

   b) 16×16, 16^2; $(-16) \times (-16)$, $(-16)^2$; $4 \times 4 \times 4 \times 4$, 4^4; $(-4) \times (-4) \times (-4) \times (-4)$, $(-4)^4$

7. a) 1024   **b)** 625   **c)** −64

8. No. Example: $-3^6 = -729$ because the base is 3, and $(-3)^6 = 729$ because the base is −3 and a negative number multiplied by itself an even number of times results in a positive number.

9. $8^3 = 512$ mm³

10. $3^4, 4^3, 2^5, 5^2$

11. Example: $45 = 3 \times 3 \times 5$. The number 45 is not a square because there is not an equal number of prime factors that multiply to make 45. If the prime factorization had two 5s as well as two 3s, then the number would work. $3 \times 3 \times 5 \times 5 = 225$ or 15^2.

12. $1.28, $327.68, $335 544.32, $10 737 418.24

13. $9 \times 9 \times 9$; 9^3

3.2 Exponent Laws

1. b)   **2.** d)   **3.** a)   **4.** c)

5. a) $3^5 = 243$ **b)** $(-2)^7 = -128$
   c) $4^8 = 65\,536$ **d)** $(-3)^8 = 6561$

6. a) $7^2 = 49$ **b)** $(-5)^3 = -125$
   c) $8^4 = 4096$ **d)** $(-6)^3 = -216$

7. a) $(5^3)^4$ or 5^{12} **b)** $[(-9)^2]^5$ or $(-9)^{10}$

8. a) $5^4 \div 5^3 = 5^1$ **b)** $\frac{(-2)^6}{(-2)^4} = (-2)^2$

9. Tony should have subtracted the exponents in step 3, not divided them. $\frac{6^{12}}{6^2} = 6^{10}$. The correct answer is 60 466 176.

10. Example: Any number (except 0) divided by itself equals 1. Since $\frac{4^3}{4^3} = 1$ and $\frac{4^3}{4^3} = 4^{3-3}$, then 4^{3-3} (or 4^0) must also equal 1.

11. a) 25^3 or 5^6; 15 625   **b)** $(-4)^6$ or $(-64)^2$; 4096

12. $10^{17} = 100\,000\,000\,000\,000\,000$

13. Example: $6^7 \times 6^0$; $6^2 \times 6^5$; $6^4 \times 6^3$

3.3 Order of Operations

1.

Expression	Coefficient	Power	Repeated Multiplication	Value
$-3(7)^2$	-3	7^2	$-3 \times 7 \times 7$	-147
$2(5)^4$	2	5^4	$2 \times 5 \times 5 \times 5 \times 5$	1250

2. Step 1 c), Step 2 a), Step 3 d), Step 4 b)

3. a) 108 **b)** 32 **c)** 700 000 **d)** -108

4. a) $2(3)^3$ **b)** $5(-7)^5$ **c)** $-2(8)^4$ **d)** $6(9)^5$

5. a) 16 **b)** -17 **c)** 3 **d)** 0.7

6. Example: In Step 2, Juan should have multiplied 8 by 8, not by 2. The correct answer is 140.

7. a) -199 **b)** 225
   c) undefined; cannot divide by 0 **d)** 20

8. a) 136 **b)** 73

9. 216 mm²   **10.** -233

11. a) $-5^2 = -25$, $(-5)^2 = 25$

   b) Example: The expression -5^2 has an exponent of 2, a base of 5, and a coefficient of -1, so evaluating the power and then multiplying by the coefficient gives an answer of -25. The expression $(-5)^2$ has an exponent of 2, a base of -5, and a coefficient of 1, so the expression has a value of 25.

3.4 Using Exponents to Solve Problems

1. False. A power in a formula represents repeated multiplication.

2. True

3. False. Patterns involving repeated multiplication can be modelled by an expression that contains only powers.

4. 864 cm²   **5.** 5 mm

6. a) $100(2)^n$ **b)** 3200 **c)** 102 400

7. 2 m   **8.** 15.1 cm²   **9. a)** $6s^2$ **b)** $h^2 = a^2 + b^2$ **c)** s^3

10.

Power(s)	Base(s)	Exponent(s)	Coefficient
a) s^2	s	2	6
b) h^2	h	2	
a^2	a	2	1
b^2	b	2	
c) s^3	s	3	1

11. a) 3.38 m² **b)** 22.5 m²

3 Chapter Link

1.

Time (h)	Population of Bacteria in Sample	
	A	B
0	50	600
1	150	1 200
2	450	2 400
3	1 350	4 800
4	4 050	9 600
5	12 150	19 200
6	36 450	38 400
7	109 350	76 800
8	328 050	153 600

2. a) A, 6 **b)** $50(3)^6$ **c)** 50

3. a) $50(3)^n$ **b)** $600(2)^n$

4. Example: Shortly after hour 6, the populations would be equal since the population of Sample A overtakes that of Sample B during hour 7.

5. a) $600(2)^5 - 50(3)^5$ **b)** 7050

6. a) $50(3)^n + 600(2)^n$ **b)** 74 850 **c)** 3 566 850

3 Vocabulary Link

Across

6. exponential form

Down

1. factored form
2. power
3. exponent
4. base

Chapters 1–3 Review

1. $3^{10} = 59\,049$
2. vertical and horizontal symmetry, rotational symmetry of order 2

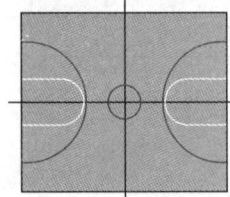

3. a) Examples: $-1, 0, 1$

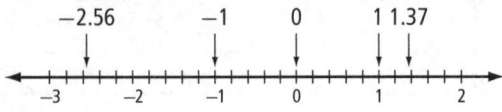

b) Examples: $-0.605, -0.602, -0.601$

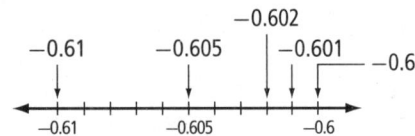

c) Examples: $-\frac{1}{2}, -\frac{1}{6}, 0$

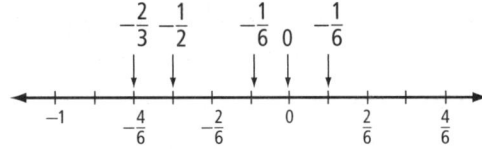

4. a) 64 b) $-\frac{61}{36}$ or $-1\frac{25}{36}$ c) $\frac{19}{243}$
5. Yes. 6, 60°
6. a) $-5\frac{14}{15}$ b) $-2\frac{145}{168}$ c) $6\frac{1}{9}$ d) $\frac{43}{72}$
7. a) $(-4)^3 + (-3)^2 = -55$
   b) $[(5)^2(2)^2(-1)^3]^2 \div (5)^3 = 80$
8. a) 474 cm² b) 186.92 cm²
   c) 583.96 cm². The surface area of the new figure is the same as the total surface area of the two figures minus the area of two of the circular ends of the cylinder.
9. 5
10. a) -3.13 b) -11.44 c) -941.12
11. a) 35.2 m² b) 7

4 Get Ready

1. a) 5:20 or 5 to 20 b) 9:27 or 9 to 27
   c) 3:18 or 3 to 18
2. a) 1:4 or 1 to 4 b) 1:3 or 1 to 3
   c) 1:6 or 1 to 6
3. a) $0.25, 25\%$ b) $0.\overline{33}, 33.\overline{3}\%$ c) $0.1\overline{6}, 16.\overline{6}\%$
4. a) 6 b) 21 c) 1 d) 2
5. Examples: a) $\frac{2\text{ cm}}{200\text{ cm}} = \frac{1\text{ cm}}{100\text{ cm}}$ b) $\frac{1\text{ cm}}{500\text{ m}} = \frac{7\text{ cm}}{3500\text{ m}}$
   c) $\frac{15\text{ cm}}{300\text{ cm}} = \frac{40\text{ cm}}{800\text{ cm}}$ or $\frac{15\text{ cm}}{3\text{ m}} = \frac{40\text{ cm}}{8\text{ m}}$
6. 0.25 m 7. 100 km

4.1 Enlargements and Reductions

1. a) enlargement, larger
   b) reduction, smaller c) scale factor, constant
2. a) 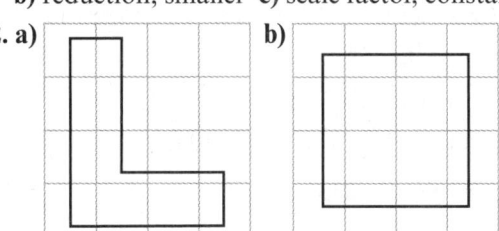 b)

3. a) 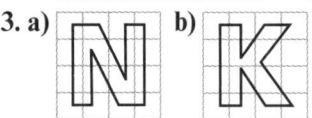 b)

4. a) equal to 1 b) less than 1 c) greater than 1
5. a) Example:

b) Example: I measured the various parts of the butterfly, multiplied that measurement by 4, and then drew the part in the new measurement. For example, the body is 5.5 mm long. I drew the larger body 22 mm long.

6.

7. a) enlargement
   b) approximately 1:2.3. Example: If you measure the A in the newspaper headline and the A in the poster headline, you can find the scale factor.

4.2 Scale Diagrams

1. d) 2. c) 3. b) 4. a)
5. a) divide 85 by 5, then multiply 1 times the answer b) divide 132 by 6
6. a) 121.5 b) 4   7. a) 130.2 cm b) 2 mm
8. a) $\frac{1}{7.5}$ b) $\frac{1}{4}$ 9. a) $\frac{1}{16.3}$ b) $\frac{1}{13\,333.3}$
10. a) approximately 1:206 or 1:207, depending on how you measure
    b) The scale drawing should be 1.1 cm by 1.5 cm.

    c) 1.65 cm²

4.3 Similar Triangles

1. a) angles b) sides
2. scale factor, proportion
3. a) Yes. They are similar because the corresponding angles are equal and the corresponding sides are proportional.
   b) No. The angles are not equal and the sides are not proportional.
4. a) ∠A and ∠J, ∠B and ∠K, ∠C and ∠L; AB and JK, BC and KL, AC and JL
   b) ∠P and ∠M, ∠Q and ∠N, ∠R and ∠L; PQ and MN, PR and ML, QR and NL

5. △PQR and △VWX are similar. Example: They are both isosceles right triangles with 45° angles on the legs. Corresponding sides are proportional.
6. No. Example: They are not similar because the corresponding sides are not proportional.
7. a) $x = 21$ b) $x = 13.8$
8. Example: Triangle reduced by half.

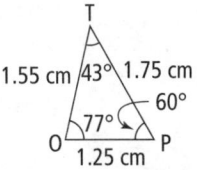

9. 167 cm

4.4 Similar Polygons

1. False. Polygons that are similar have all corresponding angles equal in measure.
2. False. Example: You can use similar polygons to determine unknown side lengths.
3. False. A polygon is a two-dimensional closed figure made of three or more line segments.
4. a) Yes. Example: They are similar because all side lengths are proportional with a scale factor of 2.
   b) Yes. Example: All side lengths are proportional with a scale factor of 1.7.
5. a)

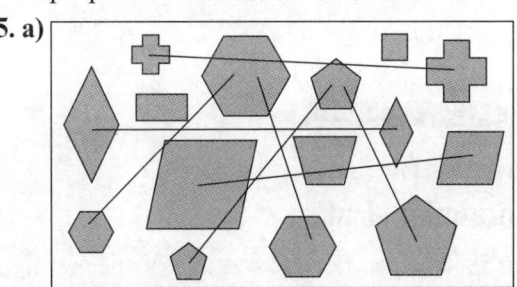

b)

c) Examples:

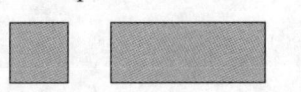 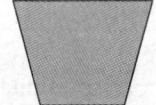

6. a) $x = 1.7$ b) $x = 2.25$, $y = 12$

7. a)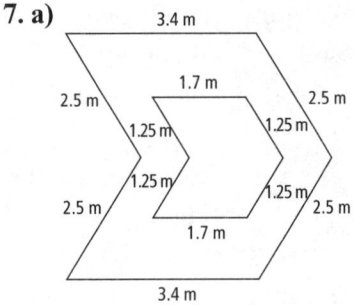

b) 25.2 m

8. $x = 6.3$; $y = 6.7$; $z = 5.0$

9. 160 cm

4 Chapter Link

1. a) Answers may vary. Examples:
   - Making every square on the small visual equal to two squares on the enlargement would double the size of the logo.
   - Making every square on the small visual equal to 1.5 squares on the enlargement would produce a logo one and a half times the original size.

   b) Examples:
   - The scale factor is 1:2. I made each dimension twice the size of the original.
   - The scale factor is 1:1.5. I made each dimension one and a half times the size of the original.

2.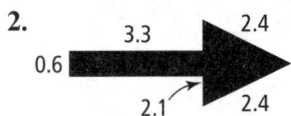

4 Vocabulary Link

1. e) ratio
2. c) polygon
3. f) reduction
4. j) similar
5. g) scale
6. a) corresponding
7. b) enlargement
8. i) scale factor
9. h) scale diagram
10. d) proportion

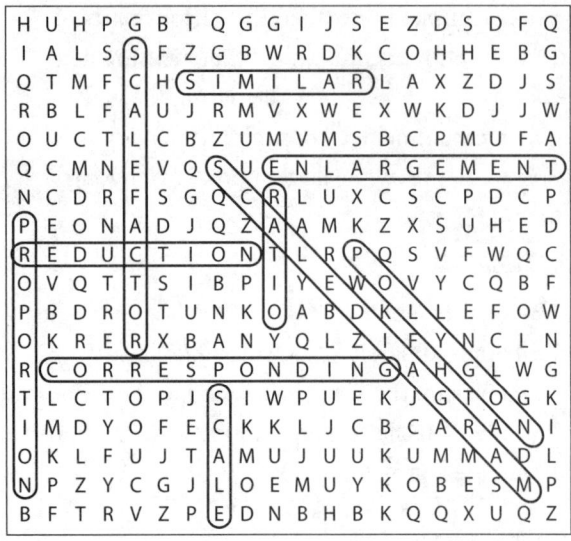

Chapters 1–4 Review

1. $4^7 = 4 \times 4 \times 4 \times 4 \times 4 \times 4 \times 4 = 16\,384$;
   $7^4 = 7 \times 7 \times 7 \times 7 = 2401$

2. There is rotational symmetry of order 2.

3.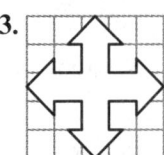

4. a) $-12\,025$ b) $-8\frac{8}{27}$

5. a) hexagon, rectangle, square, diamond, triangle
   b) hexagon: order 6, 60°, $\frac{1}{6}$; rectangle: order 2, 180°, $\frac{1}{2}$; square: order 4, 90°, $\frac{1}{4}$; diamond: order 2, 180°, $\frac{1}{6}$; triangle: order 6, 60°, $\frac{1}{6}$

6. a) $-3\frac{53}{120}$ b) $-20\frac{5}{18}$ c) $-3\frac{14}{25}$

7. $\frac{1}{3000}$ 8. a) $23 \div 53$ b) $4^4 \div 9^4$

9. 1679.18 cm² 10. a) $1759.02 b) $259.02

11. BC = 5 cm

12. Example: Calculate the surface area of one half of the roof, the front, and one side of the birdhouse. Because the other half of the roof, the back, and the other side of the birdhouse are identical to the first set of calculations, multiply the answer by two. Then, subtract the hole and add the sides of the cylindrical perch, but not the end of the perch.

13. a) 2.45 m b) 5.34 m

5 Get Ready

1. a) +3

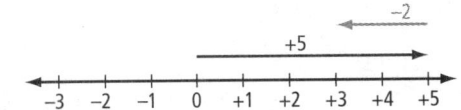

b) +5

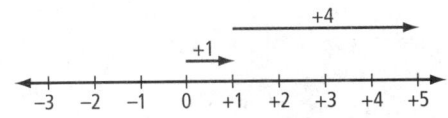

c) −5

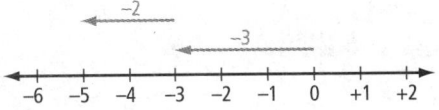

2. a) $(-2)+(+5)=+3$ b) $(-1)+(-2)=-3$
   c) $(-3)+(+7)=+4$
3. a) +5 b) −4 c) −13 d) +2
4. a) +4 b) −5 c) +3 d) +10
5. a) NC: 2, V: x, C: −7
   b) NC: −3, V: b, C: +5
   c) NC: 1, V: t, C: −4
   d) NC: −6, V: r, C: +3
6. Examples:
   a) $s-5$, where s is Sarah's sister's age
   b) $2l-3$, where l is the length
   c) $p+14$, where p is the perimeter of the triangle
   d) $\frac{1}{2}n$ or $\frac{n}{2}$, where n is the number of tickets the school expected to sell
7. a) $p+p+p+p$ or $4p$
   b) Example: The length of the rectangle is 8 units more than its width.

5.1 The Language of Mathematics

1. symbols, variables
2. polynomial, monomial, binomial, trinomial
3. exponents, highest
4. a) 2; binomial b) 1; monomial c) 3; trinomial
   d) 4; polynomial
5. a) 2; 2 b) 2; 2 c) 1; 0 d) 2; 3
6. a) $4c^2-3c+2, g+h+j$
   b) $4c^2-3c+2, 5p^2-r, 4ab$ c) −12
   d) $4ab, -12$ e) $4c^2-3c+2, 4ab$

7. a) x^2+x-4 b) $-2x^2-3$ c) x^2-3x
8. a)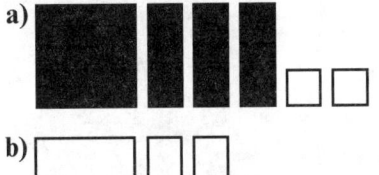
   b)

9. a) x^2+7 b) $3x-9$ c) $4x$
10. a) $5n$ b) $w(w+5)$ or w^2+5w c) $0.8x+40$

5.2 Equivalent Expressions

1. a) a, b b) −7; 1 for w, 2 for x c) No
2. x^2 should be circled in each term; $-2x^2$
3. No. They are not like terms because either the variables differ or the exponents of the variables differ.
4. a) 1; 1 b) −3; 1 c) 6; 2 d) no value; 0
   e) −1; 2 f) 1; 2
5. a) $-cd, -xy$ b) $-cd, -xy, -3jk$ c) k^2
   d) $9r, 4x$
6. a) $3r, -r$ b) $-4y, 0.3y, \frac{y}{2}$ c) $cd, 6cd$
7. Examples:
   a) $5c^2-c^2-5c+c+9-8$
   b) $3m^2+2m^2+8m-6m-9+6$
   c) $6d^2-5d^2-8d+3d+7-2$
8. The order of the terms may vary.
   a) $-b^2+5b^2+6-8+9; 4b^2+7$
   b) $4t^2-3t^2+7t+6t-5+14; t^2+13t+9$
   c) $-2n^2-3n^2+9n+5n+3-7;$
      $-5n^2+14n-4$
   d) $3y^2-6y^2+3y+2y+4-6-5;$
      $-3y^2+5y-7$
9. $3b+6$

10. a) Example:

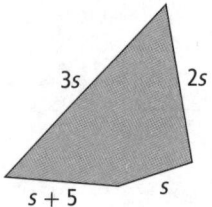

I made the shortest side, s, 10 units. If $s = 10$, then $s + 5$ is 15 units, $2s$ is 20 units, and $3s$ is the longest at 30 units.

b) $7s + 5$

11. a) $C = 70n + 215$ **b)** $460

5.3 Adding and Subtracting Polynomials

1. A 2. opposite
3. **a)** $8y - 2$ **b)** $-b^2 + 2$ **c)** $-4s^2 + 7s - 6$
4. **a)** $4d - 1$ **b)** $-6m^2 - 5$ **c)** $-r^2 + r - 9$
5. B
6. **a)**

$-x^2 + 2x$

b)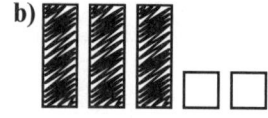

$3x - 2$

7. **a)** $3y^2$ **b)** $-6g + 3$ **c)** $-2b^2 + 4b - 7$
   d) $4d^2 + 3d + 6$ **e)** $k^2 + 8k - \frac{1}{2}$
8. **a)** $(3r - 5) + (-5r - 2)$; $-2r - 7$
   b) $(6 - 3f) + (-4 + 5f)$; $2 + 2f$
   c) $(-4n^2 + 5) + (n^2 + 9)$; $-3n^2 + 14$
   d) $(6a^2 + 2a - 5) + (-4a^2 - 5a - 7)$; $2a^2 - 3a - 12$
9. **a)** $(x + 3) + (2x + 2) + (2x)$
   b) $5x + 5$ **c)** $x = 4$; Verify: $5(4) + 5 = 25$
10. **a)** $x + 2x + (x - 10)$ **b)** $4x - 10$

5 Chapter Link

1. Examples: **a)** $5x^2 - 3x + 10$ **b)** $-3x^2 + xy$
2. **a)** $2d - 9$ **b)** $(2a^2 + a + 3)$ **c)** $(2r^2 + r + 3)$
3. **a)** Example: Let $d =$ days and $k =$ kilometres:
   $(35d + 0.2k) + (15d) + 200$
   b) $460

5 Vocabulary Link

1. polynomial
2. like terms
3. term
4. trinomial
5. binomial
6. descending
7. monomial
8. algebra
9. degree of a term
10. degree of a polynomial

Chapters 1–5 Review

1. **a)** $3x^2 - 2x + 7$; 3, 2, trinomial
   b) 3; 1, 0, monomial
   c) $9x^2 + 5y^2 + 6xy + 6x + 5y$; 5, 2, polynomial
2. **a)** -3; x, y; 1 for x, 2 for y **b)** -1; a; 3
   c) none; none; none
3. $(-4)^3$, 7, $(-2)^4$, 5^2, 2^5
4. Examples:
   a) 37, 38.44 **b)** 180, 182.25 **c)** 0.05, 0.0529
   d) 0.30, 0.3249
5. $A'(-1, 4)$, $B'(-3, 2)$, $C'(-7, 2)$, $D'(-7, 6)$, $E'(-1, 6)$
   Yes; rotational symmetry of order 2.
6. **a)** $=$ **b)** $<$ **c)** $>$ **d)** $<$
7. 462.4 cm³
8. 12; 30°, $\frac{1}{12}$
9. **a)** approximately 306 124 000
   b) approximately 11 213 333
   c) approximately $27\frac{3}{10}$
10. **a)** $\frac{469}{486}$ **b)** -0.119
11. 12 756.2 km
12. **a)** 607.5 cm² **b)** 445.5 cm² **c)** 506.3 cm²
13. No, the shapes are not similar because the corresponding angles are not equal in measure.

6 Get Ready

1. a)

Time, t (h)	Distance, d (km)
0	5
2	8
4	10

b)

Time, t (s)	Speed, s (km/h)
5	60
6	50
7	40

2. a) Yes. Example: It makes sense because there can be times and temperatures between the ones labelled on the graph.

b) No. Example: It does not make sense because you can sell only whole hamburgers, not fractions of a hamburger.

3. a) This is a linear relation because the difference between the consecutive values in each row is the same (15 m in the first row and 2.1 m/s in the second row).

b) This is not a linear relation because the difference between consecutive values of h is not consistent even though the difference between consecutive values of t is consistent.

4. (60, 10.5)

5. Examples:

a)

x	y
1	5
2	8
3	11

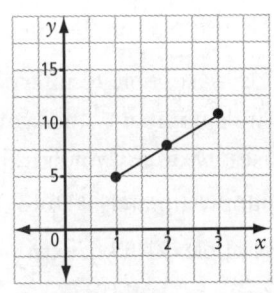

b)

n	t
1	−1
2	−5
3	−9

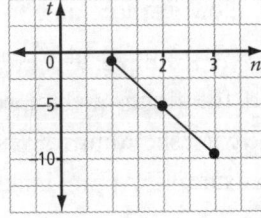

6.1 Representing Patterns

1. a) pattern, four rails, posts

b) Example:

Number of Posts, p	Number of Rails, r
1	0
2	4
3	8
4	12

c) Example: To get r, multiply p by 4 and subtract 4.

2. a) equation **b)** Example: $4p - 4 = r$

c) Example: Substitute values of p from the table.

3. a)

Figure Number, f	Perimeter, p
1	8
2	14
3	20
4	26

b) $6f + 2 = p$; f = figure number, p = perimeter

c)

Figure Number, f	Perimeter, p
5	32
6	38
7	44
8	50
9	56
10	62

4. a) Example: Multiply the figure number by 3 and add 1 to get the number of toothpicks needed.

b) $t = 3f + 1$;

Figure Number, f	Number of Toothpicks, t
1	4
2	7
3	10
4	13
5	16
6	19
7	22

c) No

5. a)

x	y
1	−4.5
2	−7
3	−9.5
4	−12
5	−14.5
6	−17
7	−19.5

b) Example: $y = -2.5x - 2$ **c)** −169.5

6. a) Example: $C = \frac{\$179.40}{12} + \frac{\$181.80}{12}$

b) $27.07

c)

Number of Players Buying	Cost per Shirt
1	$ 196.75
2	$ 105.85
3	$ 75.55
4	$ 60.40
5	$ 51.31
6	$ 45.25
7	$ 40.92
8	$ 37.68
9	$ 35.15
10	$ 33.13
11	$ 31.48
12	$ 30.10
13	$ 28.93
14	$ 27.94
15	$ 27.07

6.2 Interpreting Graphs

1. a) interpolation
b) extrapolation
c) interpolation, between
d) extrapolation, beyond

2. It is reasonable to interpolate, but only for whole numbers, since you cannot sell part of a seat. You cannot extrapolate, because the number of seats is finite.

3. Example: 21.5 kg; extrapolation

4. a) Yes. Example: It is possible to refill the tank, allowing more time to expire. **b)** 25 L

5. a) No. Example: The graph shows the upper and lower limits of the spring. **b)** 40 kg **c)** 24 cm

6. a) Example: Approximately 36 years
b) Example: Approximately 94 cm; interpolation

7. Example:

a)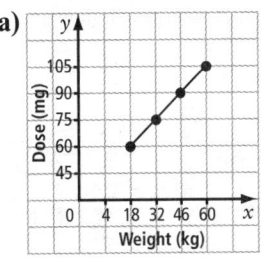

b) 40 kg: 85 mg; 100 kg: 190 mg

c) 50 mg: 8 kg; 120 mg: 74 kg

6.3 Graphing Linear Equations

1. equation
2. coordinate, linear relation
3. interpolate, extrapolate (in either order)
4. a) Example:

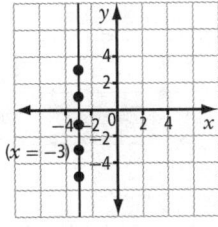

x	y
−3	−5
−3	−3
−3	−1
−3	1
−3	3

b) Example:

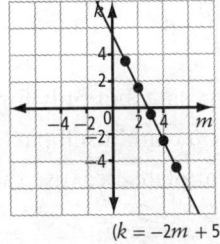

m	k
1	3.5
2	1.5
3	−0.5
4	−2.5
5	−4.5

5. a) $y = -2x + 0.25$ b) $y = -0.5x$
6. a) $y = 0.5x + 1.5$

b) Example: A line passes through points A to N; $y = 2x - 1$

c) Example: A line passes through points A, B, C, D, E, and F; $y = 1$

7. a) Example: $l = 1000 - \dfrac{99t}{60}$

b) Example: Approximately 450 min or 7.5 h; interpolation

c) Agree. Example: It takes about 7.5 h to pump out 750 L.

8. a) Example:

Alex Time (min)	Distance (km)	Zoe Time (min)	Distance (km)
9:20	1	9:45	1.25
9:40	2	10:00	2.50
10:00	3	10:15	3.75
10:20	4	10:30	5.00
10:40	5	10:45	6.25

b)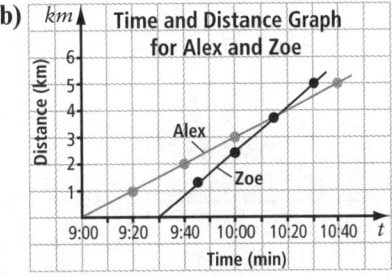

c) 10:15 a.m. d) 0.5 km

6 Chapter Link

1. Examples:

a) Air

Time, t (s)	Distance, d (m)
1	340
2	680
3	1020
4	1360
5	1700
6	2040
7	2380
8	2720
9	3060
10	3400

b) Water

Time, t (s)	Distance, d (m)
1	1450
2	2900
3	4350
4	5800
5	7250
6	8700
7	10150
8	11600
9	13050
10	14500

c) Steel

Time, t (s)	Distance, d (m)
1	5050
2	10100
3	15150
4	20200
5	25250
6	30300
7	35350
8	40400
9	45450
10	50500

2. a) $d = 340t$ **b)** $d = 1450t$ **c)** $d = 5050t$

3. a) approximately 4.26 s **b)** approximately 14.85 s

4. Examples:
  a) approximately 0.23 s
  b) approximately 3.48 s

6 Vocabulary Link

1. i) variable
2. e) extrapolate
3. b) commission
4. g) linear equation
5. d) continuous
6. a) coefficient
7. h) linear relation
8. c) constant
9. f) interpolate

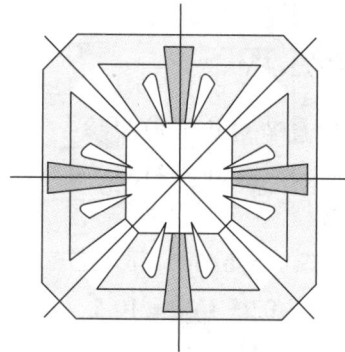

Chapters 1–6 Review

1. Example: **a)** $3x^2 + 2x$
   b) $3x^2 + 7x - 2$ **c)** $2x, 3x$
2. **a)** $y = -\frac{x}{3}$ **b)** $y = 2x + 3$
3. Example: **a)** 1.75 **b)** -0.8
4. $\frac{1}{2}$; the length and width of Picture 2 are half of the length and width of Picture 1.
5. **a)** There are 4 lines of symmetry: vertical, horizontal, and two oblique or diagonal lines.

   b) 90°; $\frac{1}{4}$ of a rotation
6. **a)** Estimate: 2.5; Actual: 2.59
   b) Estimate: 9; Actual: 8.75
   c) Estimate: 12; Actual: 12.6

7. a) 13 **b)** 0.216

8. Error in step 1 ($-2^2 = 4$, not -4).
Correct answer: 154

9. 137.33 cm²

10. a) $5a^2 - 9a - 7$ **b)** $6x^2y - 7xy^2$

11. 4.6 cm

12. a)

Distance (km)	Cost ($)
0	30
100	35
200	40
300	45
400	50
500	55

b)

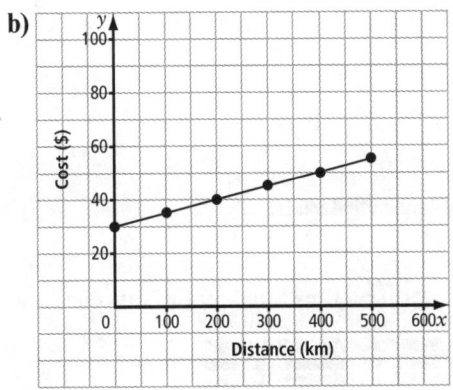

c) $42.50 **d)** 450 km

e) Example: $C = 0.05d + 30$, where C represents cost in dollars and d represents distance in km.

7 Get Ready

1. a) T; 2 **b)** B; 2 **c)** B; 1 **d)** M; 2

2. Examples: $3x^2 + 2y - 4x$, $3x + 2xy - 4y$

3. b) and d)

4. a) $3x^2 - 6x + 5$ **b)** $3p^2 - p + 2$

5. a) $7x - 10$ **b)** $2t^2 + 3t + 1$

6. a) -7 **b)** $y^2 + 5y - 2$

7. a) $3x^2 + 8x - 10$ **b)** $-y - 9$

7.1 Multiplying and Dividing Monomials

1. a) product; $-x$-tiles

b) division; dividend; x-tiles

c) numerical coefficients; exponent rules

2. Example: To divide monomials algebraically, you can divide the numerical coefficients and then use the exponent rules to divide the variables.

3. Orientation of models may vary.

a) $-8x^2$

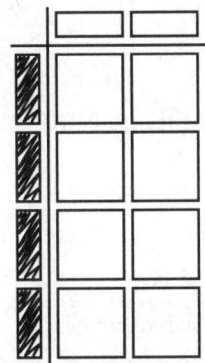

b) $12x^2$

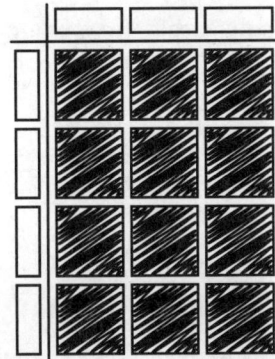

4. a) $6x^2 \div (-3x) = -2x$ **b)** $9xy \div 3x = 3y$

5. a) $2x$

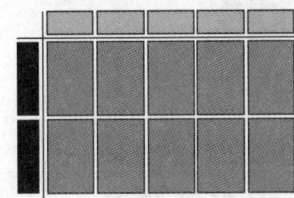

b) $3x$

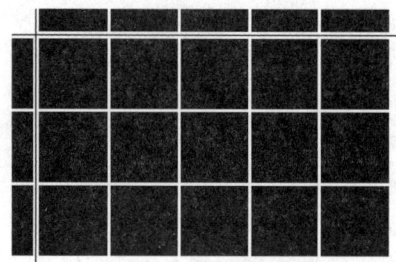

6. a) $24a^2$ b) $12x^2$ c) $-20x$ d) 4
7. a) $(12x)(4x)$; $48x^2$ b) $\frac{(3h)(4b)}{2}$; $6bh$
8. 12 m
9. a) $9x$ b) $4x$

7.2 Multiplying Polynomials by Monomials

1. a) area b) $(2x)(3x + 4) = 6x^2 + 8x$
2. $(-2x)(5x + 6) = (-2x)(5x) + (-2x)(6)$
   $= -10x^2 - 12x$
3. Order of factors may vary. Examples:
   a) $(2y)(5y + 2)$ b) $(4.5t + 2.3)(3.1t)$
   c) $(x)(x + 1)$ d) $(2x - 2)(-3x)$
4. Orientation of rectangles may vary. Examples:

   a)
	4.6g	5
2.3g		

   b)
	5	7.2f
2.1f		

5. Orientation of tiles may vary. Examples:

   a)

   b)

6. a) $(1.2z)(-4z) + (1.2z)(2y)$
   b) $(-2e)(-e) + (-3f)(-e) + (4)(-e)$

7. a) $-49v^2 - 49vx$
   b) $28x - 12xy$
   c) $-0.1ab + 8b^2 - 0.7bc$
   d) $\frac{3a^2}{2} - a$ or $\frac{3}{2a^2} - a$
8. Example:
   a) $(6w - 4)$ m b) $(2w^2 - 2w)$ m^2
9. a) $48.3 + 2m$, where m is the cost of the catch of the day
   b) $(0.15)(48.3 + 2m)$
   c) $\$89.93$

7.3 Dividing Polynomials by Monomials

1. numerical coefficients; variables; quotient or divisor; divisor or quotient; product; dividend
2. dividend; quotient; model
3. $(6x^2 + 8x) \div 2x$; $3x + 4$
4. $4x^2$; $6x$; $2x$; 3
5. $3x - 2$

6. $2x - 3$

   Orientation of tiles may vary. Example:

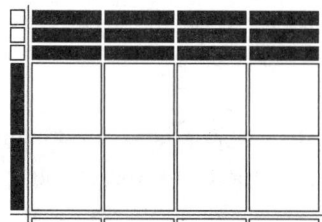

7. a) $-6y + 1.8$ b) $-0.5s + t - 1.5$ or $-\frac{s}{2} + t - \frac{3}{2}$
   c) $-0.9d^2 + 0.8d - 0.4$ d) $y + z + 1$
8. $7.5 \div (30x + 22.5)$
9. $(3.6x^2 + 7.2x)$ cm^2
10. $5t$ cm
11. a) 40π m^2 b) 5 m c) 4 m

7 Chapter Link

1. a) $768y + 216$ units **b)** $32y + 9$ units
c) $512y^2 + 288y + 40.5$ units^3 **d)** 20 bundles
e) $12\,800y^2 + 7200y + 1012.5$ units^3

2. a) $(4374d^2 + 1458dp + 972d)$ units^2
b) $(81d^2 + 27dp + 18d)$ units^2

3. Example: A square carpet with side length $7.6a + 8.2$ m is cut into 4 square carpets of equal size. What are the side lengths of the smaller carpets?
Answer: $(7.6a + 8.2) \div 4 = (1.9a + 2.05)$ m

7 Vocabulary Link

Across
5. distributive property

Down
1. polynomial
2. monomial
3. spider map
4. binomial

Chapters 1–7 Review

1. a) $5x$; -20 **b)** $5x + y$; $2x^2 - xy$
c) $2x^2 - xy$; $7d^2 - 3cd - 5c + 6$ **d)** c and d
e) -20; $5 + c + d$; $7d^2 - 3cd - 5c + 6$ **f)** 5; none

2. a) $y = 2x + 3$ **b)** $y = \frac{-3}{4}x$ or $-0.75x$ **c)** $y = 3$

3. a) $11x^3$ **b)** $15j^2 - 18j$

4. a) $-3x - 2y$ **b)** $32t + 16$

5. Example:
a)

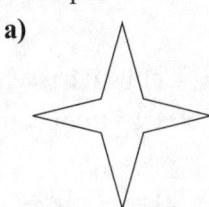

b) 4 **c)** 4 **d)** 90°; $\frac{1}{4}$

6. a) 58.27 **b)** $-\frac{2}{15}$

7. a) 24 **b)** 3 145 728 **c)** 50 331 648

8.

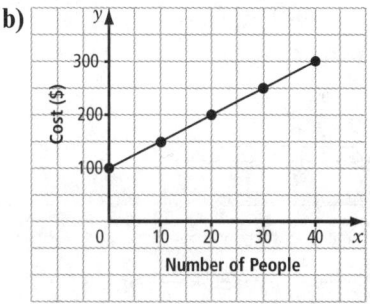

9. a) 1.3 m **b)** 8.62 cm **c)** $\frac{1}{3}$ m

10. a)

Number of People	Cost ($)
0	100
10	150
20	200
30	250
40	300

b)

c) $225 **d)** 80
e) Example: $C = 5n + 100$, where C represents the total cost in dollars and n represents the number of people.

11.

8 Get Ready

1. Examples:
a)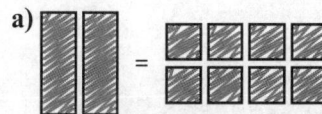

b)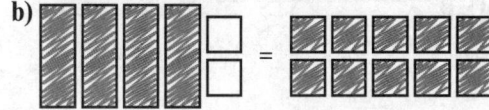

2. a) $2x - 6 = 6$ **b)** $6 = 3x - 9$
3. a) $2x + 7 = -3$, so $x = -5$
  b) $3x - 4 = 5$, so $x = 3$
4. a) $s = 6$ **b)** $x = 8$
5. a) $5(-4) + 7 = -13$, so $x = -4$ is the solution
  b) $12 - 5(-4) = 32$, so $x = -4$ is not the solution
6. a) $x = 7$; Check: $7 - 2 = 5$
  b) $t = 2$; Check: $3(2) + 4 = 10$
  c) $g = -2$; Check: $2(-2) - 7 = 11$

8.1 Solving Equations: $ax = b, \frac{x}{a} = b, \frac{a}{x} = b$

1. number lines, materials, algebraic
2. substitution **3.** solution, facts
4. $4x = 0.24$; $x = 0.06$
5.

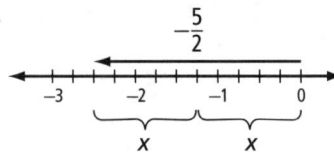

6. a) $m = \frac{7}{15}$ **b)** $x = \frac{8}{9}$ **c)** $x = -\frac{45}{4}$ or $-11\frac{1}{4}$
  d) $k = \frac{10}{9}$ or $1\frac{1}{9}$
7. a) $w = 15.36$ **b)** $d = -1.125$
  c) $x = -23.25$ **d)** $m = 0.255$
8. a) $r = 2.1$ **b)** $x = -3.5$
9. a) $t \approx 2.59$ **b)** $y \approx -9.16$
10. a) $18.5 = \frac{d}{0.75}$, so $d = 13.875$ km
  b) $90 = \frac{128}{t}$, so $t = 1.42$ h
11. $259.80 **12.** 625 mL **13.** 5 **14.** 20

8.2 Solving Equations: $ax + b = c, \frac{x}{a} + b = c$

1. model **2.** subtract, multiply **3.** denominators
4. solution, substitution, facts
5. Example: $\frac{x}{3} + \frac{3}{10} = \frac{4}{5}$, so $x = \frac{3}{2}$
6. Example:

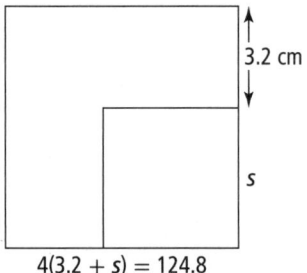

$x = 0.12$

7. No. Example: $2.5x$, should have been multiplied by the same value, 100, as the other terms.
8. a) $x = \frac{11}{20}$ **b)** $x = \frac{-3}{2}$ or $-1\frac{1}{2}$ **c)** $g = \frac{145}{24}$ or $6\frac{1}{24}$
  d) $q = \frac{51}{10}$ or $5\frac{1}{10}$
9. a) $x = 8.6$ **b)** $f = -1.8$ **c)** $b = 38.7$
10. 37.5 min **11.** 1406 km² **12.** 19.4 cm **13.** 70

8.3 Solving Equations: $a(x + b) = c$

1. divide, distributive **2.** substitute
3. Example: $(3)\left(\frac{1}{3}\right)(x - 4) = 3(2)$ or $x - 4 = 6$
4. a) $x = -0.7$ **b)** $m = 3.74$ **c)** $a = -4.1$
  d) $x = 2$
5. a) $v = -4.19$ **b)** $y = 5.32$ **c)** $u = 11.61$
  d) $w = 1.52$
6. a) $x = \frac{-9}{4}$ or $-2\frac{1}{4}$ **b)** $x = \frac{34}{5}$ or $6\frac{4}{5}$
  c) $p = \frac{27}{8}$ or $3\frac{3}{8}$ **d)** $e = \frac{-12}{5}$ or $-2\frac{2}{5}$
7. a) $K = 25.9$ **b)** $j = -16.5$
  c) $y = 4.471$ **d)** $n = 7.66$
8. a) 28 cm
  b) Example:

[Diagram: square with side 3.2 cm marked, inner square with side s, equation $4(3.2 + s) = 124.8$]

9. $8.65 **10.** $\frac{41}{8}$ or $5\frac{1}{8}$ **11. a)** 9.5 km/h **b)** 3.2 km/h

8.4 Solving Equations: $ax = b + cx$, $ax + b = cx + d$, $a(bx + c) = d(ex + f)$

1. False. To solve $7x + 5 = 3x - 11$ by the reverse order of operations, first subtract 5 from both sides of the equation.
2. False. The equation $2(4.5x + 3) = -5(3x - 1.3)$ becomes $9x + 6 = -15x + 6.5$ by using the distributive property.
3. True
4. a) $x = -1.4$ **b)** $n = 0.5$ **c)** $x = 2.5$ **d)** $y = -27.6$

5. a) $x = -\frac{3}{4}$ b) $c = \frac{10}{27}$ c) $x = \frac{13}{5}$ d) $w = \frac{7}{8}$
6. a) $x = 2.14$ b) $p = 0.56$ c) $m = -2.11$
7. a) $p = -4.5$ b) $x = -\frac{13}{5}, -2\frac{3}{5}$, or -2.6
   c) $k = 3.7$
8. 8 weeks 9. $x = 7.2$ 10. a) 15.75 min b) 3.54 km
11. 19

8 Chapter Link

1. 2.5 km 2. 283 km 3. 157 km
4. No. Example: The left and right sides of $22.50 + 0.15d = 0.28d$ are not equal when d represents 170 km.
5. 49.09 km

8 Vocabulary Link

1. g) 2. c) 3. e) 4. b) 5. d) 6. a) 7. f)

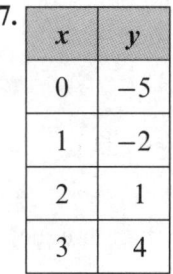

Chapters 1–8 Review

1. a) $-7x^2 + 2x + 3$; 3, 2, trinomial
   b) $2p + 15$; 2, 1, binomial
2. a) $380 b) $3\frac{3}{5}$ h or 3.6 h
3. a) 2 b) 4 c) 2 d) $\frac{1}{4}$ e) $\frac{1}{2}$
4. $6x - 2$

5.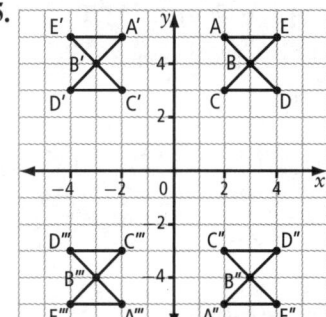

A'(−2, 5), B'(−3, 4), C'(−2, 3), D'(−4, 3)
E'(−4, 5)
A''(2, −5), B''(3, −4), C''(2, −3), D''(4, −3),
E''(4, −5)
A'''(−2, −5), B'''(−3, −4), C'''(−2, −3),
D'''(−4, −3), E'''(−4, −5)

6. Example: 10 tricycles, 1 children's bike, and 1 mountain bike; or 5 tricycles, 2 children's bikes, and 2 mountain bikes

7.
x	y
0	−5
1	−2
2	1
3	4

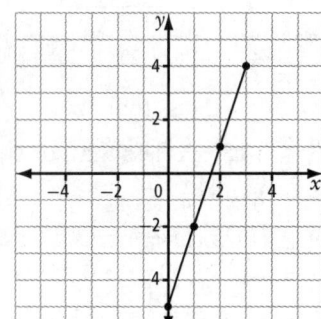

8. a) $c = \frac{35}{9}$ or $3\frac{8}{9}$ b) $g = 2$ c) $f = -1$
   d) $r = \frac{7}{3}$ or $2\frac{1}{3}$ e) $b = -34$
9. $(-5)^5 = -3125$
10. a) the number of times the coin is flipped
    b) the number of possible outcomes
    c) HHH, HHT, HTH, TTT, THH, TTH, THT
    d) $2^{10} = 1024$

9 Get Ready

1. a) $5 > 2$ b) $7 < 20$ c) 5×3 d) $9 = \frac{18}{2}$
2. a) 4 is less than 8.
   b) 8 is greater than 2.
   c) 14 divided by 2.
   d) 4 does not equal $\frac{8}{3}$.

3. a) 5, 4 **b)** −1, 0, 1 **c)** 5, 6, 7 **d)** 3, 2, 1, 0
4. a) 1 < 7, 7 > 1 **b)** 4 > −1, −1 < 4
   c) 3 < 3.5, 3.5 > 3 **d)** 0 < 1, 1 > 0
5. a) 0, 1, 2, 3 **b)** 5, 6, 7 **c)** 12, 13, 14, …
   d) 0, 1, 2, 3, 4, 5, 6, 7, 8, 9, 10, 11, 12, 13, 14
6. a) $x = 2$ **b)** $x = -4$ **c)** $x = 1$ **d)** $x = 3$

9.1 Representing Inequalities

1. algebraically; graphically; verbally
2. boundary 3. closed; left
4. open; right 5. less; equal; greater
6. combination; conditions
7. **a)** 2, 4, 6 **b)** −14, −13 **c)** −6, −2, 1
8. **a)**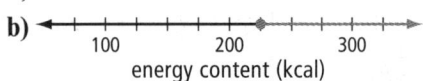
   b)
   c)
9. **a)** $x < 4$; x is less than 4.
   b) $x \leq -15$; x is less than or equal to −15.
   c) $x \geq 1.375$ (or $\frac{11}{8}$); x is greater than or equal to 1.375 (or $\frac{11}{8}$).
10. **a)** −5.6, 1.7, 3.2 **b)** −12, −4.3, 0
11. **a)**
    b)
12. **a)** $x < 3$ and $x > 9$ **b)** $x \geq -20$ and $x < 10$
13. **a)** Let t = time; $t \leq 13$
    b) Let V = volume; $V \geq 1.8$ and $V \leq 2.5$
14. **a)**
    b)
15. **a)** $c \geq 225$
    b)

16.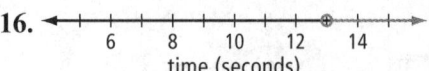

17. **a)** A combination of inequalities needs to be used because the tide height varies between two boundary values.
    b) Let h = height of tide; $h \geq 0.8$ and $h \leq 3.2$
    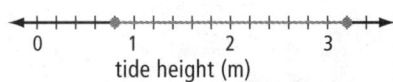

9.2 Solving Single-Step Inequalities

1. True
2. False. The inequality $10 \geq -2x$ can be solved by dividing by −2 and reversing the inequality symbol.
3. False. The inequality $\frac{x}{5} < -10$ can be solved by multiplying both sides of the equation by 5.
4. False. The two inequalities have different solutions. For $-10x < 30$, dividing by −10 causes the inequality to be reversed.
5. **a)** $x < 8$ **b)** $x \geq -5.3$ **c)** $-40 \geq x$ or $x \leq -40$
6. **a)** $x \leq -\frac{11}{4}$ or $-2\frac{3}{4}$ or $x \leq -2.75$ **b)** $x < 63$
   c) $-15 \leq x$ or $x \geq -15$
7. Reverse the inequality for two cards:
   $\div (-5)$ and $\times (-0.7)$.
8. **a)** 6, 7 **b)** 3 **c)** −10, −5, 0 **d)** −8, −4
9. Example: The solution to $10 > x + 4$ is $x < 6$. The boundary point on the number line is correct. However, the arrow should point to the left.
10. Example: Yes, you need to reverse the sign when you divide both sides of the inequality by a negative number.
11. Examples:
    a) Let b equal the number of books;
    $4b \leq 150$ or $b \leq \frac{150}{4}$.
    b) $b \leq 37.5$. Lauren can buy 37 or fewer books.
    c) $37 \times 4 < 150$, $148 < 150$. True

12. Examples:
   a) Let n equal the number of uses; $37.5n > 285$.
   b) $n > 7.6$. Eight or more uses make the members' plan cheaper.
   c) No. The boundary point of 7.6 is not a reasonable solution because only whole numbers are possible for the number of uses.
13. a) $3.49x > 49.95$
   b) It becomes cheaper to buy the game when the number of days is greater than 14.
   c) She should buy the game.

9.3 Solving Multi-Step Inequalities

1. isolate; equation; reverse; multiplying; dividing; negative
2. multi-step; left; right
3. comparing; inequalities
4. a) $x < 9$ b) $x \geq -18$
   c) $x < -\frac{12}{5}$ or $x < -2.4$
   d) $-\frac{3}{2} \leq x$ or $x \geq -\frac{3}{2}$ or $-1.5 \leq x$ or $x \geq -1.5$
5. a) $x \leq -12$ b) $x > -2$
   c) $x \leq -\frac{5}{2}$ or $x \leq -2.5$ d) $1 < x$ or $x > 1$
6. a) The solution is correct.
   b) The solution is not correct. $x > 1.5$.
   c) The solution is not correct. $3\frac{2}{5}$ is the boundary point, not part of the solution.
   d) The solution is correct.
7. a) Example: Let $d =$ number of downloads per month.
   b) $29 + 0.8d < 17 + 1.19d$
   c) $d > 30.769 \ldots$. Site A is a better deal when Ethan makes more than 30 downloads.
8. a) Example: Let $t =$ time in hours a bike is rented.
   b) $25 + 8t > 55$
   c) $t > 3.75$. The all-day plan is better if renting for at least 4 h.
9. a) Sheila will be closer after 2.6 h (2 h 36 min).
   b) Sheila would have to travel at least 89.6 km/h.

9 Chapter Link

1. Let $t =$ time (h); $t > 6$

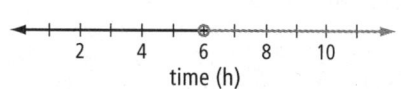
time (h)

2. Examples: a) Let $L =$ length painted on Michele's side; $L \geq 5$ and $L \leq 25$

   b)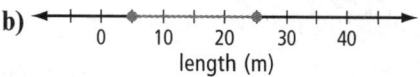
   length (m)

3. a) Let $t =$ time in hours; $3.5t \geq 5$
   b) Example: Hani can take a break after a little more than 1.4 h.
4. a) $3.5t > 3t + 5$. Hani will have painted farther after more than 10 h.
   b) Example: $3.5(11) > 3(11) + 5$, $38.5 > 38$. True

9 Vocabulary Link

1. inequality
2. open circle
3. combination of inequalities
4. closed circle
5. graphically
6. verbally
7. algebraically
8. solution of an inequality
9. boundary point

Chapters 1–9 Review

1. Example: $5x^2 - 4xy + 6$
2. a) Example: $y = -1.75$ b) Example: $x = 3$
   c) $y = \frac{3}{2}x - 4$ or $y = 1.5x - 4$
3. a) $8x - 14$ b) $4a^2 + 3a - 1$
   c) $10t^2 - 12t + 4$ d) $-2.3x + 0.2$
4. a) $\frac{1}{48}$ b) 604.8 cm
5. a) -2 b) $-14mn + 42n^2$ c) $9p - 1 + 3q$
   d) $\frac{2}{5}s^2 - \frac{4}{15}s$
6. 3.9 cm

7. a) Yes; order of 4; 90°; $\frac{1}{4}$

b) Yes; vertical, horizontal, and two oblique lines of symmetry

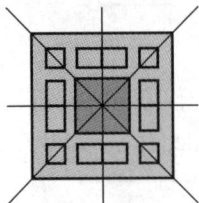

8. a) In step 2, the 5 and 81 need to be multiplied before adding −64; 341

b) In step 1, the 4 and 3 need to be added before being squared; 130

9. a) small block: 436 cm²; large block: 1048 cm²

b) 1264 cm²

10. a) $a = 81$ **b)** $p = 9$

11. a) 15.21 **b)** 0.69 **c)** Example: 3.2 **d)** 3.16

12. $x < -\frac{3}{8}$

10 Get Ready

1. a) 2 cm **b)** 1.5 cm

2. a) Examples: 6 cm, 4.5 cm

b) 6.28 cm, 4.71 cm

3. a) any estimate between 20° and 30°

b) any estimate between 45° and 60°

c) any estimate between 100° and 110°

4. a) 25° **b)** 48° **c)** 105°

5. Example: I was pretty close but a little large. My estimated angle was 58°.

6.

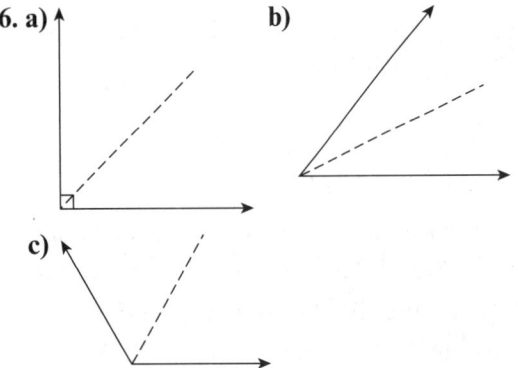

7. 45°. Example: It bisects a 90° angle and 45° is half of 90°.

8.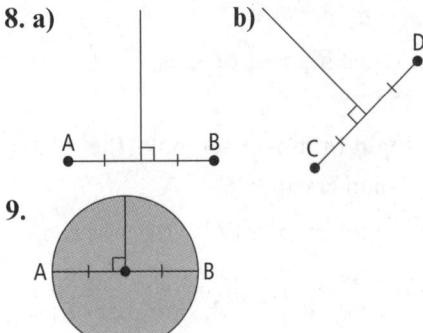

9.

Example: AB is a diameter. Its perpendicular bisector is at the centre of the circle and defines two radii.

10.1 Exploring Angles in a Circle

1. a) arc **b)** inscribed angle **c)** subtended

2. a)–d) Example:

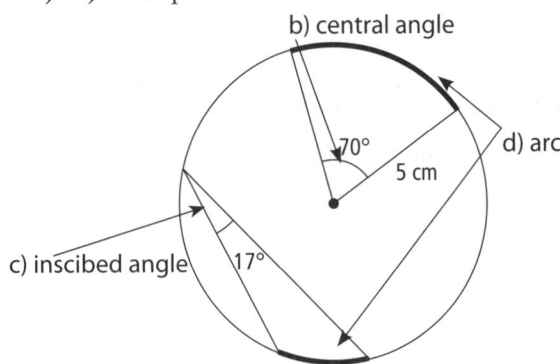

3. a) 35°. Example: ∠FIH measures 90° because it is an inscribed angle subtended by the diameter IG, therefore ∠IHF must measure 55° (total of angles in a triangle is 180° and 180 − 35 − 90 = 55); ∠GHI measures 90° for the same reason as ∠FIH, and ∠GHI − ∠IHF = 35° (90 − 55 = 35).

b) central angle. Example: It is formed by FJ and GJ, which are radii of a circle.

c) 70°. Example: It is a central angle subtended by the same arc as the inscribed ∠FHG of 35° (see answer a) above).

4. a) 90° **b)** 4 cm **5. a)** 60° **b)** Example: 1 and 7

6. a) 9.5 cm **b)** 90° **c)** 8.5 cm

7. **a)** 106°. Example: △STR is an isosceles triangle because ST and TR are both radii of the circle and therefore equal. 180 − 37 − 37 = 106

   b) 53°. Example: Since they are subtended by the same arc, inscribed angle ∠RQS must be half the measure of the central angle ∠RTS.

10.2 Exploring Chord Properties

1. **a)–c)**

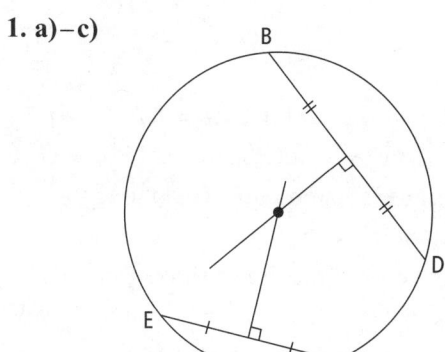

2. **a)** centre, bisectors, chords
   b) bisector, chord, centre
   c) centre, bisector, chord
   d) centre, chord, bisector

3. **a)**

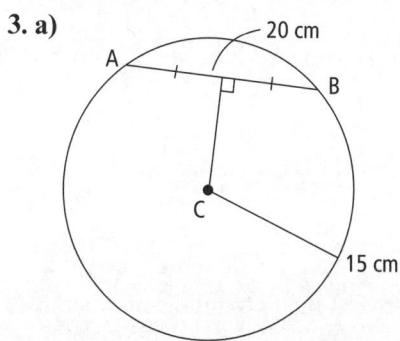

   b) 11.2 cm

4.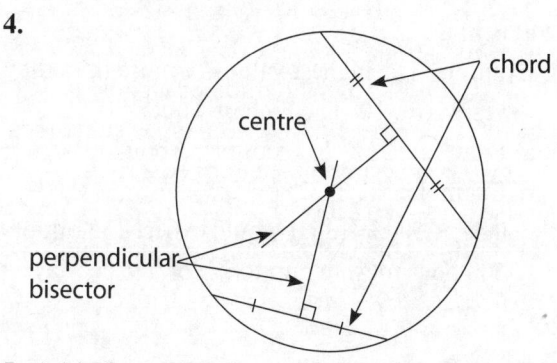

5. **a)** 14.28 cm **b)** 5.72 cm **c)** approximately 3.5 cm
6. 15.28 cm

7. **a)** Example: Use the rope to create two chords and their perpendicular bisectors; the centre of the circle is where the bisectors meet.
   b) approximately 5.3 m

10.3 Tangents to a Circle

1. False. A tangent always touches a circle once.
2. False. The place a tangent touches a circle is called the point of tangency.
3. True 4. True
5. **a)** 90°. Example: Segment FD is tangent to the circle at point F. FG is a radius. Tangents are perpendicular to the related radius.
   b) 30°. Example: △FDG is a right triangle. The sum of angles in a triangle is 180°.
   180° − 90° − 60° = 30°
   c) 75°. Example: △FGH is an isosceles triangle and ∠FGH = 30°, and (180° − 30°) ÷ 2 = 75°
6. 73 cm 7. **a)** 10.8 cm **b)** 39.5°
8. **a)** 12.03 m
   b) Example: Darcy's arm forms the radius of his turning circle. This is half the diameter. When he lets the discus go, it leaves along a tangent to the circle he made.
9. 37.5°

10 Chapter Link

1. **a)** 90° **b)** central 2. **a)** 45°
3. Yes. Example: One side of the △HED is the circle's diameter (chord HD).
4. 14.14 m
5. **a)** 2.93 m **b)** 18.47 m **c)** 7.66 m
6. 22.5°. Example: Since angle ∠BJD measures 90° or twice that of ∠BGD (being the inscribed angle subtended by the same arc), and radius JC bisects the chord resulting in ∠DJC measuring half of ∠BJD or 45°; ∠JCD = 180 − ∠DJC ÷ 2, or 67.5°; ∠JCL = 90° because CL is a tangent and GC is the diameter, so ∠DCL = 90 − ∠JCL or 22.5°.

10 Vocabulary Link

1. b) 2. a) 3. e) 4. c) 5. i)
6. d) 7. g) 8. h) 9. f)

```
T A N G E N T C G S W Q S O F S S A R C
J P E R P E N D I C U L A R V C U T C H
C I C H C V O D C H V B U T N Q P Z A Z
E X L O W M R H R U L M T U H X P A R A
N N F X X O J Y V D W V O E C Q L W P R
T S Q W H R P H Y I D J O Y N E I E C
R A I C J T K C J B D V V M U D M C N O
A T J T G K B U O I B F G J R M E N T F
L F J X R X Q M F L H H G E A X N T E A
A E B W J N R O P U W R Y J D C T V R C
N R M E O A J Z F H K V O G O L A B S I
G C I C A W M Z M X C R D B P D R X S R
L I N S C R I B E D A N G L E R Y O Q C
E B O S S A Z H R P U I G U M A S U L
C B R C I T O V C E M G C D A S N T A E
W J A K C V O H Y T A N Q S T V G H R R
E S R D O P L B S F R G P S M I L N E G
R X C T K C J V E R Q F C L U B E N A I
```

Chapters 1–10 Review

1. a) $5 + n$, n = a number added to 5
   b) $b - 6$, b = number of bicycles he started with
2. a) Example:

Weeks, w	Total Savings, S ($)
0	27
1	47
2	67
3	87
4	107
5	127

   b) $S = 20w + 27$ c) $667
3. No. Example: The figures are not proportional. Although the related angles appear to correspond, the related sides are not proportional. For example, AD is 1.5 cm and EH is 1.0 cm, but AB is 1.5 cm and EF is 1.1 cm.
4. a) $1\frac{31}{92}$ b) $-\frac{5}{6}$

5. a) Example:

   b) 6 c) 6 d) $60°$, $\frac{1}{6}$
6. 19
7. a) $a = 12$ b) $p = 7$
8. 552 cm²
9. $\angle a = \angle b = 90°$, $\angle c = 100°$, $\angle p = 80°$
10. a) $x < 57$ b) $x \geq -5$ c) $x < 3$
11. a) Yes, because the household could use more kilowatt hours (extrapolate), or a whole number between the shown values (interpolate).
    b) approximately $260 c) approximately 75 kWh
12. $\angle AED = 90°$, radius = 5 cm

11 Get Ready

1. a) mean = $7.\overline{2}$; median = 8; mode = 8
   b) mean = 5.14; median = 5; mode = 4.3
2. Example:
   - The mean is easiest. Add the values and divide by the number of values.
     $\frac{3 + 5 + 7 + 3 + 5 + 2 + 7 + 3}{8} = 4.375$
   - The mode is next easiest. The value that occurs most often is 3.
   - The median is the most difficult. The value halfway between the two middle numbers 3 and 5 (after they have been arranged in order) is 4.
3. a) 6 b) 24
4. Example: The highest value is 7 more than the lowest value, 10. The highest value is 17.
5. a) Example: 28% b) Example: About 43%
   c) Example: 5% + 22% = 27%;
   $0.27 \times 500 = 135$. I would expect 135 out of 500 boys to watch up to 2 h of TV per day.

11.1 Factors Affecting Data Collection

1. survey
2. influencing factors
3. bias
4. ethics
5. Examples:
   a) An influencing factor is the choice of people interviewed. Students should also be surveyed; not including them shows bias. When will the cafeteria customers be surveyed? Surveying them after a good meal may affect their response.
   b) There are no influencing factors. Customers at a sporting goods store may have opinions about the brand of snowboard they prefer.
   c) An influencing factor is cost. Offering a digital audio player might be quite costly for the administration.
   d) An influencing factor is ethics. Asking participants about something that they know is not allowed is unethical.
6. Examples:
   a) Bias: Yes. The bias is using language such as "fastest and smoothest" to describe one brand of snowboard. Rewrite: "What brand of snowboard would you buy?" or "What properties of a snowboard do you consider most important?"
   b) Bias: Yes. The bias is assuming that all people drink the three given beverages. Rewrite: "Which drink do you prefer? A Pop, B Coffee/tea, C Root beer, D Other _____ (Please specify.)"
7. Examples:
   a) Influencing factor: The government member may be biased in favour of the current premier. Rewrite: "Who do you think is the best premier in Canadian history?"
   b) Influencing factor: The respondents may be confused by the wording of the question. Rewrite: "What games and systems do you and your friends need?"
8. Examples:
   a) Question 1: "What is your favourite car colour?" Question 2: "What is the most popular car colour on drawings in a grade 9 art class?"
   b) Question 1: "Do you think it is important for family vehicles to have regular oil changes?" Question 2: "How often should family vehicles have an oil change? A Never, B Regularly, C Frequently, D Other _____ (Please specify.)"
9. Examples:
   a) Question: "What music group do you like best?" Whom to ask: Teens aged 13 to 19.
   b) Question: "What is the most important consideration when buying a digital music player?" Whom to ask: Customers shopping for a digital music player.
10. Example: "What is your favourite sport? A Hockey, B Soccer, C Volleyball, D Other _____ (Please specify.)"

11.2 Collecting Data

1. Example:
   - Population: All of the individuals being studied; all of the dogs in an animal shelter
   - Sample: Any group of individuals in a population; all of the mixed-breed dogs in an animal shelter
2. e) voluntary response sample
3. c) stratified sample
4. d) systematic sample
5. a) convenience sample
6. b) random sample
7. a) Population: All students at the school
   Examples:
   - Survey the population: If this is an election, everyone should be invited to vote.
   - Survey a sample: If this is an opinion poll, use a sample to determine the popular candidates.
   b) Population: All players on the lacrosse team. Example: Survey the population: Since the team is small in number, survey all team players.

Answers • MHR 179

8. Examples:
   a) Use a stratified sample by dividing the city into regions according to population. Then, survey a proportional number of people from each region.
   b) Use a systematic sample by surveying every fourth student on the class roster for each grade. Or, use a convenience sample and survey the first 50 students who enter the library on a school day.
9. Examples:
   a) Take samples: Survey the water quality in different areas of the lake. It would be impractical to survey the population since that would involve testing all of the water in the lake, which would be very costly.
   b) Survey the population: All jet engines should be tested since public safety is at stake.
10. Examples:
    a) Sample: People in the park on a certain day
    b) Population: All citizens and visitors to the city
    c) Yes, the results of the survey about the signage in the park would likely represent the population. No, the results of the survey about park use for concerts would not represent the population. The survey should include people who may not use the park but have an opinion about where concerts should be held.
    d) The same sample should not be used for both questions. Even though the two questions involve the park, they are unrelated. People who are not in the park should also be surveyed about whether concerts should be allowed.
11. Examples:
    a) "Which mascot do you prefer to represent our new school? A Bear, B Cougar, C Lion, D Other _____ (Please specify.)" The original question is too open-ended and may result in many different responses. It may take more time to sort out the responses.

b) If Dhara uses a stratified sample that is larger than 30, then this sampling method may be better. Also, using a stratified sample would ensure representation from each grade. Anya's sample of 30 students may be too small to represent all students. Ian's survey of the population may take too much time.

11.3 Probability in Society

1. biased sample
2. generalize
3. experimental; theoretical
4. Examples:
   a) • The random sample is large enough to represent the entire population.
      • The defect occurs on a regular basis.
   b) Yes. The random sample indicates $\frac{1}{40} = 2.5\%$. In a run of 3200 chips, you could expect $3200 \times 2.5\% = 80$ computer chips to be defective.
5. Example: $0.002 \times 100\,000 = 200$
   I predict that 200 decks of cards will be damaged. I assume that the sample represents the population.
6. Examples:
   a) The prediction may be false since only 20 batteries were tested. The survey results may have allowed students to overestimate the number of batteries that would not last longer than 100 h.
   b) Test more than 20 batteries and purchase a quantity of the same battery from different stores.
7. a)

Candidate A	Candidate B	Candidate C	Total
45%	15%	40%	100%
2430	810	2160	5400

b) experimental probability: 40%; theoretical probability: $33\frac{1}{3}$%
Sample Assumptions:
- Each candidate has the same chance of winning.
- The sample represents the population of students who will vote in the election.

c) No. If the poll represents the population of voters, then candidate A will win, not candidate C.

8. a) 72.9 **b)** 70 **c)** 75.67

d) Example: Neither of the samples is a close predictor of the overall score. The mean of the first three games is significantly lower than the mean for the overall score. The mean of the last three games is significantly higher than the mean for the overall score.

9. The experimental probability of having blue eyes is 14.75%. This is slightly less than the article's claim for 16.67%, but more than Karen's prediction of 10%. The experimental results are closer to the article's claim.

11.4 Developing and Implementing a Project Plan

The purpose of this section is to assist you in developing and implementing a project plan. Responses will vary according to the research you plan.

11 Chapter Link

1. a) 250 **b)** 95%

c) The theoretical probability is 25%. This assumes that each category of browser has the same chance of being chosen.

d) The theoretical probability of 25% is less than the experimental probability of 27%.

e) Example: Yes. Since a stratified sample of 5000 Canadians was used, the sample appears to represent the population of grade 9 students. Therefore, the result indicating that Internet Explorer is the preferred choice can be generalized to the population.

2. Examples:

a) All grade 9 students in Canada who use the Internet

b) Use a sample. It would be impractical, costly, and time consuming to survey the population.

c)
- Use a random sample by putting all the names of grade 9 students in the school in a box and drawing 50 names.
- Use a systematic sample by selecting every fifth student from a student roster.

d) What is your preferred online activity?
A E-mail/instant messaging, B Browsing, C Downloading and saving music, D Playing games, E Downloading or watching movies/TV, F Other _____ (Please specify.)

11 Vocabulary Link

1. influencing factors
2. stratified sample
3. convenience sample
4. random sample
5. population
6. survey
7. biased sample
8. systematic sample
9. voluntary response sample
10. sample
11. generalize

Practice Final Exam

1. C 2. B 3. B 4. 1 5. C 6. A 7. C
8. D 9. A 10. A 11. B 12. 0.25 13. C 14. 18
15. C 16. 12 17. D 18. C 19. B 20. D 21. B
22. D 23. B 24. A 25. B 26. A 27. $-2\frac{1}{4}, -0.3, \frac{3}{4}, 2\frac{1}{8}$
28. D 29. D 30. B 31. B
32. Example: The owner could survey every tenth person who comes into the store, and ask the following questions:
    1. Which is your age range?
        a) 30 years old or younger
        b) older than 30 years old
    2. What is your favourite brand of jeans? The owner can ignore the responses of those greater than 30 years old.

33. Let n be the number of pairs of jeans sold, and R be the revenue from the sale of jeans, in dollars.
$R = 89.99n$

34.

n	R
1	89.99
2	179.98
3	269.97
4	359.96
5	449.95

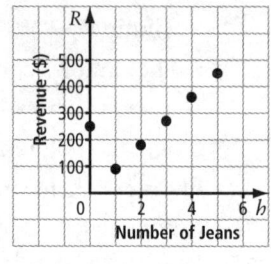

35. Let n be the number of pairs of jeans sold.
$89.99n \geq 1000$

36. At least 12 pairs of jeans must be sold.